Economic Growth and Inequality

In an era of increasing inequalities, and also of deep anxieties about the consequences of two major economic crises, economists are faced with a major question: can economic growth be achieved without inequalities? *Economic Growth and Inequality* critically evaluates the economic literature on this question from a pragmatic perspective, seeking to reconcile those who regard economic liberties as a paramount value, and critics who object that prioritizing these liberties leads to inequitable outcomes.

The book presents an overview of the models used by economists to define and measure inequalities and the ongoing dialogues between political philosophers and economists in an effort to find solutions to the problems. It explores Rawlsian justice, Sen's capability theory, and the theory of rent and compares and contrasts the most often discussed institutions and policies designed for remedying poverty and reducing inequalities.

This book marks a significant contribution to the literature on some of the most pressing problems of our time and will be of great interest to readers of political economy, public policy, moral philosophy, and history of economic and political thought.

Laurent Dobuzinskis teaches Political Science at Simon Fraser University. He has written on a wide range of issues relevant to political economy. His most recent contribution to the field is *Moral Discourse in the History of Economic Thought* (Routledge 2022).

Routledge Frontiers of Political Economy

Globalization and the Decline of American Power
The Political Economy of the American Fall
Cyrus Bina

Marx and *Le Capital*
Evaluation, History, Reception
Edited by Marcello Musto

Permanent Economic Disorder
Shahzavar Karimzadi

Temporary Economic Crises
Shahzavar Karimzadi

Money and Capital
A Critique of Monetary Thought, the Dollar and Post-Capitalism
Laurent Baronian

Modern Money and the Rise and Fall of Capitalist Finance
The Institutionalization of Trusts, Personae, and Indebtedness
Jongchul Kim

Innovation, Complexity and Economic Evolution
From Theory to Policy
Pier Paolo Saviotti

Economic Growth and Inequality
The Economists' Dilemma
Laurent Dobuzinskis

For more information about this series, please visit: www.routledge.com/Routledge-Frontiers-of-Political-Economy/book-series/SE0345

Economic Growth and Inequality

The Economists' Dilemma

Laurent Dobuzinskis

Routledge
Taylor & Francis Group
LONDON AND NEW YORK

First published 2023
by Routledge
4 Park Square, Milton Park, Abingdon, Oxon OX14 4RN

and by Routledge
605 Third Avenue, New York, NY 10158

Routledge is an imprint of the Taylor & Francis Group, an informa business

British Library Cataloguing-in-Publication Data
A catalogue record for this book is available from the British Library

ISBN: 9781032106144 (hbk)
ISBN: 9781032106199 (pbk)
ISBN: 9781003216247 (ebk)

DOI: 10.4324/9781003216247

Typeset in Bembo
by Newgen Publishing UK

Contents

Preface

This book complements my previously published *Moral Discourse in the History of Economic Thought*. Although the two works can be read separately, *Moral Discourse* being more historical and this one more focused on current scholarship and policy debates, they are both concerned in a broad sense with the economists' discourse and how this discourse intersects with that of moral philosophers on the subject of justice. Both works pay serious attention to the theoretical as well as practical obstacles that stand in the path of remedying injustices even though, in both books, I resist the temptation of specifying what an ideal political economy might look like, either at the level of abstract theory or political practice. With respect to the intersection of economics and moral or political philosophy, the difference between the two books is that *Moral Discourse* is mostly concerned with the ideas of economists who were themselves philosophers, such as Adam Smith or John Stuart Mill, whereas the present book provides more room for an analysis of the dialogue that not particularly philosophically minded economists and philosophers have been able (or sometimes not able) to establish on the subject of economic inequalities. The historical approach in *Moral Discourse* meant that this work left little room for dealing with contemporary perspectives and theoretical innovations such as feminist economics; the present volume is an attempt to fill some of these gaps.

My original motivation for writing the present volume is to bring to light and analyze the unique quality of the economists' discourse on inequalities. I view it as a sometimes insistent, sometimes more implicit, admonition not to lose sight of the potential impact on economic efficiency of any move in the direction of a fairer allocation of a society's resources. The economic literature is replete with cautionary tales about the risk of slowing economic growth by going too far in the direction of an egalitarian allocation of resources. Hence my choice of the term "dilemma" in the title. More than any other disciplines, economics values the goal of enhancing the "welfare" of everyone—that is to say ensuring that everyone's preferences are met, with the more or less tacit assumptions that such preferences are mostly oriented toward increased standards of living. I would even go as far as saying that most economists, even the "non-welfarist" ones who look beyond the satisfaction of preferences for material rewards, refuse to believe that a poorer society could ever be fairer or more just than a more prosperous one. The more progressive economists aim for achieving both prosperity and fairness *concurrently*, often arguing that failure to do so actually reduces the prospect of furthering growth; the more conservative ones claim that in the long run, everyone will be better off by prioritizing even unequal growth in the short term. I would *not* say that most social scientists and philosophers are any fonder of the ascetic life;[1] but those among them who seek to achieve egalitarian goals are far less explicitly worried about the risk of postponing an immediate increase in the collective wealth, let alone the wealth of the mythical "job creators," if the cause of justice can better be served by this sort of trade-off. For them, the trade-offs are more complex and involve a wider diversity of values (e.g., human rights, freedom, personal autonomy, self-respect, reciprocity, redressing past wrongs, etc.).

I feel compelled to add two caveats. The first is that although the contrast I have outlined above holds true in a large measure throughout the rest of this volume, it does suffer interesting exceptions, such as the renowned economist Amartya Sen. I only propose it as a hypothesis to guide my explorations through the relevant literature and not as a Procrustean bed on which I intend to fit the works of all the theorists I critically examine hereafter. My second remark is that I while I find the economists' fetishization of efficiency somewhat narrow-minded, as a pragmatist I believe that a relatively unencumbered market economy works best at realizing most of the values that liberal minded, democratically oriented egalitarians are committed to, including autonomy and self-respect. Therefore, even though I regard the current level of economic inequalities as deeply troubling from both an ethical and a practical standpoint, my comments reflect a skeptical stance toward costly redistributive schemes and utopian egalitarian visions.

Note

1 Apologists of the concept of "degrowth," which include a few heterodox economists, but consists mostly of environmentalist social scientists or activists being the obvious exception.

Acknowledgments

This book is the outcome of many years of intensive research but also of teaching a course on "states and markets" which gave me opportunities to test my grasp of complex concepts by trying to explain them to students. Theirquestions helped me to develop my own thinking on what economic well-being means and how to achieve it. Over the years I have also had occasions to discuss my project and exchange ideas with more colleagues and friends than I can list here, although I want to thank my two children, Alex and Caroline, whose professional experiences of how "the real world" works has been very salutary. I especially want to thank colleagues who have taken the time to write insightful comments on various drafts of my manuscript: Genevieve Fuji Johnson, David Laycock, Claudio Katz, Krishna Pendakur and John Richards. I also want to thank Ella McFarlane at Routledge for steering this project to its completion.

1 Introduction

One cannot help but be impressed with the number of books written by economists on the subject of economic inequalities since the financial crisis of 2007–08 unfolded (Milanovic 2010, 2016; Bowles 2012; Piketty 2014, 2015a, 2020; Stiglitz 2012, 2015, 2020; Noah 2012; Church et al. 2015; Drennan 2015; Ostry et al. 2017; Boushey 2019; Novak 2018); all are written for the general public, although some (e.g., Piketty 2014) are also addressed to social science researchers and policy analysts. Indeed, many of these works have transformed the nature of the debates on income distribution, taxation, and so on. This is somewhat ironic, however, considering that for quite some time, economists have paid relatively little attention to inequalities.[1] I argue in this book that some of the reasons why this was so continue to infiltrate the discourse of economists on inequality. It would be wrong to claim that what economists have to say on this subject is uninformed by concepts and theories originating in other disciplines. Inversely, it would be wrong to claim that philosophers and social theorists have always remained indifferent to the significance of economic incentives, or the problem posed by the scarcity of resources. Nevertheless, the discourses of economists and noneconomists have their own tropes and emphases. The intellectual silos within which many scholars work more or less unconsciously are still standing. This book is a modest attempt to chip at them by bringing to the fore exemplars of economists and/or philosophers who already have analyzed economic inequalities in innovative, transgressive (i.e., not narrowly economistic) ways, or by underlining opportunities for productive engagement across disciplinary boundaries. I aim for two goals. One is more intellectual in nature and consists of identifying areas where economists and philosophers—or, for that matter, other scholars—already have learned or could learn more from each other to produce innovative ways of theorizing inequalities, poverty, and injustice. The other is more practical: What can be done about economic inequalities that would be feasible, that is to say, not prosperity-reducing or otherwise harmful to the general welfare, and yet normatively defensible?

Note however that when I allude to the need for a deeper engagement among economists and other scholars concerned with economic inequalities, I am not advocating the discarding of disciplinary boundaries altogether. There is at least one fundamental premise of the economists' discourse that I am not

DOI: 10.4324/9781003216247-1

challenging—and which I use throughout the rest of this book as a normative criterion. I am referring here to the centrality of the notion of feasibility in economic analysis. Geoffrey Brenan (1993, 124) is right to suggest that what "the economist identifies as the primary weakness of traditional political philosophy" is "the failure … to take feasibility seriously." All I am suggesting by arguing in favor of a lowering of intellectual barriers is that an honest debate among scholars coming from different horizons should produce a richer notion of feasibility that is informed by parallel (i.e., resolutely nonutopian) reflections in political philosophy, political science, and the lessons that can be learned from the emerging synthesis of experimental economics, social psychology, and the cognitive sciences; the latter provide good reasons for not holding on dogmatically to a narrow definition of rationality.[2]

What were the reasons for the mainstream economists' relative neglect of inequalities until relatively recently? Three of them deserve particular attention. They are all interconnected but can de differentiated for didactic purposes. The first is that most mainstream economists since the origins of mathematical economics in the late nineteenth century have been keen to separate the positive and normative sides of their discipline—the latter being treated more as an afterthought than as a fundamental concern. Consequently, they have been inclined to ignore the ethical and political ramifications of the inequalities inherent in their models. As Jonathan D. Ostry et al. (2019, 1) note, "Mainstream economists … have worried far more about whether average incomes are growing and much less about how growth is distributed among people." And they add that "economists generally frown on too much redistribution." Few of them, however, went as far as Robert Lucas (2003, 20), who claimed that "of all the tendencies that are harmful to sound economics, the most seductive, and in my mid the most poisonous, is the focus on the question of distribution." This was certainly not what John Stuart Mill thought of distribution;[3] but that is precisely the point: modern mathematical economics has been more focused on the technical challenges posed by the ongoing refinements of the Walrasian general economic model or similar mathematical puzzles (e.g., the chaotic nature of financial markets) than with how the economic pie is shared—something which is obviously not separable from moral philosophy and political theory. I would immediately add that not only have mainstream economists found it impossible to consistently shy away from normative issues, but in recent years, as the "mainstream" seems to have branched out in various directions, including behavioral or experimental economics, and as heterodox currents have asserted themselves more vigorously, the boundary between positive and normative concerns has become more porous.[4]

The second and third reasons for the economists' relative neglect of inequalities originate in the research priorities and theories that have shaped micro- and macroeconomics. With respect to microeconomics, the issues concerning distribution were relegated to the field of "welfare economics." As I explain in Chapter 2, welfare economics has gone through several stages, eventually ending up in what some analysts regard as a theoretical impasse. The question it posed—what ought to be the balance between efficiency and equity—was obviously important. But the answers that were provided remained either controversial or muddled in theoretical complications. As for macroeconomics, it was for a long time focused too exclusively on the subject of full employment and managing business cycles. The assumption was that increasing prosperity is "the tide that lifts all boats," and, therefore, poverty and its attendant problems would in time be resolved by continuous growth. This illusion has by now been shattered. But the belatedness of the acknowledgment (see Chapter 3) that inequalities are deepening everywhere, including in the emerging economies where growth is occurring, and that growth in the advanced economies has slowed down significantly in the twenty-first century, accounts in some measure for the longstanding neglect of inequalities to which I alluded. Now these sketchy remarks need to be clarified.

To fully grasp what economists have in mind when they debate something like a Hobson's choice between desirable efficiency and the more nebulous notion of equity requires an explanation of what economists mean by "economic efficiency." The *Oxford Dictionary* defines it as "the quality of doing something well with no waste of time or money." The "something" in question is often understood as an objectively measurable goal. A factory, for example, is efficient if it produces an optimal number of products (cars, computers, or loaves of bread, etc.) with a given amount of inputs. To a large extent, this was also how Soviet planners understood efficiency: the five-year plans were meant to be instruments for producing as much steel, electricity, and so on, with a given amount of natural resources and human capital. Whether these targets matched the Soviet citizens' subjective expectations of material welfare was not much of a concern to them—at least not until the very last decade of the Soviet Union when these concerns became unavoidable but also turned out to be impossible to meet without abandoning the planned economy model. Of course, this meaning of efficiency is not irrelevant to economic theory in a market economy. For some specific purposes, it might be necessary to measure the technical efficiency with which firms in a given sector produce certain types of goods, whether natural resources are used appropriately, and so on. But the way in which the concept of efficiency enters in economic theory, and is embodied in the presumed tension between efficiency and equity, originates in the notion of "Pareto efficiency." As explained by B. Lockwood (2008, 292), according to Vilfredo Pareto,

> an allocation of resources in the economy was optimal if there existed no other productively feasible allocation which made all individuals in the economy at least as well-off, and at least one strictly better off, than they were initially. Although Pareto actually used the word "optimal," this is really a definition of efficiency, as a Pareto-"optimal" allocation of resources is "good" only in the limited sense that not everybody can be made better off. It may in fact be very undesirable in some other way, for example, very

> unequal. It is not surprising, therefore, that the word "Pareto-optimal" has gradually been replaced by "Pareto-efficient."

And by "well-off" in this context, we must think of a subjective assessment of the extent to which an economic agent's preferences are satisfied. Pareto, however, ruled out the feasibility of comparing the *degree* to which individuals consider themselves to be better- or worse-off by moving from one allocation to another. Thus, if shifting from one state of affairs to another leaves at least one person better-off and harms no one (i.e., at least one person is more satisfied with the means at their disposal), then this shift is a "Pareto improvement." No more Pareto improvements are possible at the point where a Pareto-optimal equilibrium is reached. Indeed, as Yew-Kwang Ng (2004, 36) explains, "It is well established that, under certain classical assumptions such as nonincreasing returns, the absence of externalities and so on, a perfectly competitive economy will attain a Pareto optimum. This is the first theorem of welfare economics." To sum up, an economy is "efficient" if it meets consumer demand; what an external observer might consider to constitute an efficient output in terms of some "objective" criterion does not factor into this definition, although it is generally assumed that increasing the gross domestic product is the most effective way of making people better-off (it's a sure bet that "representative agents" prefer having more material goods than having less).

However, an efficient allocation of resources is not necessarily unbiased. For example, an allocation can be more efficient than an alternative even though only a small minority of individuals benefit from the shift. As long as no one is worse-off in absolute terms, economic growth that is unequally shared would be a Pareto improvement. And, of course, taking away from the most affluent to redistribute some of their gains to the less privileged would *not* be Pareto-efficient since the more affluent individuals would be less well-off as a result. But the same could be said of an endogenous or spontaneous change in economic circumstances that would improve the living conditions of one group (not necessarily the richest) at the expense of another group, for example, as a result of a technological advancement that benefits people working in one sector of the economy but deprives others of their livelihood. That is the crux of the neglect of inequalities in microeconomics and where the concept of equity comes into the picture.[5] Are there ways of ensuring that resources are allocated in a way that can be considered "fair"? For example, if moving from situation A to situation B leaves some people better-off and some people worse-off, but the "winners" are able to compensate the "losers" and still come out ahead, then the move is both equitable and efficient. These transfers were originally formulated by Nicholas Kaldor and Michael Hicks in strictly theoretical terms since their models do *not* even require that actual transfer should take place, only that the potentiality of a compensation could be shown to exist (for a more in-depth look at the issue of compensation, see Chapter 2). Welfare economists have analyzed compensation as a rational way of refining the concept of a Pareto-superior outcome (Ng 2004: 47–64). However, the theorists' perspective on this problem is rather narrow-minded. According to Mark D. White (2019, 80),

> Economists rarely account for compensation, arguing that it is a technicality or not their responsibility, falling instead on those who will implement the change, such as government or corporate bureaucrats. This division of labor may be reasonable in theory, but in effect, it absolves economists of their responsibility to take account of all of the effects of their actions (and harms deliberately imposed can hardly be considered an "unforeseen consequence"). If compensation is to be taken seriously, it should be incorporated into any proposal submitted to a Kaldor-Hicks test, and if that test shows compensation itself to be too costly, this should be taken as a criticism of the proposal itself, not an excuse to ignore it or pass the buck. Treating compensation as an afterthought allows the economist to sweep it under the rug, compounding their moral culpability in Kaldor-Hicks decisions.

Cost–benefit analysis is a practical method grounded in welfare economics for evaluating the merits of alternative government policies or specific programs. Many experts in cost–benefit analysis who work for public agencies take this issue seriously, but there are thorny empirical difficulties to be solved when compensation is treated not merely as a hypothetical test of feasibility but as something that must actually be implemented. And, as economics becomes more pluralistic, more and more theorists are interested in pushing the boundaries of what constitutes an equitable allocation of resources beyond the technical parameters of cost–benefit analysis. Some among them (e.g., feminist economists) pay much attention to nonmonetary values that more orthodox economists tend to neglect and voice criticism of the utilitarian premises within which equity is often framed. But one might say that the furthest away from Pareto efficiency a policy tends to shift the rules of the competitive game, the more critically many, if not most, economists will look at it.

Returning to what I briefly said about macroeconomics, we observe a rather seamless continuation of the same reasoning. The discourse of modern economics has privileged positive analysis over normative considerations, and distribution is clearly an issue that inevitably veers into a confrontation among opposing values. But, implicitly, economists have also placed much faith in the ethics of utilitarianism. From that standpoint, maximizing the common welfare is the greatest good, and stimulating economic growth is the best way to achieve that goal. From that angle, insisting on redistributive policies is counterproductive because it erodes the social-economic and cultural conditions that facilitate growth: respect for property rights, rewarding the risks associated with entrepreneurial initiatives, competitive innovations, and so on. (This was the logic behind Robert Lucas' previously cited remark.) And, again from that macroeconomic standpoint, while absolute poverty might be a problem that needs to be addressed, *relative* inequalities among groups of individuals who progress at different paces along the path that leads to prosperity is less of a problem in itself. It is merely the consequence of the otherwise healthy "creative destruction" extolled by Joseph Schumpeter. What has changed in recent years, however, is that economists have started to seriously consider the question raised by Joseph Stiglitz (2012) and some others (e.g., Gründler and Scheuermeyer 2018; Boushey 2019) that inequalities, rather than merely being an unfortunate but neutral side-effect of growth, actually act as a brake on it. This is a complicated issue on which there is no consensus (see Barro 2002), but this new angle, together with the fact that the extraordinary level reached by inequalities in much of the world has become a hotly debated political issue, has forced economists to become less indifferent to how the proverbial pie is divided.[6] This new context has also opened opportunities for economists to look beyond the efficiency–equity trade-off and to initiate a conversation with philosophers about the meaning and implications of justice in a deeper sense (Kolm 2005; Sen 2009; Sugden 2018; Hodgson 2021; Smith and Wilson 2019; McCloskey 2021).

Moral philosophers have been concerned about the meaning of justice since the very beginning of the philosophical tradition. They have posed the problem in more general terms, but the specific question of the equitable distribution of resources occupies an important place in their enquiries. Now that economists seem willing to explore normative questions beyond the narrow meaning of equity they started from, there exist many opportunities for a deep conversation among all the scholars interested in the normative implications of inequalities. But, as I hinted above, one can still discern some distinctive features in the rhetoric of economists, without implying that economists all speak with the same voice even if they often start from the same assumptions. The latter, as I have so far sketched out, include the importance of efficiency and the priority given to growth.

Having thus far established the reasons that account for the economists' neglect of inequalities until recently, I now want to raise the question of what is troublesome about inequalities in general, and economic inequalities in particular. And here again, we can discern some specificities of the economists' discourse, although it is prudent to avoid overgeneralizing.

David Graeber and David Wengrow (2021) provide a fascinating account of the trajectory of the idea of equality since the dawn of humanity. According to them, the conventional story of a trajectory from egalitarian bands of hunter-gatherers to hierarchical civilization is misrepresentation of the complexity of human evolution. Rather than a linear progression, it seems that humans have gone back and forth between equality and hierarchy. But if we limit our inquiry to the Western tradition, it is clear that the ancients accepted inequality as the natural state of affairs. Plato defined justice as an arrangement according to which the members of the three classes constituting his ideal city states (artisans, auxiliaries or "guardians," and the "philosopher kings") each keep their place in a rigid hierarchy. Aristotle's polity was a little less hierarchical as far as male citizens were concerned, but he regarded slaves and women as unfit to play any public role. Although in medieval times the church affirmed the equality of all human beings in the eyes of God, marked differences in status and power were unquestioned until the dawn of the age of Enlightenment. Equality is a modern idea. But it is also a defining feature of modernity. The modern idea of equality was forcefully put forward by Thomas Hobbes in his description of an imagined state of nature; it is precisely this original equality that is the source of conflicts and rivalries, which the creation of a sovereign state is supposed to put an end to. The whole history of political thought since the early beginnings of the Enlightenment is pithily summed up by the economist Serge-Christophe Kolm (1996, 38): "There is a prima facie reason in favor of equality and against inequality, which results from the very requirement of rationality." But this "equality" refers to the way in which individuals ought to be treated: they ought not be constrained in the choices they are able to make. The actual allocations of valued goods that individuals eventually obtain from participating in a market economy will, of course, be different, reflecting the choices that free individuals will make under circumstances that are not necessarily identical. There may be good reasons for making these circumstances more identical in some or even most respects, but it is neither feasible nor even desirable to impose identical circumstances on everyone (for instance, access to education ought to be as equal as possible, but individuals can decide for themselves whether they wish to avail themselves of the educational opportunities offered to them).

Kenneth Binmore (2005, 2014) provides a game-theoretic explanation of why equality is rational, that is, why inequalities *a priori* need to be justified. Binmore demonstrates that the optimal solution to a two-player bargaining game is the egalitarian solution (2005, 31–32). But Binmore qualifies this conclusion in two ways. The first is that the payoffs of the game need to be weighed by "social indices"; such indices take into account differences in status that are relevant to the problem at hand: "For example, a person's social index increases with need, provided that need is equated with the risks people are willing to take to satisfy their wants" (Binmore 2014, 10787). It would be unfair to deny disabled individuals a greater share of some resources that the rest of the population would need less of. The second qualification is that this formal solution to a bargaining game is valid only if interpersonal comparisons of utility are allowed. Now this is a technical concept that needs to be clarified. Interpersonal comparisons of utility are possible when utilities are measured cardinally and not merely ordinally. If one assumes that individuals can only rank their preferences but cannot compare the degree to which one option is preferred over another, then interpersonal comparisons are not feasible. Lionel Robbins in the 1930s claimed that only ordinal rankings are compatible with the fact that individuals' preferences are purely subjective and, therefore, that there can be no comparison of the ways in which specific values are assigned to the choices they make (*de gustibus non est disputandum*, as the saying goes). But plausible as this principle is in many instances, such as consumer choices, it is far from being convincing in all situations. As Adam Smith already insisted in his *Theory of*

Moral Sentiments, people spontaneously experience sympathy for the pains and pleasures of other. To some extent at least, some things (e.g., good health) are experienced by most people as being intrinsically more valuable than others (e.g., smoking). This is indeed obvious in many instances concerning policy choices (e.g., prioritizing relief for the victims of a natural disaster over other uses of public funds), and nowadays most economists more or less grudgingly concede that ruling out interpersonal comparisons in all situations is untenable (Fleurbaey and Hammond 2004). But this is still a controversial matter, and, therefore, a minority of economists might refuse, on principle, to agree with Binmore's game-theoretic argument in favor of equal sharing, even with the qualification introduced above that "equal" must also be fair.

But let us accept that equality is prima facie rational. This tells us little about what it entails, whether it should be prioritized over other values, and so on. What equality ought to mean is a question that has been debated for a long time, and even if we look only at the contemporary literature, there are many interpretations to consider, as Richard Arneson (1995) makes clear. At the risk of oversimplifying, one can say that most theorists agree that a distinction should be made between, on the one hand, equality of outcomes or conditions of existence in a market economy and, on the other hand, equality of opportunity. The latter can itself be subdivided into several competing definitions and theories, but all are focused on what needs to be done to equalize the likelihood that individuals or groups will succeed in reaching their goals rather than on the final results of these efforts. In recent years, arguments in support of equality of opportunity have come mostly from the camp of "luck egalitarians" who claim that inequalities that deserve to be rectified are those due to "brute luck," that is, those circumstances for which individuals cannot be held responsible. One should note, however, that some theorists (e.g., Sen 1980; Anderson 1999) have famously attempted to find alternatives to or at least qualify the dichotomy between outcomes and opportunities. But for the moment, I set those aside (see Chapter 4, however). Equality of opportunity in different guises has been defended by most economists who have waded into the philosophical arena. It is, however, a complex, multilayered notion that builds upon many ideas that are not easily measurable. Equality of opportunity comes into play when the question is raised of what ought to be done to rectify the injustices caused by deep inequalities (see Chapters 4 and 5). But in trying to ascertain what these inequalities look like in practice, the concept of equality of conditions is more germane—not as an ideal that ought to be achieved but simply as a benchmark. I further note that in the economists' discourse, conditions usually refer to levels of "welfare," that is, the degree to which individuals or households are capable of satisfying their preferences for the goods and services they can choose from. A crude approximation of a level of welfare is income (wages, returns on investment, etc.), which obviously is the most effective way of satisfying one's preferences in a market economy. This is why the next two chapters are more focused on the equality of welfare.

Let me now outline the organization of this book in the form of a little fable. Economists have not always been very concerned about inequalities, but now, they seem to be finally paying attention. And now they do—or at least some of them who have gained prominence—have started to engage with philosophers on this subject. This is bringing us a little closer to finding pragmatic solutions that are neither economically naïve nor hopelessly utopian. So who are the heroes and villains of this tale? A long time ago, an eccentric economist named Arthur Pigou urged his colleagues to think about ways of reducing inequalities of welfare (income) and proposed a way of doing it, which he called "welfare economics." But his colleagues preferred to listen to what Vilfredo Pareto was telling and concluded that Pigou had badly posed the problem in the first place (see Chapter 2). But then an Italian economist named Corrado Gini was heard suggesting that it would be a good idea to define what constitutes inequalities of welfare more precisely and to use his index to measure them; a French economist named Thomas Piketty has been up to the challenge and has built an impressive dataset that, he claims, shows the depth of these inequalities of welfare/income (see Chapter 3). But, so what? Isn't equality of opportunity a better way of posing the problem than equality of outcomes? Neoclassical economists and their classical liberal friends among philosophers are telling us not to worry too much about these data. Economic freedom generates growth, which, in the end, lifts up all boats. If the rule of law effectively protects all property rights, everyone should endeavor to take advantage of the opportunities offered by an efficient market economy (see Chapter 4). Not so fast, reply egalitarian philosophers and those in the economists' camp who care to listen to them, pointing out that equality of opportunity is not a given—it must be enhanced by appropriate socioeconomic reforms, although they differ among themselves about the goals and contents of such reforms (see Chapter 5). But then a pragmatist political economist comes along to ask the question of what can realistically be done in practice to remedy unjust inequalities (see Chapter 6). Much interest is paid to a new *ex ante* asset-based, "predistributive" approach as an alternative to the current *ex post* redistributive welfare state (and this book provides arguments in its favor), but there is no consensus on this matter, although in the end everyone agrees that "more research should be done." To recap what I said above, my hope is that this book provides reasons for insisting that such future research should be conducted in a manner that facilitates exchanges of ideas across a wide range of fields and disciplines.

Notes

1 I admit that this is a rhetorical overstatement. It would be wrong to claim that the subject of inequalities was never addressed. Respected economists such as Simon Kuznets (1955) or Amartya Sen ([1973] 1997) made decisive contribution to the literature on economic inequalities many years before it became a topical subject. My point is rather that macroeconomics was, for a long time, more focused on growth than on inequality, and to the extent it was, inequality was downplayed because it

was not generally regarded as an economic problem, that is, an obstacle to growth. Consequently, it tended to be viewed as a problem for social policy. The title of Matthew Drennan's (2015) book is telling in this regard: *Income Inequality: Why It Matters and Why Most Economists Didn't Notice.*

2 On this point, see Dobuzinskis (2022, chapter 8).

3 The sixteen chapters of Book II of Mill's *Principles of Political Economy* (the first edition of which was published in 1848) are devoted to the subject of distribution. Interestingly, two of these chapters address the question of remedying low wages. Neither was Adam Smith indifferent to distribution: "It is but equity, besides, that they who feed, cloath and lodge the whole body of the people, should have such a share of the produce of their own labour as to be themselves tolerably well fed, cloathed and lodged" ([1776] 1981, vol. 1, 96).

4 See Dobuzinskis (2022).

5 Serge-Christophe Kolm ([1971] 1997, 69) defines equity as follows: "A state of society is called equitable if each person prefers to be in her own situation rather than in any other person's situation, that is, if each thinks of everyone else: 'I'd rather be in my place than in hers'. We will add the possibility of indifference to this preference. In other words, equity implies that no one can be jealous of anyone else; there is equity when no one has a possible reason to be envious."

6 Samuel Bowles and Wendy Carlin (2020, 178) report that when asked to answer the question "what is the most pressing problem economists should be addressing?" the majority economics students responded by choosing "inequality."

2 Equality of Welfare

Theoretical Foundations*

Introduction

What is specific about economic inequalities? The policies designed and implemented to deal with pressing issues such as poverty, homelessness, poor health, and so on, inevitably require taking into account a multiplicity of factors above and beyond economic data about income, employment, and similar "economic" factors. But considering the aim of this book, the theoretical frames within which economists have posed the problem must be examined closely. Where should we look for such frames? The rather obvious answer is "welfare economics." This discipline was established for precisely the purpose of finding answers to the question of how to make people, individually and collectively, better-off. Antoinette Baujard (2016, 611) provides a more complete definition:

> Welfare economics is the economic study of the definition and the measure of the social welfare; it offers the theoretical framework used in public economics to help collective decision making, to design public policies, and to make social evaluations. Questions usually tackled by welfare economics are the following: what is social welfare? Is there a reliable and satisfying way to measure it? If social welfare is based on individual preferences, can we derive a social preference from the preferences of individuals? Are competitive equilibrium outcomes optimal in the sense that they lead to the highest social welfare? Can any optimal outcome be achieved by a modified market mechanism? Can we really formulate recommendations for public policies on the basis of such welfare analyses?

These questions are indeed central to this chapter. But whether welfare economics provides the most convincing answers is debatable. There are at least two reasons to be somewhat skeptical. The first is that, as I show hereafter, welfare economics has gone through a few crises since it was first founded in the early decades of the twentieth century. Some would even argue that welfare economics as a research program has run its course, that it belongs more to the history of economic ideas than to contemporary economics, and thus that it is time to move on to other methods.[1] The second and related reason is that it is

DOI: 10.4324/9781003216247-2

in fact possible and justifiable to approach economic inequalities from different angles, such as macroeconomics, behavioral economics, neo-institutionalism, and so on, not to mention more descriptive/empirical perspectives within a generic literature on political economy broadly defined. Consequently, many noneconomists concerned with inequalities may not be familiar with welfare economics.

Nevertheless, I contend that examining how welfare economics evolved and could be revived is a good way to start my inquiry into how historically questions centered on growth, distribution and inequalities have been posed by economists. I intend to argue that even if welfare economics offer only incomplete answers to the problem of balancing efficiency and equity, more recent innovative attempts at building "non-welfarist" approaches that, for instance, attempt to track the correlation between economic performance and happiness are well worth examining, at least briefly. In any event, welfare economics should not be written off since its applied version, known as "cost–benefit analysis," continues to be widely used. And from this standpoint of the history of ideas, it shed light on how economists have grappled with the dilemma of addressing normative issues while not abandoning the hope of continually strengthening the scientific credentials of economics.

The next section retraces the birth of welfare economics. This historical detour is justified in part by the recent interest shown in the life and works of Arthur Pigou, who, as this latest scholarship suggests, might have been ahead of his times instead of merely being remembered as the distant founder of welfare economics (Aslanbeigui and Oakes 2015; Kumekawa 2017; Knight 2018). It is followed by an account of the transition from "old" to the "new" welfare economics and the reasons why the latter eventually reached an impasse; I then provide a more hopeful conclusion on the opportunities for a renewal of the tradition by building upon a critical reframing of "welfare" as multidimensional well-being and, more ambitiously, happiness.

The Birth of Welfare Economics

The subject matter of welfare economics was part and parcel of the works of the great classical political economists, from Adam Smith (and even some of his French predecessors) to J. S. Mill. But it is generally acknowledged that Arthur Cecil Pigou (1877–1959) established welfare economics as a distinct research program. Pigou was firmly anchored in the neoclassical Cambridge tradition. He succeeded Alfred Marshall in the Chair of Political Economy in 1908 and held it until his retirement in 1943. He owed an intellectual debt to his beloved teacher and mentor Marshall and, to a lesser extent, to Francis Edgeworth. But his neoclassical economics was not the only influence on his thought. As a student at Cambridge, Pigou studied philosophy, history and literature. He was drawn toward the utilitarian moral theory of Henry Sidgwick, who was held in as much esteem at Cambridge as Marshall. As Aslanbeigui and Oakes (2015, 4) explain, "If Pigou became an economist by studying the techniques of marginalism and partial equilibrium analysis with Marshall, he became a logician of policy analysis by reading Book IV of Sidgwick's *The Methods of Ethics* on utilitarianism and its extension into economics in his *Principles of Political Economy*." In the latter volume, Sidgwick displayed a less skeptical attitude toward government intervention than Marshall's opinion on this subject, and in this respect, Pigou owed more to Sidgwick than to Marshall. Pigou declared that in writing *The Economics of Welfare*, he intended "to bring into clearer light some of the ways it now is, or eventually may become, feasible for governments to control the play of economic forces in such wise as to promote the economic welfare, and thought that, the total welfare of their citizens as a whole" ([1952] 2002, 129–130). For this reason but also, as I explain further below, because Pigou agreed with Sidgwick's efforts to ground utilitarian ethics on more than a self-centered conception of utility, one could say that "Pigou modernized Sidgwick's thoughts by imposing Marshallian analytics on them" (O'Donnell 1979, 589).

The other noteworthy influence was more practical. Although he grew up in an affluent middle-class family, went to prestigious schools, and never experienced hardship, Pigou was personally very concerned with poverty. He was motivated by Charles Booth's meticulous research on the living conditions of the poor families in London to write an essay titled "Some Aspects of the Problem of Charity" (1901). In it he wrote that although progress had been made in the nineteenth century, there was still "a vast problem before the statesman and the philanthropist" (cited by Hongo 2013, 210).[2]

Pigou envisioned welfare economics as being both a positive and a normative research program. Normative because it was intended to address practical problems; as he put it, economics must ultimately lead to "practical results in social improvement" (Pigou [1952] 2002, 4). It can do so by providing information to policymakers about the consequences of the options they have to choose from. Note in that respect that Pigou did not advocate for economists to act as partisan supporters of specific reforms, but to consider all policy proposals equanimously (Aslanbeigui and Oakes 2015, 99). The object of their concern should be to increase the "economic welfare of the population" measured by using the "measuring rod of money" (Pigou [1952] 2002, 11). Pigou was a sophisticated thinker who fully realized that "economic welfare" is only one aspect of the "total welfare," but he believed that "there is a presumption that qualitative conclusions about effects on economic welfare will hold good also of effects upon total welfare" (ix).[3] But these normative views must be consistent with the findings of positive science; in that respect, welfare economics is also a positive discipline. (In fact, Pigou himself made several contributions to pure theory.) Indeed, the history of welfare economics and the various research programs that branched out from its original core has been characterized by a distinctive oscillation between concerns for theory and concerns for practical applications. This shifting focus is noticeable in Pigou's own works.

Pigou was a very productive scholar. I only want to highlight here the works that are most relevant to my purpose, namely, *Wealth and Welfare* (1912), *The*

Economics of Welfare (originally published in 1920 and revised three times, the fourth revised edition dating from 1952), *The Theory of Unemployment* (1933), and *Socialism versus Capitalism* (1937). The foundational principles for welfare economics were laid out in *Wealth and Welfare*, but he felt the need to expand on them; *The Economics of Welfare* does not innovate much as compared to his earlier book, but goes in much more detail (and is arguably a little too long and verbose). I mentioned the two other works because they illustrate two trends in Pigou's thought, which are also a reflection on intellectual and political developments happening in Britain during his lifetime. As economists became more adept at using mathematics, Marshall's practice of keeping mathematical formulas in appendices and only using ordinary language in the main text went out of fashion. Pigou was willing to go with the flow and used mathematics extensively, albeit not exclusively, in his very dense and very-challenging-to-read *Theory of Unemployment*,[4] which incidentally was severely criticized by Keynes, who presented it as an exemplar of the "classical" approach he rejected in his famous *The General Theory of Employment, Interest and Money* (1936). The second trend throws light on the evolution of Pigous' political values and commitments. On social policy, Pigou was always moderately egalitarian. On other issues, including free trade, he very much leaned toward laissez faire. But in the 1930s and 1940s, he warmed up to the idea of socialist planning; this is made evident in his *Socialism versus Capitalism*. Even in this work, he was still skeptical about its feasibility in principle and very critical of the ways in which it had been implemented in the Soviet Union. But he suggested that gradual steps could be taken to achieve greater control of the economy by a progressive government and endorsed more far-reaching social reforms than he previously had, including the nationalization of public utilities. Pigou never was an active member of any political party, but it could be said that his political allegiance leaned toward the British Liberal party before the Great Depression, but then he sided with Labour in the 1940s.

I now turn to an analysis of the major themes in Pigou's welfare economics. Everyone today is at least vaguely familiar with the macroeconomic concept of "gross domestic product" (GDP), which used to be called "gross national product" (GNP). The media frequently report changes in the GDP as the economy grows or contracts depending on the phases of the business cycle. No precise statistical measurement of this sort was available to Pigou, but the concept itself was not unknown; he coined the term "national dividend," which is defined as follows: "The national dividend is that part of the objective income of the community, including, of course, income derived from abroad, which can be measured in money" ([1952] 2002, 31). The two themes I want to focus on are: (1) Pigou's views on the distribution of the national dividend, and (2) his analysis of the structure of the national dividend or, to be more specific, the causes and effects of "externalities," to use the term contemporary economists employ when discussing this question. These aspects overlap to some extent, but they call for somewhat different policy solutions.

With respect to income, Pigou argued that an increase in the size of the national dividend is welfare-enhancing *if it does not negatively affect the poor.* Alternatively, maintaining the national dividend constant but transferring resources from the rich to the poor is also welfare-enhancing. He was even prepared to accept a *small* negative effect of transfers on the national dividend (Pigou [1952] 2002, 719), but he optimistically expected that improvements in the living conditions of the poor would contribute to an increase in the national dividend over time (e.g., better health boosts productivity). Ever the elitist, however, he was worried that the state might need to monitor the ways in which disadvantaged people use their increased income to prevent them from wasting it in injurious ways ([1952] 2002, 756–757; Kumekawa 2017, 78–82). I want to underline the significance of this divergence from a literal definition of the utilitarian doctrine; for Pigou, the welfare of the poor overrides other permutations of the economic welfare of a society for ethical rather than consequentialist reasons. In this respect, Pigou drew his inspiration from Henry Sidgwick, who insisted that the pursuit of self-interest must be tempered by "a sympathetic aversion to the pain of other men" (1901, 460). It would be wrong, of course, to imply that Benthamite utilitarianism promoted individual selfishness since Bentham emphatically stressed the ideal of the "greatest good for the greatest number" and argued that this should be achieved by the intervention of the legislator enacting rules that encourage socially beneficial choices and punish antisocial behaviors. But from where do legislators get their other-regarding values since Bentham did not have an ethics, properly speaking? And this ethical gap is also evident in the endlessly discussed question of whether the greatest good requires sacrificing those who stand in the path of that goal (something that every student of philosophy has encountered by reading about Bernard Williams' infamous "trolley problem"). Thus, Sidgwick felt compelled to address "the profoundest problem of ethics" (386), namely, the relationship between rational egoism and rational benevolence as a moral problem in itself. Ultimately, however, Sidgwick (506) reached the pessimistic conclusion that there is no purely *rational* solution to this problem. Utilitarianism as a doctrine, in other words, does not provide final answers to our deepest ethical dilemmas. But political economy does not have to be consistently utilitarian; it can be guided by a more pragmatic mix of values. Margaret O'Donnell (1979, 591) sums up Sidgwick's more pragmatic approach to the question of how to raise the level of happiness in a community in his *Principles of Political Economy*: "(1) to make 'the proportion of produce to population a maximum, taking generally as a measure the ordinary exchange value, so far as it can be applied,' and (2) to 'rightly' distribute 'produce among members of the community, whether on any principle of equity or justice, or on the economic principle of making the whole product as useful as possible.'" The parallels with Pigou's previously cited maxims are clear, except that Pigou improved upon Sidgwick's vague phraseology by specifying that what is right is not to sacrifice the interest of the poor when seeking to increase the overall economic welfare.

(I believe that in writing about this issue, Pigou was at least as concerned about the ethical choices that economists must make as he was with the adequacy of public policies.)

On the more specific ways in which the "national dividend" is best allocated, Pigou paid special attention to "industrial peace" and the labor market (see Part III of *The Economics of Welfare*). He addressed two sets of questions concerning (1) frictions that can occur in the labor market and how governments can ease them by means of more or less indirect interventions, and (2) whether, more directly, interventions intended to assist workers living on unfair low wages can be justified. In principle, a market economy should achieve an equilibrium in which "the wages offered for each class of working people [tend to] approximate the value of the marginal net product for that class" (Pigou [1952] 2002, 473). That is to say, wages reflect the limit beyond which remunerating workers for additional outputs ceases to yield a net benefit. But in practice, one cannot expect that self-correcting markets will always work effectively, nor that employers will always treat their employees fairly. Pigou was particularly concerned with the potential "exploitation" of wage earners (483, 486, 556). By using this loaded term, Pigou did not suggest that he was taking on board the whole Marxist theory of class struggle. Far from it, in fact, he made no reference to Marx. His definition was more circumspect, "an attempt to pay the workpeople less than their marginal worth" (483). It is not a systemic flaw but an abuse of power under specific circumstances. Nevertheless, it is undoubtable that Pigou was aware of the rhetorical connotation of this term and used it to convey the strength of his conviction that unfair employment practices ought to be remedied. The best remedy for this problem is collective bargaining. In other words, Pigou was certainly not advocating repressive legislation against unions, although he argued that regulations might be needed to prevent unions from engaging in practices that would be a source of economic inefficiencies. More generally, he thought that government might have a role to play in mediation and arbitration of labor disputes, for example, by establishing "labour boards" (421). But if mediation or arbitration fails, governments would be justified in intervening coercively to preserve industrial peace.

Pigou consistently demonstrated a concern for fairness. As mentioned previously, he was even prepared to use the term "exploitation" to characterize wages less than proportional to the workers' productivity. But he argued against a policy that would raise all "unfair wages" to their proper level for it could push some low-wage earners out of their jobs. Instead, he rather cryptically alluded to the possibility of "the direct action of the state, in securing for all families of its citizens, with the help, if necessary, of State funds, an adequate minimum standard in every department of life" (Pigou [1952] 2002, 618). He elaborated on this point in Part IV of *The Economics of Welfare*, and in other writings, he advocated publicly funded old-age pensions, unemployment insurance, and health insurance (Aslanbeigui and Oakes 2019). The net effects of the taxes used to fund such programs (e.g., a progressive income tax that would exclude savings) on the welfare of the community should be positive. Although, as I indicated above, Pigou became more and more interventionist, he never argued that the only way to increase welfare and, in particular, reduce poverty was to rely on government interventions. Well-functioning open markets should be the primary motor of growth and prosperity. But in order to be well functioning, markets occasionally need to be corrected by measures designed to rectify "market failures"[5] caused by monopolies and externalities. This brings me to the second facet of Pigou's theory of welfare economics.

Externalities can be defined in the broadest sense as the indirect, and generally unintended, effects of decisions made by economic agents. This definition captures both the "external economies" realized at the level of a firm or an industrial branch (e.g., reduction in costs through economies of scale, diffusion of technology) and "externalities" affecting third parties on a wider, possibly even global, scale. External economies were intuited by Marshall, but Pigou systematized his ideas. Roger McCain (2019, 37) provides a useful typology of Pigou's treatment of these issues:

Ia. economies of scale (of the firm)
Ib. diseconomies of scale (of the firm)
IIa. external economies of scale (of the industry)
IIb. external diseconomies of scale (of the industry)
IIIa. positive externalities to third parties
IIIb. negative externalities to third parties.

For my purpose here, I focus on type IIIb. Using examples such as sparks from railway engines doing damage to the surrounding woods (Pigou [1952] 2002, 134), or the dense fog covering London throughout much of the year in the early twentieth century because of coal-burning (184), Pigou raised the problem of costs "thrown [by the users of a service or consumers of certain goods] unto people not directly concerned" (134). Because the private product does not factor in the negative externalities, there exists a difference between the private and social net products. The overall societal welfare depends on the size of the social product, and governments can take corrective actions to reduce the effects of negative externalities. The policy option that Pigou favored was the use of "bounties and taxes" (192), in other words, rewards (subsidies) to encourage positive externalities and adverse incentives intended to discourage negative externalities. By raising the costs of production for polluters, for example, a tax may reduce the amount of pollution. Pigou did not rule out the regulatory imposition of specific production targets or other coercive measures, but "bounties and taxes" was his preferred solution. While constraining, it still leaves room for a range of choices on the part of the affected economic agents.

No solution is perfect, and Pigouvian taxes, as they are usually called, have been criticized for a variety of reasons. The Hayekian argument is that state authorities do not have sufficient knowledge to calibrate the tax rate at the level where it will produce exactly the desired result. A more pointed critique came from James Buchanan (1969), who argued that taxes could actually make things worse. Ronald Coase (1960) argued that taxes may not be necessary in the first place. Coase's insight, for which he is justly famous, is that in situations where the activities of one economic agent negatively affect the interests of another, the parties themselves can negotiate a mutually satisfying solution without the intervention of external authorities (be they a regulatory agency, the tax collector, or the courts if a liability regime exists). Rather than formulating a mathematical model, Coase used stories, some of which are inspired by actual court cases. Here are two of them. A physician's office is located near a noisy candy and cake factory. (This is an actual case in British jurisprudence: *Sturges v Bridgman* [1879], in which the plaintiff was Dr. Octavius Sturges and the defendant the well-established confectioner Frederic Bridgman.) The physician could sue the confectioner, and if the court finds the latter liable, he will have to invest in new, less noisy machinery. But the confectioner could, instead, offer to insulate the doctor's office, and both would be better-off (less noise for one, lower cost—as compared to new machines—for the other). The other story goes as follows. A cattle rancher's cows are grazing in a field adjacent to one owned by a farmer who grows lettuces. The *status quo ante* is such that the cattle causes no or negligible damage to the farmer's crop. But the rancher now decides to increase the size of his herd, and more cows will wander off into the farmer's field. If the cattle rancher is held liable, he is obligated to compensate the farmer for the damage caused by his cows. Nevertheless, he might still wish to increase the size of his herd if it is more profitable (i.e., if the marginal benefits exceed the marginal costs) than paying the compensation he owes to the farmer. But the farmer may not wish to continue farming the parcel of land adjacent to the ranch if he is offered a deal from the rancher. That deal is as follows: the rancher offers to pay a rent for the land (which will no longer be cultivated), which is *greater than the net benefit the farmer used to get* from cultivating the land (i.e., sale of the crops minus the corresponding production costs) but costs the rancher less than the net benefit from the sale of the additional meat *after compensating* the farmer. Not only are both individuals better-off, but the economy as a whole is more efficient because the farmer will use his gain to increase his production of a different crop elsewhere; in the end, there will be more meat and at least as much produce being offered for sale.[6]

The principle illustrated by these examples, however, depends on two conditions: (1) property rights are clearly defined, and (2) the transactions are negligible (e.g., no need to hire lawyers). The latter condition is a somewhat exceptional case, as Coase acknowledged. Even though, however Coase having established a benchmark—direct negotiations between the parties—he faulted Pigou for having assumed that government regulation is the opposite default position: "The central tendency in [Pigou's] thought … was that, when defects were found in the working of the economic system, the way to put things right was through some form of government action" (Coase 1988, 20). But Coase was arguably unfair to Pigou, as several authors have pointed out (e.g., Simpson 1996; Hovenkamp 2009). To begin with, Coase was in fact building upon a foundation set up by Pigou. The very notion of transaction cost had already been articulated by Pigou who, however, used the phrase "cost of movement" ([1952] 2002, 158). Admittedly, Pigou was more inclined to assume that these costs are *not* negligible, which is a defensible pragmatic position. Moreover, it is not the case that Pigou dismissed the possibility that the parties could negotiate an arrangement among themselves (Hovenkamp 2009, 639). He was, however, more attentive to the uncertainties that characterize these bargaining opportunities.

I do not wish to dwell any further on this controversy. The point I want to underline, however, is that this can be interpreted as yet another instance of the extent to which economists value the self-correcting properties of free markets. It could be alleged that Coase was reacting somewhat too harshly to what he perceived as a misdirected attempt on Pigou's part to undermine this fundamental axiom even if, all things considered, he casted Pigou as a straw man. Moreover, it has been demonstrated that when the Coase theorem is modeled as a cooperative game, which is plausible, the "core" of the game, that is, the resource allocation to which all parties can agree, remains empty when there are more than two parties involved in bringing externalities to the negotiation table even if the transaction costs are nil (Aivazian and Callen 2003).

Climate change seems also to have vindicated Pigou. He did not think of cases where it would be appropriate to tax consumers rather than producers. But the issue of climate change has created a new wrinkle in the form of the much discussed—and increasingly applied—"carbon tax," which penalizes either both the producers and the consumers, or just the consumers of fossil fuels. This tax is generally supported by economists, including very orthodox, and promarket analysts, because it is less coercive than direct regulation and, therefore, has occasioned a renewal of interest in Pigou's economic theory. (Coase's critique does not apply in this case since the transaction costs of reaching an agreement about carbon emissions among property owners in some, let alone all, nations are prohibitive.) But carbon taxes have been met with fierce political opposition in many jurisdictions (e.g., violent demonstrations by the "gilets jaunes" protesters in France). Economists need to think about perfecting their rhetorical skills if they hope to convince a skeptical public that being environmentally virtuous can also increase the general welfare in the long run.

In brief, Pigou built his theory of welfare economics on orthodox neoclassical foundations, but his policy recommendations were inspired by relatively egalitarian beliefs. His critics were to chip away at this particular combination of positive and normative tenets, as I explain hereafter.

The "Ordinalist Revolution"

While posterity has been rather favorable to Pigou on the subject of externalities, the same cannot be said of his redistributive scheme. Pigou's reliance on Marshall's concept of marginal utility, which he assumed meant roughly the same thing to most people, that is, are "comparable," and, therefore, can be combined to estimate the costs and benefits of changes in the distribution of the national dividend, came under attack in the 1930s.

Pigou extensively used the concept of marginal utility. Even though utilities are subjectively experienced, he assumed they are roughly comparable across all individuals using the "measuring rod of money." Therefore, they can be combined to formulate a criterion for evaluating income support policies:

> It is evident that any transference of income from a relatively rich man to a relatively poor man of similar temperament, since it enables more intense wants to be satisfied at the expense of less intense wants, must increase the aggregate sum of satisfaction. The old "law of diminishing utility" thus leads securely to the proposition: Any cause which increases the absolute share of reel income in the hands of the poor, provided that it does not lead to a contraction in the size of the national dividend from any point of view, will, in general, increase economic welfare.
>
> (Pigou [1952] 2002, 89)

His critics deployed arguments that were purportedly technical but raised serious normative questions. The attack was launched by Lionel Robbins who had no intellectual connection to Cambridge (he taught at the London School of Economics). As he made clear in his *Essay on the Nature and Significance of Economic Science* (1932 and revised in 1935), even if Pigou's welfare economics followed in the footsteps of Marshall's effort to make economics into a science, it still was not sufficiently scientific. What Robbins understood by "scientific" was somewhat inconsistent insofar as his epistemological views were drawn from both the Vienna Circle's logical positivism and Austrian economics (Aslanbeigui 1987), in spite of the fact that the Austrians, and Ludwig von Mises most notably, rejected the Vienna Circle's thesis that all sciences should be closely modeled on the methods of the natural sciences. Robbins drew arguments from both schools of thought as a way to leave absolutely no doubt that Pigou's reliance on cardinal, that is, measurable and, therefore, comparable utilities, was wrong. From positivism, Robbins borrowed the idea that propositions that cannot be empirically verified are meaningless. While those who buy a good prefer it to the money they spend doing so, the intensity of preferences cannot be operationalized: one cannot determine whether a good is preferred *n* times more than another one (just as 20°C is not twice as warm as 10°C). And from Mises, Robbins took the idea that Pigou's welfare economics was not sufficiently subjectivist—that it did not pay sufficient attention to the significance of the *choices* made by individuals. Economics is essentially concerned with the logic of the choice of means that individuals make to achieve their goals, but it precludes the use of empirical tools because using such tools would imply that economic agents' choices depend on their historical/social circumstances instead of being explainable in terms of an *a priori* rational, "economizing" reasoning. Aslanbeigui (1987, 328) sums up Robbins' epistemological position on this point:

> Fundamental postulates of economics are not mere tautologies… . They have an a priori-synthetic character in being "simple" and "indisputable" facts of experience, so much so that "they have only to be stated to be recognized as obvious" (Robbins 1935, 79). These postulates are, however, subjective truths and cannot be verified empirically. "It is really not possible to understand the concepts of choice, of the relation? ship of means and ends, the central concepts of our science, in terms of observation of external data."
>
> (89–90)

Robbins' essay was the manifesto for the so-called ordinalist revolution,[7] out of which the New Welfare economics emerged. Since the concept of preference ordering is central to this paradigm, it is necessary to go over a few technical points. Individual preferences so defined are supposed to have the following characteristics:

- Individuals know how to rank-order all possible combinations of alternatives open to them; if, for example, there are two such alternatives, *a* and *b*, individual *i* will know whether he or she prefers *a* to *b*, or *b* to *a*, or is indifferent between the two; a strict preference excludes the possibility of indifference, but a weak preference leaves room for it.
- Preferences are supposed to be transitive; that is, if individual *i* prefers *a* to *b*, and *b* to *c*, then *i* prefers *a* to *c*.[8]
- Choices are made independently of irrelevant alternatives: if *a* is preferred to *b* in the set $\{a, b\}$, then *a* is still preferred to *b* in the set $\{a, b, c\}$.[9]

These assumptions are not always empirically true. Real flesh-and-blood people do not spend much time evaluating and carefully rank-ordering all the alternatives that are open to them. Sometimes, they do not even know what all the alternatives are. We tend to make routine decisions on the basis of various "rules of thumb" or intuitive guesses.[10] This is why advertisers bombard us with images that are not intended to appeal to our more rational selves. The world being a complex place, it may also be the case that the criteria that a person sees as relevant for choosing *a* over *b* are different from those they may apply to a choice between *b* and *c*, and then between *a* and *c*. In other words, people may respond to a variety of psychological motivations that detract them from making consistently transitive choices. But there may still be a good normative reason why these assumptions *ought* to be true.

In the long run, one may prefer *a* to *b*, then *b* to *c*, but also *c* to a. However, in the short term, this is not a pattern that is likely to improve the welfare of those who follow it. Why? Because a person whose preferences are not transitive can easily be fleeced. This is known as the "money pump" or the "Dutch book" argument. If I exchange *c* (which could be a set of old but newly fashionable vinyl LPs) for *b* and an additional $10 shipping fee, then exchange *b* (which could be a faddish item I'm no longer interested in) for *a* (say a guitar) plus a fee of $10, and then can be persuaded to trade my guitar for the same LPs again plus the same $10 fee (perhaps I'm not as good a guitar player as I thought I was), I'm back where I started from, except that I'm now poorer by $30! It is conceivable that under more complex circumstances, even reasonable individuals could be exploited by traders or auctioneers who gain something from each trade and benefit more if the parties are stuck in intransitive cycles. If the intransitivity of the choices is not immediately apparent, it would take some time for the victims to realize that they have been taken advantage of. Transitivity ought to guide our choices because "intransitivity makes us vulnerable to being used by others in ways that, upon informed and careful reflection, we would not freely accept" (King 2011, 655). This being granted, it is not certain that the same can be said about collective preferences. A group or an entire nation can probably afford to pursue intransitive preferences with relative immunity. But at this point, I cannot explore this issue any further.[11]

Vilfredo Pareto put the concept of preferences at the core of his theoretical economics. He reformulated the concept of equilibrium by dispensing with the more traditional approach in terms of supply and demand, replacing it with an approach based on the use of "indifference curves" (the graphical representation by means of convex curves of how individual preferences over two or more goods yield different combinations of these goods among which an economic agent is indifferent). I do not wish to elaborate on this point (but see Bruni 2009 for more details). I mention this only to provide a context that explains how Pareto came to propose his celebrated concepts of optimality and efficiency. The New Welfare economics rests squarely on the notion of Pareto efficiency or, depending on how it is expressed, Pareto optimality. An improvement is efficient if it makes it possible to move from an allocation of resources *A* to allocation *B* in such a way that at least one person prefers *B* to *A* and nobody prefers *A* to *B*, although some may be indifferent. Pareto optimality *B** is reached when moving away from *B** would make some people worse-off (even if it would make other people better-off). To be more specific, three principles define Pareto efficiency:

1. "*Consumer sovereignty*: the preferences of individuals are autonomous and are respected as such (consequently there are no 'good' or 'bad' preferences)" (Mathis 2009, 32).
2. "*Non-paternalism:* all that matters to society is the utility of individuals; the state does not require any additional consideration as an end in itself" (32).
3. "*Unanimity*: changes of allocation require the consent of all, i.e., everyone has a right of veto" (32).

It is on this foundation that "great castles of theory have been built" (Hicks 1975, 310). The strength of the New Welfare economics owes much to the fact that the Pareto optimum fits well within the conceptual apparatus of the neoclassical theory of economic equilibrium. Two "fundamental theorems of welfare economics" are evidence of this congruence (several economists worked on them independently, but the most general proof was provided by Arrow [1951]). The first is that "every competitive equilibrium is also a Pareto-optimal state" (Ng 1983, 56). When externalities are present, however, as when the cost of environmental pollution is not carried by the polluters, the link between Pareto optimality and competitive equilibrium is weakened.[12] The second theorem states that "every Pareto-optimal state can be sustained as a competitive equilibrium by an appropriate distribution of resource endowments" (56);[13] in other words, policymakers can use social policy to rectify an unfair initial allocation of resources, but once this correction has taken place, the market will bring about a desirable equilibrium on its own without further intervention. (It is important to remember that what economists call "efficiency" refers to preference satisfaction rather than, as is more common in ordinary uses of the term, optimizing the use of one's resources or time, as I explained in Chapter 1.)

Sen (1970; see also Mueller 2003, 643–646) has raised an intriguing question about the implication of the Pareto optimum for the liberal democracies' commitment to the sovereignty of the individual. This is what he calls "the liberal paradox." Is individual liberty compatible with the Pareto optimum? To answer that question, Sen proposes the following thought experiment. Can two individuals, Lewd and Prude, abide by a rule that would apply to both of them collectively regarding who, if anyone, should read D. H. Lawrence's novel *Lady Chatterley's Lover*? There are three possible states of the world: (x) in which Prude reads it; (y) in which Lewd reads it; and (z) in which none of them does. The rule in order to be rational should satisfy three conditions:

- U (Universal domain): *all* possible alternative orderings of individual choices are allowed.
- P (Pareto condition): if *everyone* prefers x to y (just for the sake of our example), then x preferred over y is the *collective* choice of society.
- L (Liberalism): "For each individual i, there is at least one pair of alternatives, say (x, y), such that if this individual prefers x to y, then society should prefer x to y, and if the individual prefers y to x, then society should prefer y to x" (Sen 1970, 153).

Liberalism would seem to require that over certain choices (e.g., reading a novel), any individual's choice should be "decisive," meaning that the collective choice should be that society must not decide otherwise (i.e., denying that individual the right to read the novel). J. S. Mill's apt phrase "experiment in living" is a case in point: even if society disapproves of an individual's intention to live his or her life in a certain way, it should not interfere with that individual's plans. Sen logically demonstrates that when the individual rankings are as follows: Prude (who prefers to be a censor rather than be censored) prefers z to x to y, and Lewd, who thinks that Prude could learn something from reading the novel, prefers y to x to z, then conditions U, P, and L cannot be met simultaneously because they result in a collective choice that is not transitive (x

> $y > z > x$, and so on); in other words, it is irrational. Sen also considers the hypothesis of replacing L by L* in which only some individuals enjoy a given freedom ("There are at least two individuals such that for each of them there is at least one pair of alternatives over which he is decisive, that is, there is a pair of *x, y*, such that if he prefers *x* [respectively *y*] to *y* [respectively *x*], then society should prefer *x* [respectively *y*] to *y* [respectively *x*]"). But he goes on to prove that L* still results in an intransitive cycle.

Some aspects of Sen's paradox have been challenged by Brian Barry (1986), who argues that L is not really what liberalism is all about—the paradox does not really exist. Barry (1995, 135) admits, however, that the existence of illiberal preferences poses a serious problem to utilitarianism: "It is possible to imagine illiberal preferences (e.g., for the suppression of beliefs or actions that are found offensive by a large majority of the population) giving rise to a state of affairs in which it might be that aggregate preference—satisfaction could be secured by illiberal public policies."

Sen's analysis opened the way to a "non-welfarist" or "extra-welfarist" paradigm.[14] It pays more attention to factors other than individual utilities (i.e., income) than welfarist models; these other factors include abstract values, such as rights, but also more concrete aspects of ordinary life, such as being able to take advantage of opportunities. It can be shown that most, and possibly all, non-welfarist methods of policy assessment violate the Pareto principle (Kaplow and Shavell 2001, 2001.[15] This is one reason why many economists are reluctant to adopt the non-welfarist paradigm without reservations.[16] Their reluctance to move beyond utilitarian welfarism, however, leaves most noneconomists perplexed, for, as Serge Kolm (1994, 721) notes, "the economists' advice justified by 'maximizing social welfare' meet the incomprehension of the public who … thinks in terms of interrelated concepts of rights, duties, equalities, merits, needs, global social aims, etc." Before analyzing these contemporary trends, however, I must first explain how New Welfare economics displaced Pigou's theory.

Pareto Optimality and Social Ordering

The old utilitarian paradigm rested on admittedly oversimplifying assumptions, yet it had the advantage of making it rather easy to formulate policy recommendations since it presumed that an aggregate measure of a community's welfare is attainable, at least in principle. The Pareto criterion, upon which the by-now-not-so-new "New Welfare economics" was founded, made it harder to formulate unambiguous societal objectives since there always is a plurality of optima, and unanimity can never be achieved. Moreover, it is a rather vague notion: rather than speaking of an optimum, it is better to think of a "region" in which more efficient solutions to a range of problems defined by multiple constraints reflecting different value judgments can be located (Frisch 1959). But this is not to say that the Pareto optimum is a meaningless concept. It is a useful antidote to technocratic delusions—the tendency of experts to recommend "solutions" to problems that few people recognize as being urgent, which could leave some people unjustifiably worse-off. Urban renewal in past decades provides many examples of such suboptimal "solutions" that end up harming the community, as Jane Jacobs (1961) has memorably documented. The most obvious weakness of the Pareto optimum, however, is that it is not constructed with a view to achieve a *fair* allocation of resources; it is too narrowly confined within a world where self-interest rules[17] (Sen 1987, 52–53). Very privileged individuals could veto a move away from the status quo even though such a change might be very advantageous to people experiencing serious socioeconomic difficulties.

It is possible to move away from an unfair Pareto optimum, by applying the Kaldor–Hicks compensation principle. The idea here (separately proposed by Nicholas Kaldor and John Hicks) is to find equilibria that are theoretically more equitable than available Pareto optima. If Pareto-superiority is defined as a preference relation of a certain kind, whereby $x P y$ if x is strictly preferred to y by at least one individual, while all others only weakly prefer x to y, then the Kaldor criterion is another preference relation defined this time in terms of the capacity of those who benefit from the change to *compensate* the losers. (The alternative proposed by Hicks would be for the potential losers to dissuade [bribe] the potential winners if they still end up better-off.) That is to say, $x K y$ if at least one individual prefers x to y because at x that individual's benefits are still larger than at y, after *subtracting the amount of compensation* he or she owes to the "losers," and everyone else remains indifferent because, after receiving a lump-sum payment, no one is worse-off than before. But this is only a hypothetical model: there is no formal requirement that a payment be made by the winner(s) to the loser(s). Policymakers *may decide* to effect such transfers through the tax system, but welfare economics is silent about whether or not this ought to be the case. In fact, "most studies of efficient policies preclude by assumption the existence of lump-sum taxation" (Correia 1999, 582). If the payments are not actually carried out, economists may try to justify the Kaldor criterion on utilitarian and psychological grounds: (1) since more resources in total are made available at x than at y (i.e., it is not simply a case of Peter robbing Paul), then potentially everyone might benefit indirectly from this increased total wealth (e.g., more investments may be generated resulting in the creation of additional jobs); and (2), psychologically, it could be said that the losers might prefer to live in a society where they may themselves become big winners at some point.

The Kaldor compensation criterion has been criticized on a variety of grounds. For example, Sandra Peart and David Levy (2005) see in this device an example of a broader moral problem that afflicts the whole of the neoclassical school. Ethically, it is a step back, they claim (947), because "unlike the twentieth century version of 'possible' compensation, classical utilitarians employed a compensation principle in which monetary compensation was actually paid." Moreover, even if one accepts the argument in favor of hypothetical compensations, there still remains the issue that changes that disproportionally advantage a small minority of very well-off individuals will meet the compensation criterion (even relatively large compensation payments from few winners concentrated at the top of the income scale will amount to a pittance if the losers are far more numerous).

It also happens that the Kaldor criterion is flawed theoretically. The reason is that it can be shown[18] that it is not transitive; in other words, there is *no* assurance that if $x\ K\ y$ and $y\ K\ z$ then $x\ K\ z$. Tibor Scitovsky (1941) proposed a solution to that problem; his revised criterion—let's call it the Scitovsky criterion S—adds the following condition: in the preceding example, $x\ S\ z$ if $x\ K\ z$ but not $z\ K\ x$. One way to achieve this result is to combine the Kaldor and Hicks criteria (recall that the Hicks criterion selects cases where the losers cannot dissuade the potential winners by bribing them to stay with the status quo). Unfortunately, it has also been shown (Gorman 1955) that the Scitovsky criterion itself is not always transitive. Paul Samuelson (1950) has defined a criterion that escapes all these criticisms, but it is arguably too restrictive.

Fair or not, the Pareto optimum is also a rather ambiguous concept because there could be many such equilibriums to choose from. To illustrate the existence of multiple Pareto optimums, I use the Edgeworth box (see Figure 2.1). Let us imagine a very simplified economy where there are only two individuals, namely Isabella, or *i* for short, and Jim, or *j* for short. In this economy no goods are produced, but let us further assume that goods *X* and *Y* are available in certain quantities. How are *i* and *j* going to allocate these goods by exchanging one for the other so as to reach a Pareto optimum? The lower axis, read from left to right, shows the increasing quantity of good *X* owned by *i*; the vertical axis, on the left, shows from the bottom up the increasing quantity of good *Y* owned by *i*; the upper axis, read from right to left, shows

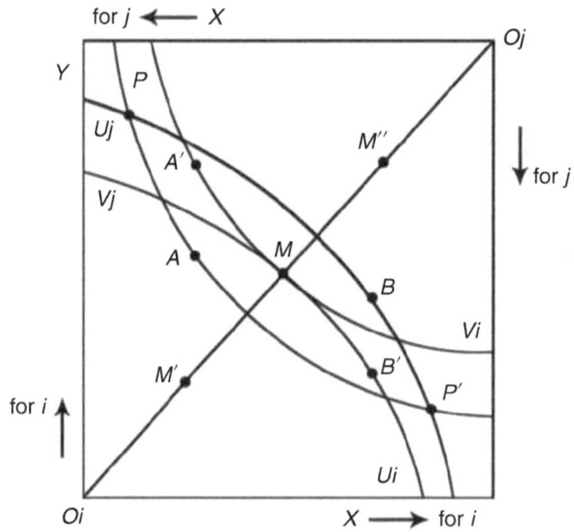

Figure 2.1 The Edgeworth box.

the increasing quantity of good X owned by j; and the vertical axis on the right shows from the top down the increasing quantity of good Y owned by j. The indifference curve U_i represents all the points (including P and P') among which i is indifferent for a given initial allocation of goods X and Y. From Isabella's standpoint, all points located in the convex space northeast of U_i are desirable but beyond her reach if U_i stands for the maximum amount of either X or Y she can get with her initial allocation. Similarly, given Jim's initial allocation, his indifference curve is U_j. If they both start at P, they can move along their respective indifference curves by trading some of their *X*s for some *Y*s and vice versa. They could respectively end up at A and B. Every point in the space delineated by the two curves intersecting in P and P' would be a Pareto improvement over A or B. Now let us assume that for some reason more of goods X and Y become available to both Isabella and Jim, allowing them to use up the amounts corresponding to the curves V_i and V_j. Is there a point on these curves that would be equally satisfactory to *both* of them? It is obviously not B' or A': B' is satisfactory for i but not for j who could use more of Y with the same amount of X; and A' would be satisfactory for j but not for i who could use more of X with the same amount of Y. The only point that would be equally satisfactory to both and from which it would not be possible to move without one of them ending up worse-off is M. But this is only for one specific allocation of total resources. There are potentially many more distributions, some of which would be more advantageous to Isabella, and some to Jim. In the end, all the Pareto optimums compatible with the particular productive mechanism that resulted in the total amount of goods to be shared in this (over)simplified economy would be aligned along the line that goes through O^i, M', M, M'', O^j (it is usually called the "contact curve," but some authors [e.g., Feldman and Serrano 2006, 38] call it the "core"). Thus, there are a multiplicity of Pareto optimums.

Using different axes, the contact curve can be represented as in Figure 2.2, which is now called a "Utility Possibilities Frontier" (UPF). Points southwest of the UPF are found unsatisfactory by the agents, while points northeast of it are beyond their reach. The simplified economy modeled by the Edgeworth box does not take production into account. It is clear that many different such boxes can be created depending on the amounts and types of resources produced and made available to the agents; in other words, several UPFs can be traced, as in Figure 2.3. In order now to evaluate the overall potentials of this (still very simplified) two-agent economic system, we have to trace the tangents to all these UPFs; this new frontier is called the "Grand Utility Possibility Frontier" (GUPF) (e.g., Furubotn 1971, 409–410). Evidently, all the points on the GUPF are Pareto optimums.

Given that there are many Pareto optimums, two questions arise: (1) can policymakers reasonably choose among the options, if by "reasonably" we mean publicly defensible; and (2) if "publicly defensible" means not only consistent with societal norms but actually in line with priorities supported by a majority, can such priorities be democratically established? The answers that

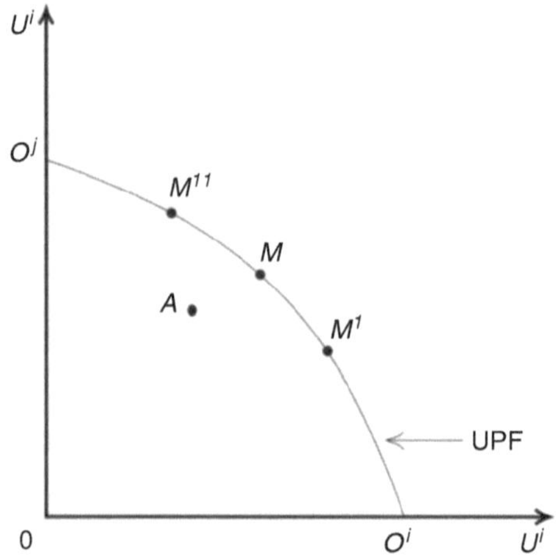

Figure 2.2 The possibility frontier (contact curve).

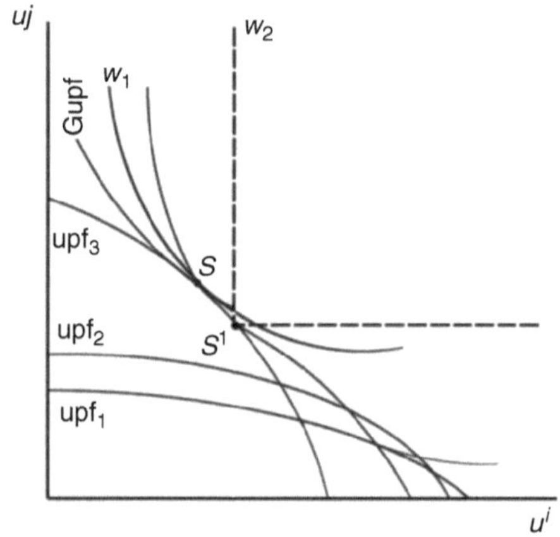

Figure 2.3 The Bergson–Samuelson social welfare function.

economists give to these questions is: possibly yes, to the first, but the second question elicits a more pessimistic response. When choosing among more than two options, democratic procedures can fail to convert individual preferences into nonparadoxical collective preferences. I elaborate on the latter issue in the next section. Let me for now deal with the first.

Assuming that some allocations on the GUPF match generally acceptable social norms, while other do not—for example, we may assume that it is not socially acceptable for one agent to accumulate all the resources even if he or she could—the question becomes: which allocation is socially desirable? Now it is important to stress that we are no longer dealing with the two-person model described above but with a generalization of this particular case. It is theoretically feasible to define a social welfare function (SWF) W such that $W = U(U^1, U^2, \ldots, U^h)$.[19]

In other words, there exists a function W that combines the utilities of all agents $\{1, 2, \ldots, h\}$. The variables that enter into that function, such as the utilities U^i and U^j, must be interpersonally comparable, which means that these values are not merely ordinal but satisfy the requirement that their marginal rate of substitution remains equal: $(\delta W/\delta U^i)/(\delta W/\delta U^j)$ is a constant.[20]

The shape of W will vary depending on the values that the member of society applies (or are assumed to apply) to the choices they make. In other words, economists can model the implications of different norms. For example, if $W = \prod_{h=1}^{H} (U^h) \alpha^h$, where h varies from 1 to H, α^h are the weights attached to each household (the symbol $\prod$ meaning the product of all terms to which it applies), the recommended optimum would be point S in Figure 2.3; this is known as the "Bernoulli–Nash" SWF. If, however, we apply the Rawlsian maximin criterion (i.e., maximizing the utility of the least advantaged members of society), then we would have W_2 that cuts the GUPF at point S' in Figure 2.3.

The previously discussed method used to model a two-agent economy can be applied to a larger community: the problem is to maximize a given SWF that includes the chosen norm of justice, subject to constraints such as what is known about the distribution of individual preferences, the availability of factors of production, and so on.[21] The idea is that once a normative principle has been adopted, it is not theoretically impossible to locate a corresponding Pareto optimum. But, as Eirik Furubotn (1971, 412) notes, "Whether one approves or disapproves of [the] special ethical judgment [implied by the shape of the welfare curve], there can be no doubt about the fact that a value bias is present. When market capitalism is the organizational means used to conduct economic activity, the resulting welfare distribution will normally be shaped by the 'windfall ethic.'" That is to say, those who benefit from exogenously generated technological advances deserve the (more or less large and unexpected) gains they obtain.

What could be the relevance of an SWF to policymakers? The Bergson–Samuelson SWF can be used to model the implications, for example, of their electoral promises. As Bergson (1954, 233) posed the problem, this "criterion must be given by some rule of collective decision-making, according to which the values of different members of the community on alternative social states are aggregated." Note that the value judgments implied here need not be restricted to the old welfare economics' utilitarian ethics (McCain 2019, 77). The welfare function then becomes (Rosefielde and Pfouts 2015, 153): $W = F(U_1, U_2 \ldots U_n; x, y, z)$. In this equation, U_1 is the utility of individual 1 among n; the variables x, y, and z stand for the social values ("relational determinants of utility") considered to be the most relevant to the policy issue at stake; and F

is "a value forming function aggregating individual utilities generated directly from consumption and indirectly from the relational variables." It is obvious, however, that one quickly runs into all sorts of problems in trying to find practical applications for this very abstract formula.[22]

Kenneth Arrow ([1951] 1963) threw a huge stone in the pond of welfare economics, and the ripples are still being felt. Arrow's so-called impossibility theorem[23] rules out the possibility of *democratically* identifying the relational variables (such as x above) that policymakers could use to formulate a socially acceptable W. Arrow proved that if certain conditions that he presents as eminently reasonable in a democracy are met, then there is no way to reach a transitive (noncycling) collective decision aggregating all preferences over more than two options without violating at least one of these conditions. They are:

- Unrestricted (or Universal) Domain (U): the SWF "is defined for every admissible individual pair of individual orderings"; in other words, voters are not *a priori* restricted in the choices they can make, even though some preference orderings could be considered improbable.
- The Pareto Property (P): if all individuals in society share the same preference profile (e.g., $a \succ b \succ c$), then the collective preference is identical (i.e., $a \succ b \succ c$).
- Independence of Irrelevant Alternatives (I): as previously explained, if a is preferred to b in a set of three options $\{a, b, c\}$, the addition of one (or more) options, for example, d, to that set, which now becomes $\{a, b, c, d\}$, does not change the fact that a is preferred to b. (This does not mean that if a was the first choice in the set $\{a, b, c\}$, it remains necessarily the first choice in the set $\{a, b, c, d\}$, but it does mean that the *relative* ordering of a and b remains the same: if I prefer chocolate to vanilla ice cream, and vanilla to butterscotch when these are my only three choices, I *still* prefer chocolate to vanilla when I can choose among four flavors, although this time I might prefer pistachio to chocolate.)
- No dictatorship (ND): No individual's preferences are "decisive" over the preferences of all other individuals; in other words, no one can impose his or her preferences on all other members of society.

The Arrovian objection obviously raises serious doubts about the relevance of welfare economics since it no longer seems permissible to claim that its methods can assist policymakers in identifying the most efficient ways of implementing democratically established priorities. Not surprisingly, many critics have sought to find ways around Arrow's theorem. One of the first was Bergson himself, who observed peremptorily that "Arrow's theorem is unrelated to welfare economics" (1954, 240), the reason being that what welfare economics is concerned with is giving advice to public officials about the consequences of implementing social policies derived from certain value choices (which public officials might happen to hold dear). As Herrade Igersheim (2019, 840), quoting from an interview Samuelson gave in 1993, explains, "Samuelson was even clearer on this point: 'understand that every Bergson–Samuelson SWF is "imposed" in the same sense that this is implied by all ethical systems.'" Arrow, by contrast, was concerned with the problem—or impossibility—of arriving at a procedure that would *adequately* reflect the values of a majority of the members of society. In fact, Samuelson and Arrow debated this difference in their respective definitions of an SWF throughout much of their lives in family gatherings (one of Arrow's sister married one of Samuelson's brothers). But even if Samuelson was right that Arrow's attempt to undermine the concept of SWF was missing its target, the effect in the scholarly literature was rather devastating: it nearly succeeded in convincing most scholars more or less vaguely knowledgeable about welfare economics that this approach had reached a dead end.

The aforementioned conditions that Arrow assumed must be met in a democracy seem *a priori* reasonable, but upon further analysis, there could be plausible reasons for relaxing some of them. There is a vast literature about how some of the exaggeratedly restrictive conditions Arrow places on collective decision-making procedures in the name of rationality can be relaxed (see Mackie 2003). But the most far-reaching and effective way of relativizing Arrow's doubts about the rationality of collective decision-making procedures has been advanced by Amartya Sen (1995), who challenged Arrow's acceptance of the dogmatic assertion that interpersonal comparisons of utility (ICUs) are not permissible.[24] Once that restriction is lifted, collective decision-making procedures no longer run the risk of being irrational. And, indeed, a growing number of economists and philosophers are questioning the premise of the ordinalist revolution. Stavros A. Drakopoulos (1989) helpfully distinguishes three groups in that debate. The first—the "positivists"—categorically oppose the view that ICUs are permissible; for them, such comparisons can only be based on nonscientific value judgments and, therefore, have no place in the science of economics. The second group includes theorists who concede that ICUs are not, properly speaking, scientific but recognize that they are unavoidable for designing any kind of social policy and, therefore, are pragmatically justifiable. The third group is prepared to accept that ICUs are not necessarily unscientific if suitable qualifications are introduced. Since Robbins published his *Essay*, the ranks of the last two groups have slowly increased, even though those who still defend the positivist thesis constitute a sizable contingent. Robbins (1938) himself joined the second group later in his career. To this typology, I would add another category: those who side with Donald Davidson's (1986) credible, but controverted, thesis that the interpretation of rationality that underlies the concept of preference orderings itself presupposes interpersonal comparisons.[25] Once we allow for some degree of interpersonal comparisons, both the New Welfare economics and Arrow's theorem beg for new interpretations. An even more fundamental challenge targets the very notion of welfare by arguing that human well-being and flourishing cannot be reduced to utilitarian conceptions of welfare improvements. I turn to these objections in the next two sections.

Has the Ordinalist Revolution Run Its Course?

For didactic purposes, it is useful to contrast two opposites: the classical utilitarian view that everyone experiences pain and pleasure in roughly comparable ways, making it possible to measure and compare utilities; and the preference-based approach typical of the New Welfare economics, according to which preferences can be rank-ordered but do not correspond to measurable and comparable utilities. In the latter case, the *only* admissible distribution is the one that meets the Pareto criterion. There are, however, many plausible intermediary positions between these polar opposites, which are not necessarily rendered irrelevant by Arrow's impossibility theorem. This all hinges on whether ICUs are workable in at least some circumstances. From here on, I assume that this is the case; returning to the typology proposed by Drakopoulos (1989), I lean toward the last two groups, which I would rename as the pragmatists and the resolute antipositivists.

It is difficult to imagine that there could ever be complete agreement across all individuals and groups on what matters in all societal contexts and in allocating resources accordingly. However, working toward a *legitimate* distribution (*not* limited to reaching Pareto optima) necessitates the identification of agreed-upon benefits. Whether one prefers more income or more leisure, more green space or more urban chaos is, indeed, a matter of personal taste, but addressing injustices in, for example, the allocation of clean and safe parks or recreational areas implies a minimum agreement on what counts as "too little" or "too costly." Note that in this instance we would be comparing *levels* of utility. But there is another sort of comparison that is equally problematic, namely, those involving *incremental* differences: do different people derive the same welfare improvement from a similar increase in their utility levels? Not all theorists who accept the validity of interpersonal comparisons argue that both types of comparisons are important or permissible (Harsanyi 2008, 529–530). This and other challenges explain why interpersonal comparability represents "a notoriously intractable issue" (Elster and Roemer 1991, 1). Pigou was arguably too naïve about it, but welfare economics or, for that matter, any discussion of the ways of balancing individual choices and Pareto efficiency with normative considerations runs into this obstacle. Upon further analysis, the availability of information about how people make choices lies at the root of the problem. Purely abstract conceptual exercises, such as the proofs of the two fundamental theorems of welfare economics, can be pursued without invoking interpersonal comparisons, but practical applications require them. The problem, however, is that relevant information may be lacking. Purists fear that to go around that obstacle, political economists tend to rely on unsubstantiated subjective assumptions that undermine the "scientific" character of economic analysis. I look at a few ways of addressing that challenge, without claiming that there exists a single answer that fully reconciles the imperative of respecting individual preferences (i.e., the nondictatorship principle) and the need to design justifiable policies for remedying unfair allocations of resources.

It is one thing to criticize the dubious assumption that economists know precisely, and in every case, how economic agents value changes affecting their welfare, and it is another thing to claim that it is impossible to find out something about their overall priorities, the direction of these changes, and so on. Political economists should not forget Smith's lesson in the *Theory of Moral Sentiments*: human beings share an ability to express and develop a sense of situational "propriety." From that angle, it should be clear that people can remain rational while also imagining what other people think or feel in many situations, albeit not in all circumstances, and not with absolute certainty. Of course, we sometimes encounter personal idiosyncrasies, cultural and ideological differences that make it difficult to reach a universally shared understanding of what is at stake when deciding how to allocate resources. But (1) there are ethical clues and psychological dispositions that allow us to converge toward a common opinion on at least some crucial issues (e.g., disaster relief, public health); and (2) where there is disagreement, deliberation and efforts to achieve more transparency about the relevant data can go a long way toward removing some of the remaining obstacles. My first point is strongly argued by John Harsanyi (1955, 1977, 48–83) and reinforced by more recent discoveries in evolutionary psychology and behavioral economics (Binmore 2005, 2009). By definition, moral judgments must be impartial. As John Harsanyi (1977, 49) puts it, if an individual *i* wants to make a moral value judgment about the merits of alternative social situations *A*, *B*, *C*, and so on, he must make a serious attempt not to assess these social situations in terms of his own personal preferences and personal interests, but rather in terms of some impersonal and impartial criteria. There are several ways of formulating such criteria for the purpose of ranking social arrangements, institutions, policies, and so on. Harsanyi (1977, 50) recommends an averaging procedure: "[in our model,] individual *i* would evaluate each social situation *A* in terms of the *average* utility level the *n* individual members would enjoy in that situation." Even if one wishes to use some other criterion (e.g., prioritizing those who are worse-off), interpersonal comparisons must enter into the expression of that criterion. The mechanism proposed by Harsanyi to carry out that operation is consistent with the classical political economy standpoint, the merits of which I have previously stressed: moral judgments are more feasibly made when they are not expected to be grounded in abstract *a priori* rules, but when they utilize our ability to imagine what other people experience and desire. Harsanyi (51) suggests using "imaginative empathy":

> Our model is based on the assumption that, in order to construct his social function W_i, each individual *i* will try to assess the utilities $U_j(A)$ of any *other* individual *j* would derive from alternative situation *A* and try to compare these with the utilities $U_i(A)$ that he *himself* would revive from these (or from other) social situations. That is, he will try to make *interpersonal utility comparisons*. Moreover, we have assumed that *i* will attempt to assess these utilities $U_i(A)$ by some process of *imaginative empathy*, i.e., by imagining himself to be *put in the place* of individual *j* in situation *A*.

There still remains the problem of moving from *individual* welfare functions (which include interpersonal comparisons, as described above by Harsanyi) to a *collective/societal* welfare function. Only the latter can guide policymakers in framing regulatory, taxation, or redistributive policies. Aggregation of individual preferences is not an easy problem to solve. We can assume that Arrow's impossibility theorem is not a serious obstacle here because interpersonal comparisons are allowed,[26] but Harsanyi (1977, 51) himself stipulates the following conditions that should ideally be met:

1. All individuals *i* have full information about the [expected] utility functions of all individuals *j* making up the society.
2. All individuals *i* agree on how to make interpersonal comparisons among different members *j* of society.
3. All individuals *i* agree on which particular individuals *j* are "members of society."

Of course, a perfect consensus can never be achieved, and it seems unrealistic to expect that all these conditions are fully met most of the time. For example, the current resurgence of xenophobic populism in many countries creates new obstacles to the realization of the third condition, since these movements oppose the more liberal, and until recently unquestioned, premise that immigrants, refugees, and possibly even undocumented migrants should have access to social programs. When there is disagreement in such issues and when, therefore, bargaining over institutional rules, the distribution of positions of authority, material resources, and so on, economists are prone to recommend using the instruments provided by game theory. How to analyze conflicts through the lenses of game theory is indeed question that Harsanyi (1977) clearly addressed. Harsanyi (83) notes, however, that interpersonal comparisons are usually not admissible in game theoretic models. But he argues that, in practice, they are often used in combination with the purely analytical results provided by game theoretic models.

Another economist who has devoted a great deal of attention to social bargaining is Ken Binmore (1994, 1998, 2005); nothing less than the negotiation of a new social contract is at stake for him. The most appropriate tool for that purpose, Binmore claims, is game theory. He, too, argues that the skepticism evidenced by prior generations of economists toward the use of interpersonal comparisons was ill-founded. Recent advances in evolutionary game theory and behavioral economics have undermined the reasons for this skepticism. Consensus about values and distributive programs can never be complete. However, conflicts can be handled within the framework of a social contract, which can hypothetically include both actual institutions and/or informal rules and more informal rules. Game theory can illuminate the process of updating these frameworks. Binmore (2005, chapter 12) suggests that it is best to proceed on a smaller scale in a decentralized manner rather than through top-down, paternalistic, and bureaucratic channels. Pilot studies, for example, can provide avenues for testing new ideas—indeed, there have been many pilot studies of the feasibility of a basic income that have been conducted in several jurisdictions, including Canada, Finland, Israel, or the US (although they yielded encouraging results, they were not regarded as sufficiently convincing to justify full implementation of the scheme). Bargaining over changes to established societal rules and norms will inevitably lead to a questioning of narrowly constructed notions of "welfare."

Beyond the Efficiency–Equity Trade-Off?

Mainstream welfare economics addressed the following questions: What constitutes a maximally efficient equilibrium given a chosen degree of equity, or what constitutes an equitable distribution of the wealth generated by an efficient economy? But this narrow way of framing the efficiency–equity dilemma has been challenged by economists and philosophers intent on moving beyond the parameters of this debate. The previous section has already prepared the ground, but here I want to engage in a more far-reaching exploration of emerging "non-welfarist approaches." Hereafter, I briefly summarize the efficiency–equity dilemma before moving on to a discussion of non-welfarist approaches.

Economic efficiency is and ought to remain a crucial consideration in policymaking. Before embarking on a course of action that could threaten the general welfare of society, one has to pause. Increasing inequality in order to achieve a higher rate of economic growth and greater average living standards may not always be an unreasonable trade-off. But most people would agree that there are limits to how far this argument can be pushed, and it is widely recognized that these limits have been reached. Efficiency, in other words, is a very relative value. Giuseppe Dari-Mattiacci and Nuno Garoupa (2008) do not deny that economic efficiency is an important criterion, nor do they challenge the idea that one must sometimes choose between efficiency and equity. But they claim that adhering to the Pareto principle in all circumstances makes it impossible to rank all available policy options.

> For example, under certain conditions the welfarist method may be unable to assess non-trivial policies, such as education or freedom of religion ... which require the aggregation of individual preferences over a social welfare function. The reason is that, when individuals have preferences over a certain social welfare function, the problem becomes recursive and may admit no solution or an infinite number of solutions.
>
> (117)

Pareto optimality fails the test of completeness, in other words. This is because individual preferences are dependent on aggregated preferences and vice versa; education, for example, influences the future preferences of individuals, who, in turn, acquire preferences for certain education policies. To break this circle, policymakers will inevitably have to rely on criteria other than individuals' preferences. Julian Legrand (1990) has advanced a more pointed criticism. He argues that efficiency is simply not something that can be "traded off" for something else, like equity. That is because efficiency is measured with respect to the achievement of a given objective, such as maximizing economic growth. But efficiency in itself cannot be a primary objective.

A burgeoning literature on "social capital" also suggests that efficiency and equity are not always inimical values. Social capital refers to the existence and availability of social networks through which individual members acquire and exchange goods or services (in the form of gifts, for example) as well as, more importantly, information; develop social and political skills; enter into more or less durable relations of reciprocal interaction; and internalize norms of appropriate conduct. (Social capital can be studied at the micro level, e.g., neighborhoods, or the macro level, e.g., regions or countries; whether such different perspectives are complementary, however, is not always clear.)

As Jane Friesen (2003, 183) notes:

> Social interactions that do not have an explicit economic purpose may affect economic productivity… . Face-to-face social contract produces and supports basic social norms that are economically important… . Supportive social relations may improve psychological and emotional health, which in turn affects productivity.

Friesen further explains that the literature that deals with such phenomena roughly falls into one of two categories: studies on community social interactions, and studies of the impact of education. Social norms, like trust[27] and reciprocity, facilitate social interactions contribute to economic prosperity while, at the same time, they dampen the effect externalities that often result in inequitable situations. There is much empirical evidence to support this point (see Dayton-Jonson 2001). Prosperous countries like Norway, Sweden, or Canada are characterized by measures of trust and social cooperation that are markedly higher than in less prosperous countries like Romania, Turkey, or Brazil.[28] Significant differences may also exist across cities in the same country.[29] And yet, some authors (e.g., Putnam 2000, 2002) are worried about what they perceive as a gradual erosion of social capital in the US and other countries, which could be due to a constellation of factors, including technology; indeed, since Putnam wrote his often-cited works, social media have contributed to transform person-to-person interactions into virtual ones with consequences that are nowadays generally recognized to be negative. It has become almost trite to observe that users of social media end up trapped in "bubbles" where they are only exposed to the opinions of like-minded individuals, thanks to the filtering of information performed by the algorithms built into the social media platforms they use.

The very same cohesive and homogeneous communities where trust and reciprocity are common occurrences are also the kind of communities that tend to show intolerance toward other groups. These negative dispositions often prove to be economically disadvantageous and can cause serious harm to the ideal of a just society. Education can play a significant role in mitigating these dysfunctional tendencies by increasing the degree of acceptance of cultural differences. Urbanization has also produced a rich diversity of cultural practices and the degree of cultural "métissage" that can be observed in such places (e.g., New York, Los Angeles, Toronto, London, Paris, Berlin, Singapore). But in more rural areas, these trends have given rise to various forms of nativist reactions, partly because the social capital people have built in more traditional settings appears to be less valued in a globalized world.

To sum up, the concept of social capital captures some important aspects of the socioeconomic nexus, but it is fraught with theoretical paradoxes and hence difficult to deploy empirically. My point is not that social capital is an irremediably flawed idea. It is rather that it must be used in conjunction with other concepts and with due care being paid to the political context in which social capital is generated and applied. The nature of social capital changes over time, and new arrangements must be renegotiated. Civil society organizations have a crucial role to play in this regard, but their strategies need to be coordinated at the political level. For example, environmental groups may be pushing for initiatives that are likely to enhance the social capital of the residents of dense urban centers (e.g., discouraging the use of cars, encouraging more pedestrian traffic, supporting local shops), but these could in turn negatively affect the residents of a semirural periphery. Reconciling these impacts is a challenge for "good governance."

(Economists in) the Pursuit of Happiness

With its narrow focus on preference satisfaction, welfare economics can only offer incomplete analyses of the socioeconomic problems that form the overall context within which economic inequalities emerge. As Yew-Kwang Ng (2004, 257) claims, it "should be expanded to make the analysis more complete, and hence more useful." This call has been answered to a large extent. As Andrew Clark (2018, 245) observes:

> Much has changed in Economics over the past 40 years. One such notable change… has been the remarkable rise in the interest shown in by economists in subjective variables in general and in particular measures of subjective well-being.

I argue hereafter that this could be a very beneficial move assuming, however, that some thorny methodological problems can be solved. Noneconomists, of course, have always understood welfare in a broader sense and often prefer the term "well-being":

> Well-being is not used [by social theorists] in the sense understood by welfare economists. It is not a question of preferences, manifested by the way

> in which individuals indicate their "choices" in their market behaviour. Well-being is a much fuller account of embodied, material life.
>
> (Gearey 2012, 14)

A growing number of economists are moving in that direction, finding some common ground with social theorists and philosophers. Non-welfarist theories are diverse and appeal to a broad range of norms, values, and intellectual traditions The field is very vast and branches into many directions, some of which are fascinating, such as analyses of the interface between religion and economics (e.g., on catholic personalism, see O'Boyle 1998; on Buddhism, see Kolm 1994), but which I will not explore here. What follows is not a comprehensive discussion of "non-welfarism" but a brief overview of the currently very topical research on happiness as a way to underline the limitations of the previous discussion of welfare economics in the contemporary context.

The concept of well-being is not as rhetorically evocative as that of "happiness." Deploying that term immediately suggests a bolder departure from the welfare economics of yesterday. Beginning in the 1990s, economists intent on rejuvenating the tradition have proposed to use happiness as a new anchoring point. Perhaps the most vocal advocate of this move is Bruno S. Frey (2008; Frey and Stutzer 2001, 2013), but he is certainly not alone in defending this position (see also Layard 2005; Ng 1997, 2004; Di Tella et al 2003; Graham 2011). The point of this still-growing literature is that policymakers should design policies that enhance the happiness of their citizens, and not just maximize the kind of preference satisfaction that is assumed to be facilitated by the purchase of private goods and services that can be bought and owned by individuals acting separately. Thus, among other implications of a shift toward happiness economics, public goods (health, education, recreational facilities, etc.) should receive more attention because they often contribute to enhancing the levels of happiness in a community. This does not mean that the new perspective should be any less empirical; in fact, the economics of happiness already is an empirical approach, which makes use of a vast amount of data from surveys about life satisfaction conducted in many countries (see, for example, the *World Happiness Report*, which has been published yearly since 2012). Considering the difficulty of measuring "utility," the new approach is arguably *more* empirical than mainstream welfare economics. It is also more holistic since the life satisfaction surveys tap into many dimensions of ordinary life. Thus, they open avenues for collaboration between economists and other social scientists. Happiness studies rely heavily on concept, theories, and empirical instruments borrowed from psychology.[30] Economists and other social scientists who are favorably disposed to interdisciplinary topics find it stimulating. Specialists who are less at ease with this type of research are more reluctant to change their research priorities. Be it as it may, economists have made decisive contribution to the study of happiness, and there is a new field of "happiness economics" (Frey and Stutzer 2001; Bruni and Porta 2007; Dutt and Radcliff 2009; Bruni et al. 2021). What are the most salient questions and worthwhile findings? Let us start with the so-called Easterlin paradox.

The paradox in question was first proposed by Richard Easterlin (1974), but was largely ignored or treated merely as a curiosity for decades. It has become by now, however, a subject of much attention and a catalyst for the progress of the economics of happiness. The paradox consists in observing that, at least in the US (and I return to this proviso later), the reported level of life satisfaction has remained more or less constant through long periods of economic growth. In other words, as people's living standards improve, they do not feel much happier as a result. This is a paradox for two reasons: (1) with respect to economic theory, it has always been assumed that preference satisfaction is rendered possible by increasing incomes: economic agents are motivated by the prospect of being able to acquire more of the goods they desire; and (2) empirically we know from surveys that people with higher incomes in every country are generally more satisfied with their living conditions than poorer individuals, and the same is true for countries: happiness levels generally trend upward when comparing countries with low GDP per capita to counties with higher GDP per capita. Interestingly, however, both the interpersonal and cross-country curves flatten at the top: as individuals or countries become more affluent, the level of satisfaction begins to vary less significantly.

There are several explanations for the Easterlin paradox. The first is a process of adaptation. The satisfaction one derives from a pay raise decreases as one gets accustomed to what can be done with the additional income. Becoming able to, say, buy a second car may be exciting at the moment, but over time the novelty wears off.[31] Most people do not dwell on their life trajectories; they feel happy or unhappy with respect to the conditions they are familiar with, and even if these are much better than where they started from, this does not change the fact that there is always something else to aspire to. It could also be that increased wealth creates its own happiness-reducing countereffects: now that every household has a second car, traffic gets worse, pollution increases, and so on. In the case of the US, relatively fast growth has been achieved through increased time spent on work. Not having the free time to enjoy their rising incomes, Americans may not report higher levels of happiness. Indeed, the Easterlin paradox does not seem to be universally valid. It seems to hold for the US and even more spectacularly for Japan where during the postwar decades, economic growth was very rapid but without causing a significant change in the levels of life satisfaction. But it has been reported that "the medium term variant of the [Easterlin] paradox … is rejected for Greece, Ireland, Italy, Spain, Bulgaria, Lithuania and Poland" (Kaiser and Vendrik 2019, 27; see also Frey and Stutzer 2013, 435). France is another country where growth has been positively correlated with increased happiness. And here a plausible explanation is the direction of change in working hours. In the US, working hours have increased alongside rising incomes but with flat levels of satisfaction. By contrast, in France where increased productivity has made possible a reduction in the time spent at work, growth has been accompanied by an *increase* in the reported level of life satisfaction. (To compensate for the longer working hours, the GDP per capita would have had to increase significantly more than it actually did [Di Tella and MacCullogh 2008, 35–36]).[32]

Moreover, as was already argued by Thorstein Veblen ([1899] 2007), people evaluate their living conditions by comparing with those of others. If most of my peers are also better-off as a result of economic growth, I feel no improvement in my own status even though, objectively, my situation might have improved. Well-to-do individuals who acquired expensive laptops decades ago might have experienced a jolt from being the first ones, but as nearly everyone owns a laptop today, one does not feel much better-off owning one. Worse still, if someone seems to move up much faster than I could, my happiness may decrease. I use the conditional tense here because even though person-to-person comparisons influence happiness and other significant societal processes everywhere and have done so since the dawn of humanity,[33] the impact of these comparisons is mediated by cultural differences. In many countries, subjects responding to surveys indicate that they feel negatively about large income inequalities, and this affects their perceived happiness. But in the US, the cultural influence of the "American dream" myth tends to counteract this tendency: insofar as Americans strongly value the prospect of getting rich themselves, unrealistic as it may be, they do not respond as negatively to income inequalities (Tachibanaki and Sakoda 2016, 115). This is not to say, however, that the consequences of immense gaps in wealth and access to political power are equanimously accepted by all Americans.

Many other interesting findings relevant to the topic of this book can be gleaned from the economics of happiness literature, but space lacks to examine them all. I want to focus on two issues. The first is the impact of gender on happiness. This question is receiving an increasing amount of attention, but it is difficult to summarize the findings. Depending on the measuring instruments used and depending on the particular aspects of life under consideration (health, employment, age, etc.), the gender-based differences in reported satisfaction vary in different directions (Clark 2018, 248). Another important question concerns the direction of causality. The initial focus on the Easterlin paradox led researchers to design studies examining the determinants of happiness (income, employment, life trajectories, etc.). But policymakers might also be keen to know whether happiness levels affect growth and efficiency. There is some evidence that happier individuals are more productive, build more social capital, and so on (Pikalkiewicz 2017). Thus, the feedback loop between efficiency and equity is not always a negative one, as is often assumed in classical welfare economics, but can also be positive (self-reinforcing). Indeed, the challenge for policymakers is to bring about these sorts of "virtuous circles":

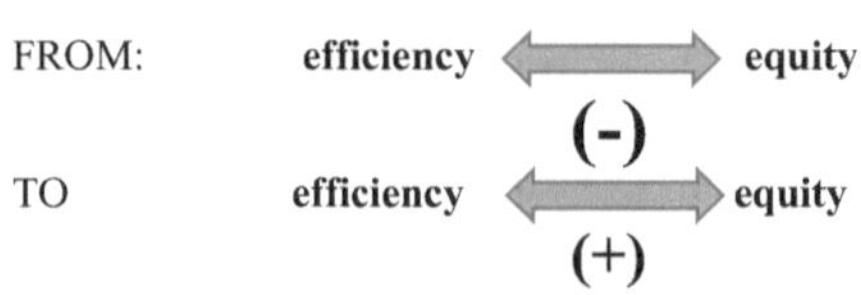

Critics of the economics of happiness (e.g., Johns and Ormerod 2007) have raised objections that deserve to be addressed. I consider two such objections: a methodological one and a normative one. The first concerns the difficulties attendant to the measurement of happiness a well as the interpretation of the significance of the available data. (I leave aside the philosophical question of whether it makes sense in the first place to measure such a thing as happiness, noting simply in passing that this point should be dealt with pragmatically: some aspects of happiness are ineffable, but data about life satisfaction in the general public is meaningful not only for democratic debates but also for political philosophers who wish to check the extent to which their ideas of the good are realistic.) Are the survey instruments sophisticated enough to capture all the nuances of public opinion? The answer is that they are continually being perfected and that some of the limitations of outdated instruments have been corrected. The scientific community (social psychologists, statisticians, economists, etc.) has of late devoted much attention to these methodological questions. But there is arguably a difficulty that remains unsolved, namely, the problem of tracking the evolution of perception over time: if a respondent locates him/herself at the top of the scale in answering a survey question at time t_1 and then again at time t_2, it is not possible to know whether, in fact, the same respondent (or possibly even any representative agent) is or is not *more* satisfied at time t_2. That is, in stating that I am happy or despondent at a given time, I cannot anticipate how much happier or more despondent I might become, but the scale itself remains the same. This could be a problem in analyzing long-term trends and might account in some (albeit probably small) measure for not only the Easterlin paradox but also the fact that happiness levels do not seem to be correlated very strongly with other upward-moving trends such as life longevity.

The second critique concerns the potential for abuse of this sort of information. If one is skeptical about the need for government intervention in the economy and suspects that the more governments try to improve collective welfare, the more they run into the risk of causing "government failures" when correcting market failures, then potentially the economics of happiness is a temptation to take one more step in the wrong direction. At the very least, attempting to improve life satisfaction scores could justify unduly paternalistic measures and, at the very worst, become a pretext for Orwellian authoritarianism. Is this even a risk? It must be conceded that the terms well-being or happiness have become more central to political discourse in most democratic countries in recent decades, and bureaucratic instruments have been adapted to respond to this new reality. The UK government seems to have taken the lead in that respect; it launched a Measuring National Well-being Program within the Office for National Statistics in 2010 and continues to issue a stream of reports on this topic. Similar developments have been observed in the EU and Canada (Sanmartin et al. 2021), to name only some examples. But while, in the early twenty-first century, a rhetorical move in the direction of a politics of happiness emerged alongside the economics of happiness (to be arguably snuffed by the doom and gloom of the early 2020s), practical policy innovations beyond initiatives in statistical accounting have lagged, with the exception of health policy. Well-being is a central theme in health policy. Some critics (Dalingwater 2019) have argued that this is a manifestation of a "neoliberal" shift from collective responsibility to individual responsibility. The recent pandemic has shown, however, that governments can still prioritize public health when needed. In fact, to come back to my earlier comment about the Orwellian undertones of the economics of happiness, the rather widespread populist revolt against government mandates (vaccination, mask-wearing, etc.) shows that this threat is taken seriously—indeed irrationally so—by some segment of the population. How to improve the quality of life of citizens without either being accused of shifting too much responsibility toward individuals (maintain a healthy lifestyle, retrain for a new job, etc.)[34] or too much paternalism (enforced confinement to prevent contagion) is a dilemma that has become the corollary of extending welfare beyond the rather narrow limits within which welfare economics and the early development of the welfare state were contained.

Conclusion

Starting from a rather simple utilitarian paradigm, welfare economics evolved into an analysis of the trade-offs between Paretian efficiency and equity. This became a sort of conceptual straitjacket. Jonathan B. Wight (2015, xv) characterized the problem thus:

> Economists regularly engage in policy discussions using normative concepts like welfare and efficiency. Many are unaware that these practices involve a particular form of ethical analysis, one that has evolved in a controversial way. As a result, policy advice about economic efficiency becomes questionable in some settings.

While this assessment is still apt to some extent, I have argued that welfare economics is evolving and branching out in several directions, which indicate a growing awareness of the problem. One of these new departures, albeit perhaps not the most far-reaching, is the current reevaluation of Pigou's legacy. As I have shown, a careful rereading of the founder's writings suggests that he tried to come to grips with the need to ground the study of resource allocation in a version of utilitarianism that was more subtle than (at least the conventional interpretation of) Bentham's utilitarianism and was aware of the complexity of the practical questions that ensue (e.g., the power imbalance that low-wage earners face). The New Welfare economics was arguably a step back from a normative or philosophical standpoint even if analytically more rigorous.

But the most significant advances originate in the various ways in which theorists, having taken note of the flaws in the Kaldor–Hicks compensation models, the attacks from Arrow, Coase, and others, among other much-discussed weaknesses of the whole paradigm, have sought to rebuild normative economics on a more explicitly non-welfarist foundation. Without in any way claiming to have provided an exhaustive treatment of the subject, I have brought to light the current trend toward reinventing welfare economics as the economics of happiness. The new paradigm holds the promise of achieving a synthesis of the individualistic subjectivism of the ordinalist New Welfare economics and the quantification of welfare that classical welfare economics assumed was possible. Whether this project has entirely succeeded in meeting that promise is still a contentious matter.

Amartya Sen's major contributions to normative economics fit rather well within the trend toward non-welfarism. Insofar, however, as all the theories discussed so far are primarily concerned with inequalities of *outcomes*, I am postponing a discussion of his capabilities approach to Chapter 5, not because it is any less significant than the economics of happiness, but because it fits better within a comparison of different conceptions of the ideal of equality of *opportunity*. What remains to be discussed is how these theoretical and highly abstract perspectives on human well-being have been operationalized and how the available data on inequalities of outcomes can be analyzed, which I do in the next chapter.

Notes

* A few passages in this chapter are reprinted from Dobuzinskis (2022).

1 The issue of the so-called death of welfare economics is discussed in Atkinson (2001), Fleurbaey and Mongin (2005), and Igersheim (2019).

2 It is precisely because of Pigou's deeply felt concern for the living conditions of the underprivileged that the philosopher and economist Amartya Sen, who is well known for his research on inequality and famines, confessed that he personally feels more sympathetic toward Pigou than Keynes, in spite of the fact that the latter is generally held in much greater esteem among progressives (Sen et al. 2020, 8).

3 Pigou admitted that there could be instances in which this is not the case; lengthening the average workday would increase economic welfare, but could have negative consequences for the quality of life of working people ([1952] 2002, 14).

4 Unfortunately, the first edition of this book was marred by many mathematical errors—which were described as "slips" by several well-intended reviewers; it is not entirely clear whether they were Pigou's own mistakes or typos or some combination of both—as well as by the disconcerting practice of using the same symbols to mean different things throughout the entire book. The publisher released a "corrigenda," but it still did not correct all the errors. On this matter, see Knight (2018, 230–243 and appendices D–H).

5 The contemporary phrase "market failure" was not coined by Pigou, but he wrote about the "failures and imperfections" ([1952] 2002, 129) of institutions to channel self-interest in the direction of socially beneficial outcomes.

6 Some critics of Coase have questioned the ethical implications of his thesis. The bargaining that takes place between parties involved in a dispute could be described as a form of extortion when there are asymmetries of information. Take a case where the initial legal rule does not hold a person or firm liable for the nuisance they create; they can threaten to cause more and more damage to their "victims," if the latter have

agreed initially to pay the individual or firm in question in exchange for a promise to desist, and, thus, extract more and more resources from them. Potential entrants may also use extortion to their own advantage by simply threatening to enter the market (Medema and Zerbe 2000, 853). But, if one would like to believe that strict legal protection against negative externalities might seem to be socially and ethically preferable in such cases, it remains that the logic of the theorem is unsullied: if there are gains to be made by bargaining around such rules, it is logical to expect that such bargaining will take place.

7 As Robert Cooter and Peter Rappoport (1984, 507) explain, "The term 'ordinalist revolution' refers to the rejection of cardinal notions of utility and to the general acceptance of the position that utility was not comparable across individuals."

8 Technically, transitivity implies all of the following:

If $a \, P_i \, b$ and $b \, P_i \, c$, then $a \, P_i \, c$.
If $a \, P_i \, b$ and $b \, I_i \, c$, then $a \, P_i \, c$.
If $a \, I_i \, b$ and $b \, Pi \, c$, then $a \, P_i \, c$.
If $a \, I_i \, b$ and $b \, I_i \, c$, then $a \, I_i \, c$.

where $a \, P_i \, b$ means "*a* is strictly preferred to *b* by individual *i*" and $a \, I_i \, b$ means "individual *i* is indifferent between *a* and *b*" (and so on for *b* and *c*).

9 Think I am in a restaurant. I ask the waiter what is my choice of desserts, and the waiter replies "apple pie or strawberry pie." If I say "strawberry" and shortly the waiter rushes back to inform me that a rhubarb pie is also on the menu, then it would be irrational for me to say "Oh, in that case I'll have the apple pie!"

10 In the literature on decision theory, this behavior is said to be guided by "bounded rationality."

11 The question of whether there can exist rationally defensible instances of intransitivity is insightfully examined by Philippe Mongin (2000).

12 "But all is not lost." Feldman and Serrano (2006, 150) add: taxes can be designed so as to remedy the market failures caused by externalities.

13 What the second theorem means is that if there exists a distribution of endowments that is consistent with a Pareto-optimal state. All that is required to bring about a competitive equilibrium, that is, Pareto-optimal, is to redistribute endowments among people and let the market run its course.

14 Extra-welfarist alludes to an approach that looks beyond the horizon of welfarism without necessarily implying a complete rejection of welfarism.

15 Kaplow and Shavell's assertion that *any* non-welfarist method violates the Pareto principle is contested (see Fleurbaey et al. 2003), although not the idea that, generally speaking, non-welfarist methods do.

16 What seems to have happened, however, is that discussions of the principles of welfare economics have become a rather specialized topic, and while there may be a renewal of interest in normative questions among a growing group of scholars, students are no longer taught the basics of welfare economics (see Atkinson 2001).

17 Walter Schultz (2001) has raised the interesting question: Are rational individuals likely to move toward a Pareto optimum by acting strictly on their self-interest? He provides a logical proof of the fact that it cannot be the case; the mechanism of the "invisible hand" and even social conventions cannot, on their own, prevent the occurrence of noncompetitive behaviors (e.g., firms trying to circumvent the prices that would result from the unimpeded balancing of supply and demand among

"price-takers") that create obstacle to the maximization of efficiency. In the absence of effectively enforced moral rules, the equilibrium reached will be suboptimal. What sort of rules? The answer is respect for essential rights, such as property rights (of which Schultz [2001, 100] provided a detailed breakdown), a right to "true information," a right to welfare, a right to autonomy, and a wide range of economic liberties (Schultz 2001, 99–104). But John Evensky (2003) aptly points out that Schultz's definition of the "right to welfare" is extraordinarily narrow, considering that it is limited to the claims that victims of accidents or crimes can proffer. The school of "luck egalitarianism" has built a solid case for protecting individuals against a much wider range of societal dysfunctions that unfairly prevent them from gaining access to the resources they need (e.g., education) to enjoy decent lives. I analyze luck egalitarianism in Chapter 5.

18 For a more technical discussion of this problem, I refer the reader to standard texts in welfare economics, for example, Feldman and Serrano (2006, 199–204) or Ng (2004, 47–52).

19 Note that the superscript signs are *not* exponents; they designate, instead, the various members of the set of individuals being considered. Such signs could just as well be denoted by subscripts, as, indeed, some authors choose to do. The seminal idea for such a model was originally advanced by Abram Bergson/Burk (1938) when he was still an undergraduate student and had not yet changed his name from Burk to Bergson. In turn, this idea was further developed and popularized by Paul Samuelson in the first edition of his famous textbook (1947, 219–236). But Bergson (1983, 40) traces the idea back to an essay written by Pareto himself in 1913.

20 To put it succinctly, without this requirement, it would not be possible to rank the different values of W in a continually increasing or decreasing order.

21 The criterion recommended by Bergson, as restated by J. Legrand (1990, 568), is such that "the welfare weight attached in the social welfare function to a change in a given individual's utility varies inversely with the individual's marginal utility of income. If there is a diminishing marginal utility of income, then this implies that the higher an individual's income, the higher the welfare weight. In other words, the social welfare function implicit in the compensation principle favors the better off."

22 For an example of the application of this method of analysis to health policy, see Adler (2019).

23 Arrow himself proposed a "possibility theorem," but it is commonly referred to as the "impossibility theorem" because that phrase better conveys the logic of the argument.

24 Arrow ([1951] 1963, 9) was clear on this point: "The viewpoint will be taken here that interpersonal comparisons of utilities has no meaning and, in fact, there is no meaning relevant to welfare comparisons in the measurability of individual utility."

25 For a sympathetic critique and refinement of this thesis, see Rossi (2011).

26 Using interpersonal comparisons greatly reduces the probability of running into intransitive preferences resulting in an irrational cycling of desired policy goals.

27 On trust, see Putnam (1993), Fukuyama (1995), and McCracken (2003).

28 Of course, the question of whether social norms are a *cause* of this difference is a difficult one. We return to this question when we examine the literature on social capital at greater length in Chapter 6. Suffice to say for the moment that while the causal arrow may run in both directions, very low measures of trust definitely are signs of social conditions that impede sustained economic growth. This is one of the reasons why education helps to promote economic growth: not only does it

disseminate literacy and useful technical knowledge, but it socializes children who thus learn to interact cooperatively and be less fearful of the unknown.

29 The empirical evidence on this point, however, is somewhat ambiguous. Putnam (1993) found marked differences in social capital between regions in northern and southern Italy, which correlate with differences in the quality of democratic politics and levels of economic development, but Glaeser and Redlick (2009) report that in the US the main difference between declining and thriving cities is not so much in the amount of social capital, which can be high in declining areas, than in the quality of human capital: declining areas are not successful at retaining skilled workers.

30 See Boniwell et al. (2013).

31 As Tibor Scitovsky (1992) very perceptively remarked, this habituation more typically happens when we buy goods that are meant to perform some rather trivial function—which is the case of all mass-produced goods—but not when we consume goods or services that are far more exciting and from which we derive more intense and lasting pleasure, such as reading a novel, or learning to play a musical instrument, or competing in sport events. Inequalities exist with regard to both the means of accessing these goods or the motivation to acquire them. Much practical work has been done on how to facilitate access to cultural activities, life-long education, and so on. The rationale for supporting the "creative industries" is largely accepted. And urban planners in many metropolitan centers have enthusiastically adopted Jane Jacob's (1961) vision of lively neighborhoods where commerce and culture thrive, which stands in sharp contrast with the rationalist modernism of mid-twentieth-century urban planning with its focus on building more highways, "slum clearance," and rigid zoning rules that create sterile urban environments. But, it is far from clear whether these new priorities benefit everyone equally. Indeed, to take just one example, the new urbanism can also be accused of worsening inequalities between the few who can afford to move into "gentrified" neighborhoods where life is more exciting, by making housing increasingly unaffordable not only for the very poor but also for many middle-class families. As for subsidizing culture, the benefits of such policies are also not always fairly distributed.

32 All the same, for complex cultural and sociological reasons, the French remain the least happy people in Europe (Perena and Senik 2020). They may be satisfied with the gains they have made in leisure time, but they report being singularly unsatisfied with their work environment (e.g., prospects for advancement).

33 On the centrality of imitation or "mimetism" in anthropology, see the works of René Girard (e.g., 1987).

34 The individualist connotation of a comprehensive/holistic definition of well-being reaches beyond these practical examples. Since only individuals subjectively know whether they are satisfied with their lives, objective standards of collective progress (national income, number of homeless persons, etc.) lose some of their significance. I revisit the problem of responsibilizing individuals when discussing "luck egalitarianism" in Chapter 5.

3 Equality of Welfare

Empirical Perspectives

The previous chapter probed the theoretical foundations of the economists' discourse on inequalities. The New Welfare economics paradigm betrays a relative neglect for the gravity of the problem since it is content with a hypothetical compensation of disadvantaged individuals who would be left behind by economic progress. But, as I have argued, other approaches recommend more vigorous measures to equalize welfare and/or some more broadly based conceptions of happiness. The questions I now turn to are: How can progress toward that goal be measured? And what evidence do we have of such progress (or lack thereof)? The next section addresses the first of these questions. The rest of this chapter examines the most often debated data-based answers to the second one. The concluding section opens a discussion of what is not fully captured by these otherwise crucially important empirical analyses.

Measuring Inequalities: Methodological Overview

The economic literature on the question of inequalities can be divided into two categories. On the one hand, we find methodological analyses of the conceptual steps required for measuring inequalities; this literature deploys sophisticated mathematical techniques (e.g. Atkinson 1970). It yields valuable tools for distinguishing among several aspects of what is at stake when people casually speak about economic inequalities. Although these concepts use variables such as pre- or post-tax income that are accessible, the mathematical models developed in that literature have not always proved easy to apply in practice, and technical discussions continue to unfold on various points (e.g., which indices are the most appropriate; whether Bayesian statistics provide new insights on how to model and measure income distribution[1]). There is another stream of literature that starts from available statistics about the rate of economic growth, income and tax revenues, and similar data with a view to infer from them policy recommendations. The divide between these deductive and inductive approaches is far from absolute, and the two bodies of literature are closely linked because empirical research makes extensive use of the concepts and methods developed by theorists. But it still makes sense to proceed from the more abstract to the more empirical aspects of the problem at hand. That

DOI: 10.4324/9781003216247-3

second stream is discussed in the next section. I begin, therefore, with an examination of the methodological challenges facing scholars interested in economic inequality.

Some of the questions posed by this line of research include:

- Is inequality to be measured with reference to individuals or households? If the latter, what is the composition of a household; how can one compute the income of individuals within a household, and so on?
- What indices can be constructed to efficiently compare different distributions of income (e.g., before and after tax, across countries or regions)?
- Are inequalities of income the only ones that matter?
- How to factor in the income-equivalent benefits resulting from the provision of public goods?
- What happens to income inequalities as income grows?
- At what point does equalization through a progressive income tax begins to affect economic growth?
- What is the relationship between inequalities and welfare?

A mathematical analysis of income inequalities starts with the specification of a vector comprising values corresponding to the chosen definition of income. For instance, let x_i be the value of individual *i*'s income, the vector

$$X = (x_1, x_2, \ldots, x_i, \ldots, x_n)$$

includes the incomes of a population of *n* individuals. If we are interested in household incomes, then we could specify a vector

$$Y = (y_1, y_2, \ldots, y_i, \ldots, y_m)$$

for a population of *m* households. (We would need also a formula for expressing the relationship between the variables *x* and *y*.) Such data can be obtained from a variety of sources, but generally consist of survey data or income tax records.

Raw data, however, tell us little about inequality. It is the *distribution* characteristics of income across a population that needs to be investigated. A step in that direction consists of formulating a function that accounts for how many individuals have incomes below any level one may wish to specify, as in Figure 3.1.

All points on the curve up to $F(x_0)$ represent the proportion of the population earning x_0 or less. This is an important conceptual building block. As F. A. Cowell (2000, 95) explains, the "function *F* is our fundamental concept for economic and statistical approaches to [the measurement of income]." For comparative purposes, it is preferable to standardize the data in terms of quantile shares. "If we evaluate the percentage of total income accruing to the top *decile* (10 percent of income units) in the distribution, rather than beginning with

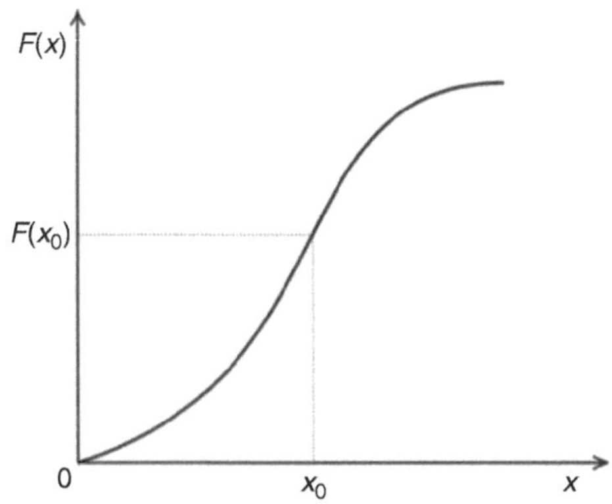

Figure 3.1 Income distribution.

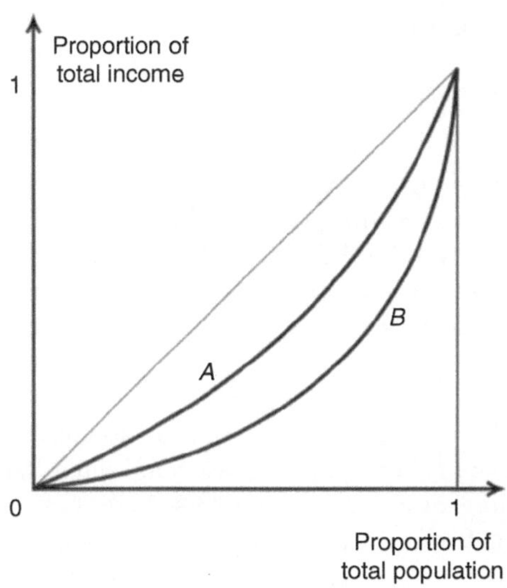

Figure 3.2 The Lorenz curve.

an income level like £15,000, then the information so produced will be comparable between distributions" (Lambert 1993, 31). And two such standardized distributions can be compared visually by drawing their respective *Lorenz curves*. The idea of a Lorenz curve (see Figure 3.2) dates back to 1905, but it is central to much of the contemporary literature on the measurement of inequality. The closer to the 45° line a Lorenz curve lies, the closer that particular distribution is to a pattern of perfect equality (i.e., all incomes would be equal). In Figure 3.2, the curves *A* and *B* plot data for country A and country B; therefore, we can say that incomes are more equally distributed in country A than country B.

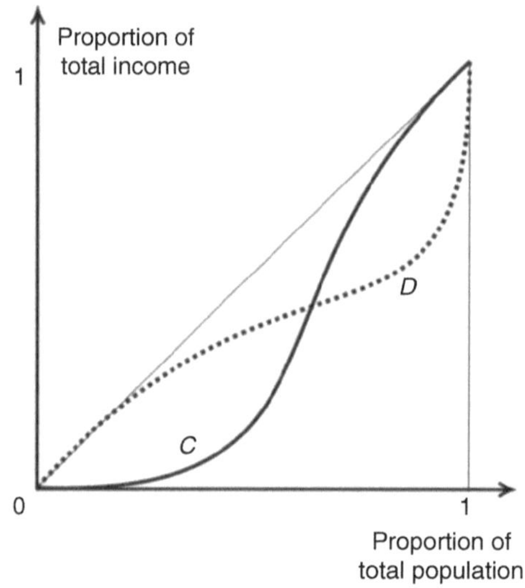

Figure 3.3 Intersecting Lorenz curves.

Matters get more complicated when the Lorenz curves intersect. This is a technically challenging question, but it does not pose a problem in most real-world situations (but see Davies and Hoy 1995; Aaberge 2008). The distribution corresponding to curve *D* seems preferable (from a more or less egalitarian standpoint) to *C* in Figure 3.3.[2] This depends on whatever set of criteria one choses to define "preferable."

From the Lorenz curve, the Italian statistician Corrado Gini deduced the now widely used *Gini index* in 1912. This index is a ratio of the area comprised between the equality line and the Lorenz curve, that is, area *S* in Figure 3.4, to the whole area below the equality line, or $S + T$ in Figure 3.4. Thus, $G = S/(S + T)$, and because $(S + T)$ is one half of the area of a square with sides measuring 1, it is equal to 0.5; it follows that $G = 2S$ or $G = 1 - 2T$. Since obviously $S < (S + T)$, *G* stands anywhere between 0 (perfect equality) and 1 (maximum inequality).

Developed countries that belong to the Organization for Economic Cooperation and Development (OECD) had a Gini average after tax and transfers of 0.3 in 1995; this has steadily climbed up to an average of 0.32 in 2011 and remained roughly stable thereafter. More erratic variations can be observed for specific countries (e.g., from 0.29 in 1995 to 0.32 in 2011 then back to 0.3 for Canada; and from 0.36 in 1995 to 0. 39 in 2012 and the years following for the US). The Nordic European countries together with Belgium, France, Germany, and the Netherlands have managed to stay below the average during this period, while Australia (except in 2004), Italy (except in 2009), the UK, and the US, among other countries, were above the average. Poorer

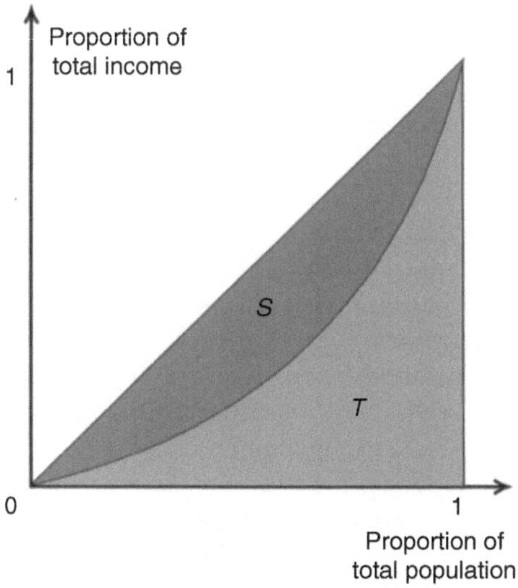

Figure 3.4 The Gini index.

countries, none of which belong to the OECD, tend to have significantly higher Gini scores. One should note, however, that in many instances there is a clear difference between pre- and post-tax Gini coefficients. In many European countries (e.g., Scandinavian countries), the pre-tax coefficients are much higher than the post-tax coefficients. In South Korea and Taiwan, where land ownership is relatively equally distributed, post-tax coefficients are somewhat higher than in Scandinavian countries, but the pre-tax coefficients are lower.

Todd Knoop (2020, 16) brings up an interesting hurdle in trying to make sense of these numbers. A Gini coefficient of 1 is practically impossible: it would mean that "everybody but one very lucky person would starve." So, what would be a feasible maximum? One plausible method would be to calculate the index only for incomes above the absolute minimum required to survive. For poor countries, the maximum would be closer to 0.5, and for more affluent one around 0.75, although if we use the "socially acceptable minimum income" rather than the absolute minimum, the maximum index for affluent countries would probably be around 0.6. The jest of this story is that the reported Gini indices reveal a higher level of inequality since they are closer to the maximum than it is commonly assumed.

The Gini index is not the only measure of inequality. The Schultz index is also derived from the Lorenz curve: it measures the maximum distance between that curve and the line of equality. N. C Kakwani (1980, 83–85) has proposed an index derived from the length of the Lorenz curve. Besides, there are several other measurements, such as those developed by H. Theil or S.-C. Kolm, which are not based on the Lorenz curve (see Cowell 2000, 109–111). One can also mention the Palma index calculated by dividing the share of the national income going to the richest 10 percent by the share going to the poorest 40 percent. Insightful as all these other indices are, it remains that the Gini index is the most frequently used.

All the indices mentioned so far are essentially descriptive in nature. They tell us little about the relationship of inequality to the welfare of society. Discussions of this issue often start from the Pigou–Dalton principle of transfer, which "says that inequality decreases (or social welfare increases) when an even transfer is made from a richer to a poorer individual without reversing their pairwise ranking (although this may alter their ranking relative to other individuals)" (Fleurbaey 2012, 7). This principle has been subjected to several criticisms,[3] including the "leaky bucket" objection raised by A. Okun (1975, 91–95): the poor will not receive all of what the rich contribute because of transaction costs traceable to administrative red tape and tax avoidance tactics. The welfare-enhancing effect of simple transfers is likely, therefore, to be less than perfect. A number of refinements or revisions of the Pigou–Dalton principle have been proposed and continue to be debated, such as Kolm's "principle of diminishing transfers," which posits that "a Pigou–Dalton transfer has a greater impact the lower it occurs in the distribution" (Fleurbaey 2012, 7). That is, even if the income difference between the donor and the recipient is the same (e.g., $50,000 vs. $10,000, or $90,000 vs. $50,000), the impact of that transfer diminishes as the income of the recipient increases (e.g., $10,000 as opposed to $50,000).

The various indices and principles discussed so far are quite abstract and oversimplifying.[4] The extent to which they match people's actual perceptions of inequality is open to question. In recent years, public opinion has focused on a single metaphor: the much-debated contrast between the super-rich "1 percent" and the rest of the population. "In the US the top 1 percent earn twice the amount of income as the poorest 50 percent of the population" (Knoop 2020, vi); the contrast is not quite as extreme in most West European countries, but the gap between the rich and poor has deepened practically everywhere as compared to what it was some fifty years ago. Although somewhat simplistic and too narrowly focused, in light of the complexities underlined above, this slogan has generated a great deal of political rhetoric but also some serious economic reflections. The French economist Thomas Piketty has provided a more fine-grained analysis of a range of inequalities than the 1-to-99 ratio while confirming its overall significance.

Trends in the Distribution of Income and Wealth

Piketty's *Capital in the Twenty-First Century* brilliantly illustrates his point that a historical approach to economics is needed to complement the abstract mathematical models that many economists are wedded to. (Piketty's intellectual journey began at the MIT Department of Economics where mathematical models are taken for granted, but he gradually embraced a more historical approach, and in his *Capital and Ideology*, he assigned an even greater role to political ideas and philosophical traditions.) The mass of data Piketty has assembled, drawing from works he undertook with his colleagues Emmanuel Saez and Anthony Atkinson for at least a decade prior to the publication of *Capital in the Twenty-First Century*, is by all accounts very impressive, and never before used with such flair. This in itself goes a long way toward explaining how a 696-page volume on a difficult subject unexpectedly became a bestseller in the English-speaking world in 2014. Indeed, it seems to have caused an even greater stir there than the original French version did in France. No doubt the book's success also had to do with the excellent translation by Arthur Goldhammer, and to the conjuncture of events that have placed economic inequalities and the plight of the middle classes at the forefront of the political agenda after decades of relative neglect. But the book also made plainly clear that economic inequalities are deeper and more spectacular in the US than almost anywhere else in the Western world today, with the exception of India (which Piketty added to his dataset in his second book).

It can be objected that this perception is not entirely accurate. For example, as Piketty (2014, 89) himself acknowledges, real purchasing power for most consumer goods has increased significantly in recent decades: it takes many less hours of work at the average wage rate today than it did in the mid-1970s to buy a whole range of products, from coffee-makers to electronics (and, of course, a comparatively cheaper computer today can do much more than the very best and costly typewriter could in 1975).[5] Importantly, however, this downward trend does not include real estate and health. Indeed, housing affordability has become a critical issue in most of the developed world metropolitan centers. Besides, even in some countries where the wealth gap has widened between the very bottom and the very top of the scale, a concurrent "hollowing out of the middle class" is not happening. For example, "Canadian households have seen a huge increase in median net-worth over the past twenty years. The median net-worth for all households reached $329,900 in 2019, up 115.48% from 1999."[6] But perception is often reality in politics, and, in any event, *American* households have reasons to feel insecure about the extent to which they truly belong to the mythical "middle class." Piketty's book understandably touched a nerve in that context. It is doubtful, however, that the policy solutions he offers for curbing growing inequalities of income and wealth stand a chance to be implemented in the foreseeable future (see below).

Piketty has made three important contributions to the extant literature on inequalities: first, an extraordinarily detailed statistical analysis of data on income and wealth extending over a very long period, concerning primarily France and Britain; second, a theoretical explanation of the trends that these data illustrate; finally, and more controversially, policy recommendations on how to address growing inequalities. Hereafter, I examine these three facets of his works and the critical reactions they have provoked.

Piketty's Statistical Tour de Force

French archives provided Piketty with a treasure trove of data, often going back to the eighteenth century (e.g., on property taxes). Where available, he also uses data from several other European countries (mostly Britain and, to a lesser extent, Germany and Sweden), the US, and Japan, although records for most of these countries do not go as far back as is the case with France. There are some obvious gaps: Piketty has little to offer with respect to China or Latin America; this is not a deliberate choice on his part but rather a consequence of political instability or the lack of transparency on incomes and taxes, which is a problem even for liberal democratic countries, but is far more acute in much of the rest of the world. From these data, Piketty extracts several U-shaped long-term trends.

The first one concerns the capital/income ratio, that is, the relative proportions of capital and national income, or β. He assumes that in the long run β tends toward *s*/*g* where *s* is the savings rate and *g* the growth rate—this he describes as the "second law of capitalism" (Piketty 2014, 170).[7] Let us consider the case of Europe first (see Figure 3.5). In the late eighteenth and early nineteenth centuries, capital, consisting mainly of the land owned by the aristocracy, accounted for between six and seven times the total value of national income in France and Britain. Around 1920, that percentage had dropped dramatically to around two to three times the value of national income. In other words, the wealth of the rich and well-off who owned capital (at any time in the history of even the richest countries, at least 50 percent of households own little or no

Figure 3.5 The capital/income ratio in Europe, 1870–2010.
Source: http://piketty.pse.ens.fr/files/capital21c/en/pdf/F0.I.2.pdf

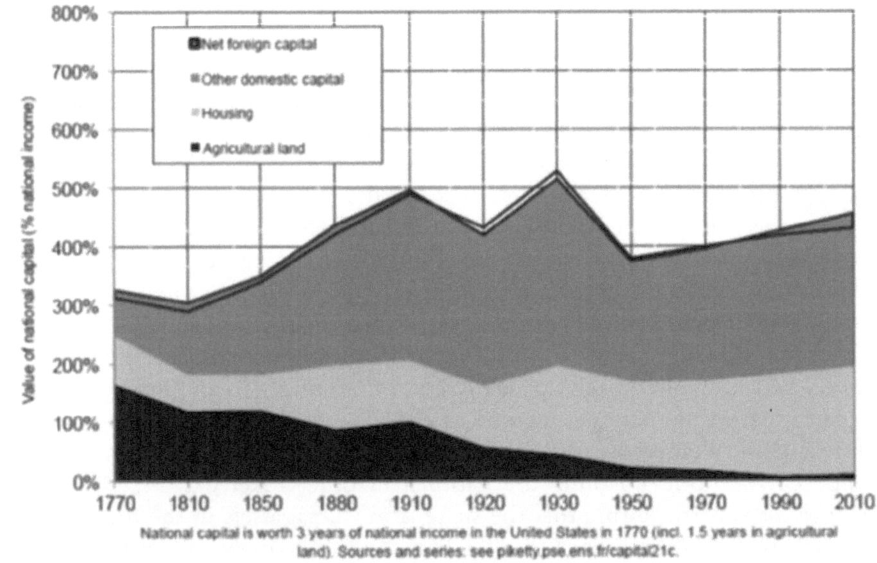

Figure 3.6 Capital in the US.
Source: http://piketty.pse.ens.fr/files/capital21c/en/pdf/F4.6.pdf

capital) had shrunk considerably. They were no longer able to earn the extravagant incomes they derived simply from the prudent placement of their capital, which they had enjoyed almost until the eve of World War I. The cause of this dramatic turn of events was, of course, the war and its economic and political aftermaths. (The French bourgeoisie, in particular, saw the enormous value of its investments in Russian bonds evaporate after the creation of the Soviet Union.) The Great Depression and World War II ensured that no recovery from that initial shock was possible. However, since the 1950s, the relative proportion of capital in the national incomes of France and Britain has climbed back up, at first slowly but much more rapidly since the 1980s. In 2010 it was back to where it was in the 1880s. But by then, of course, the composition of capital was different: the value of agricultural land has become rather trivial, especially in comparison to urban real estate/housing, which now represents the lion share of capital in these countries. The trajectory of wealth in the US is different, however (see Figure 3.6).

In the early decades of the American history, capital played a relatively insignificant role: from the time of the American Revolution to the 1850s, it accounted for only about three times the value of national income. As Alexis de Tocqueville had observed in the early 1830s, wealth was *not* dramatically unequally distributed in the US. (However, if one factors in the market value of slaves in the southern states, which was then quite considerable, the situation looks rather different [Piketty 2014, 160].) By the late nineteenth century, the famous "Gilded Age" of the Carnegies, Mellons, and Morgans, capital's share of the United States' national income had climbed significantly, and yet it was still slightly lower than in Europe, reaching a peak of five times the national income in 1910. As with Europe, the middle of the twentieth century was also a period of upheaval in North America, but, on the whole, there was more stability. The US quickly recovered from the effects of World War I; in fact, the share of capital in the national income reached an all-time high in 1929. The Great Depression followed by World War II certainly caused a big dip in the curve and much misery in real life. But capital was not destroyed to the same extent in the U than it was in Europe: the very lowest point reached in the US was a value of capital equivalent to just under four times the national income in the early 1950s, as compared to just under three times the national income in France. Then it climbed back up slowly but, interestingly, in 2010 the proportion of capital in the national income of the US was still lower than the new high reached in France and Britain in the same period, that is, about 4.5 times as opposed to about 5.5 times the national income (Piketty 2014, 116–117, 151). It is also worth noting that the share of financial assets in the total value of capital in the US is higher than in France or Britain where real estate is proportionally more significant. By themselves these trends are not worrisome. The prosperity of a nation depends in part on the availability of physical and financial capital for industrial production, housing, agricultural production, and so on. When capital is severely depleted, potential output is reduced, although a period of reconstruction is usually characterized by rapid growth favorable to labor, which is precisely what happened in the postwar years in Europe and Japan. Inversely, idle capital contributes nothing to economic growth. Thus, in order to evaluate the extent of economic inequalities, we also have to consider the relative share of labor and capital income, that is, no longer the value of capital in the national income as a whole but the relative shares of national income going to, respectively, those who earn a living from their work and those who live on the return from their investments.

On that topic, Piketty focuses on France and Britain (see Figures 3.7 and 3.8).

What we observe are, roughly speaking, two symmetrical trends: at the top, the share of labor in total income reaches its peak more or less at the points where the share of capital income (at the bottom) reaches its lowest levels. In the case of Britain, it happened first in the mid-1920s and then again in 1970; in the French case, the corresponding maximums/minimums occurred in 1940 and then 1980. The trend for labor income has been down-sloping since the 1980s in both countries, albeit not dramatically. The formula Piketty uses to account for these trends is: $\alpha = r \times \beta$, where α is the share of income from capital in the national income, r is the rate of return on capital, and β stands for the capital/income ratio, as previously defined.

To predict the evolution of the curves represented in Figure 3.7 and 3.8, we have to consider the probable values of the variables r and β. For much of the nineteenth century, r was remarkably stable, around 4–5 percent. (This allowed

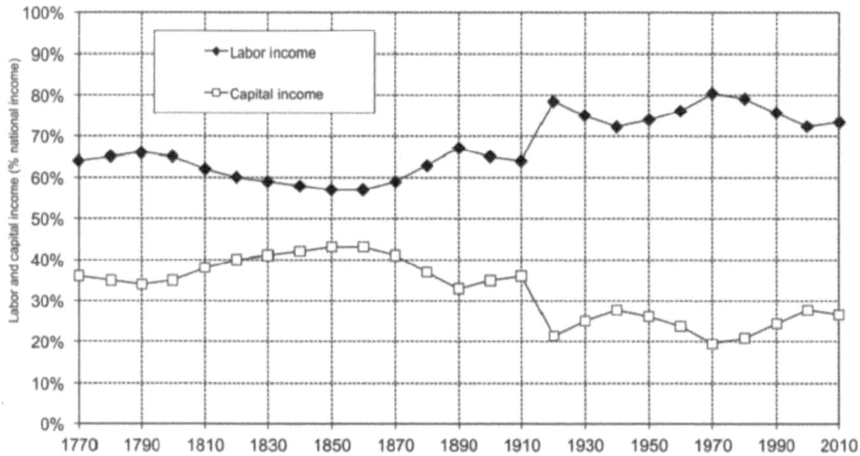

Figure 3.7 The capital–labor split in Britain, 1770–2010.
Source: http://piketty.pse.ens.fr/files/capital21c/en/pdf/F6.1.pdf

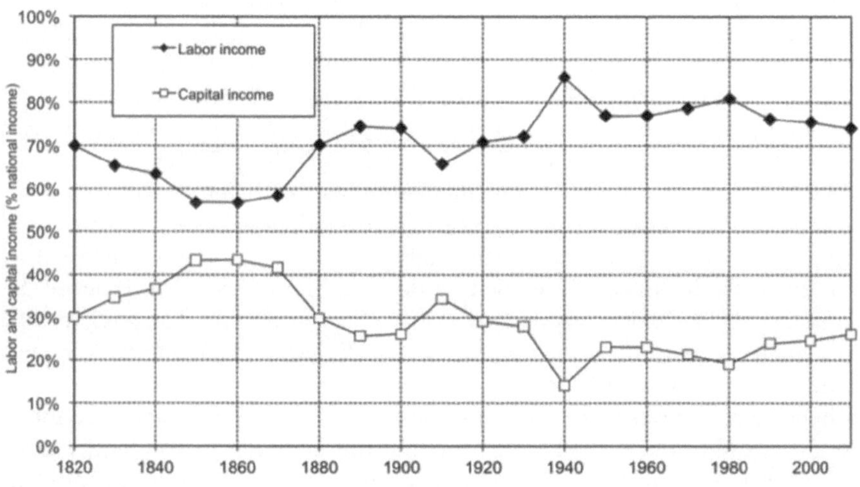

Figure 3.8 The capital–labor split in France, 1820–2010.
Source: http://piketty.pse.ens.fr/files/capital21c/en/pdf/F6.2.pdf

large estate owners in both Britain and France to enjoy high standards of living, for the times,[8] without bothering to do much more than ensuring that their estates were well run; Piketty astutely uses Jane Austen's descriptions of the ways of life of the landed gentry in mid-nineteenth-century Britain as his point of reference.) In the twentieth century and until now, *r* has been closer to the

3–4 percent mark, although this is an average that masks significant disparities (Piketty 2014, 208). The far more considerable weight of taxes on capital gains as compared to the situation in previous eras is the principal cause of this trend. In which direction is *r* likely to trend? And what consequence is it likely to have on α, that is, the share of income from capital in the national income? Much depends on the capital/income ratio, β. A key variable in that respect is the elasticity of substitution between capital and labor, in other words, the degree to which producers can use more or less of these factors as their relative productivity of cost changes. Neoclassical economics (which provide Piketty with his methodological tools) assumes that "firms can chose between various combinations of labour and capital in order to produce the same amount of output" (Meijers 2011). Piketty claims that if the elasticity of substitution is between 0 and 1, then an increase in β leads to a decrease in *r*; when it is greater than 1, the reverse occurs; and when it is equal to 1, *r* remains constant. As Piketty remarks, the most commonly used neoclassical production function is the Cobb–Douglas function, which posits that the elasticity of substitution between capital and labor is equal to 1. But this was based on data that are by now quite obsolete (Piketty 2014, 220). He hypothesizes that in the long run the elasticity of substitution is greater than 1, leading to a slight increase in α. In other words, the socioeconomic position of the owners of capital is likely to remain strong and to become even stronger. This specific prediction arguably rests on a technical mistake, as I explain below, but one can also surmise that in the 2020s the combined effects of the massive investments required to (1) fix the global supply chain destabilized by the Covid-19 pandemic and (2) the transition to clean energy sources will make capital scarce, which obviously will work to the advantage of the owners of capital (O'Sullivan 2021).

The final and most-often-commented-upon part of Piketty's statistical analysis concerns the structure of inequality at the individual level: Are the rich getting richer? Piketty uses two remarkably well-chosen windows on the distribution of wealth in the developed world. The first he found in Honoré de Balzac's novel, *Père Goriot*. Vautrin, one of the least attractive characters of this novel, explains to a still young and naïve Rastignac that he should give up studying law and puts all his efforts into marrying a heiress. That is because—and here Balzac proves to be an invaluable source of historical data—the most Rastignac could hope to get from reaching the very top of the legal establishment in France in the 1830s was a mere pittance when compared to what he could earn from sharing his prospective wife's substantial but certainly not exceptionally large inheritance. In other words, hard work even in what was even then a prestigious profession did not pay! Income earners were then at a serious disadvantage when compared to rentiers. And this continued to be the case until World War I. Conspicuously absent from the social landscape of that era was a "patrimonial middle class," that is, households whose income from labor is sufficient for them to acquire substantial assets through saving.

Through the middle decades of the twentieth century, several countertrends unfolded. First, because of the physical and economic effects of two world wars compounded by the depression of the 1930s, rentiers saw their income from capital decrease significantly and, for some of them, evaporate altogether.[9] Second, structural transformations of the economy turned out to be advantageous to those whose income is derived from labor rather than capital ownership. The growing demand for skilled labor, professional services, and managerial talents resulted in a marked increase of wages and salaries. Finally, progressive income tax rates, which especially in the US and Britain were very high at the top of the scale, placed an upper limit on wealth accumulation. By the mid-1960s, Vautrin's advice would have sounded more like "Forget marrying an heiress; get an MBA!"

On the basis of data that showed a sharp reduction in inequalities in the US between 1913 and 1948, Simon Kuznets famously augured that this trend pointed to the future of capitalism.[10] Postwar growth was a "tide that lifts all boats," and Marx was proven wrong (Piketty 2014, 11–14). Kuznets' prediction proved to be correct until the late 1970s. Indeed, what is often forgotten today is that in the postwar decades, income distribution in the US was flatter than in France and much of Western Europe. But since then, things have changed rather dramatically. The gap between the richest 1 percent Americans and the bottom 50 percent has markedly increased, reaching an astonishing level.[11] A similar trend has been observed in the UK, Australia, and Canada and, albeit less evidently so, in the rest of the OECD countries. There are many explanations for this development, but Piketty places most emphasis on changes in taxation policy. From the moment salary increases are no longer clawed back at a rate of something like 70 percent, it becomes far more worthwhile for corporate executives to devote more effort to negotiating raises. This seems to be what has happened in the US; by contrast, in Scandinavian countries where the structure of the income tax has not changed to the same extent, executive compensation packages have remained more modest. Besides, compensation packages now include stock options and very large bonuses, which executives often also invest in the stock market. Consequently, at the top of the income ladder, the distinction between income from labor (executive salaries) and revenues from capital becomes blurred (Piketty 2014, 300–301). At the other end of the income ladder, we have also witnessed a loss of well-paying manufacturing jobs and of middle management positions for a variety of reasons, including technological change and the rise of newly industrialized countries. It would be wrong to claim that all of these lost manufacturing jobs have been replaced by lower-paid ones in the service sector (retail, fast food, etc.) because college graduates and skilled technicians have benefited from the growth of the financial sector and the new information-based industries. On the whole, though, this balance is fragile; some would argue that robotization already has tipped, or definitely will tip the balance toward the lower-paid jobs, thereby accentuating the divide. Alarmist prognostications about the disappearance of the mythical "middle class" and the erosion of the American Dream must be taken with a grain of salt. Nevertheless, it is clear that opportunities for advancement are limited for people without college degrees and/or living in depressed areas.

It is already the case that social mobility is lower in the US than in all other comparable advanced economies (Corak 2013). And all over the world, well-educated "knowledge workers" face a painful dilemma: the best jobs are located in vibrant metropolitan areas (e.g., the Bay Area, New York, London, or Sidney) where real estate prices have risen to such high levels that home ownership becomes an unsurmountable challenge for most of them.

Slow growth in Europe, Japan, and, to a smaller but noticeable extent, in North America prevents any return to the era of the rising tide that lifts all boats. Although prognostications are always unreliable, it is widely believed that the rate of growth of future decades will oscillate around 2 percent or less, with the exception of a few newly industrialized countries, most notably China. (Environmental, social, and political clouds, as it were, are rising over the Chinese economy and could bring about a negative downturn there too.) This is precisely what Piketty foreshadows. But it did not take long for this prediction to be thrown off course; the dramatic events that marked the end of the second decade of the twenty-first century suggest that the global economy has become more chaotic than smoothly linear. First came the much-delayed full recovery from the 2008 financial crisis, which was characterized by growth rates in the US and several other OECD countries significantly above the 2 percent benchmark. But this was soon followed by the recession brought about by the Covid-19 pandemic, but also by a rapid and impressive V-shaped recovery; the pandemic and its complex ramifications through the global supply chain may well continue to be a cause of considerable uncertainty for an indefinite period in ways that are arguably more complex than what Piketty foresees. (After decades of stagnation,[12] wages seem to be creeping upward in most developed countries in the postpandemic era but so is inflation.)

The model he relies on consists of a comparison between r (the rate of return on capital) and g (the rate of growth) to analyze what he calls "the mechanism of wealth divergence" (Piketty 2014, 350). Quite simply (if not simplistically), if $r > g$, then the wealthy will continue to earn more and more (and the wealthiest even faster than the merely rich[13]); only if $r < g$ can growth reduce the wealth gap. Given the value of these variables in the early twenty-first century, the latter scenario looks rather improbable (especially considering that a sizable portion of income from capital goes unreported). Although r could well decrease in the long run, the expected end of demographic expansion will also negatively affect g so that the $r > g$ inequality could well continue to prevail (Piketty 2014, 375–376). This could bring back the sort of imbalance between inheritance and labor that Balzac took for granted in the 1830s, although Piketty (2014, 407–408) doubts that this could happen to the same degree. However, considering that Piketty measures r at current market prices, but relies on official statistics that report g at constant prices (corrected for inflation), the way in which he uses this formula to peer into the future is questionable. It is also interesting to note that in his subsequent (and equally massive) book, *Capital and Ideology*, Piketty dropped the formula altogether.

Piketty is obviously concerned with the impact of slower growth on inequality between social classes, but curiously he does not dwell on the question of whether inequality could be a *cause* of slower growth, contrary arguments more insistently raised by Joseph Stiglitz (2013) or Heather Boushey (2019), among others. Perhaps the most straightforward statement of that thesis can be found in an OECD report. Its key findings are:

> When income inequality rises, economic growth falls.
>
> The negative effect of inequality on growth is determined by the lower part of the income distribution: not just the poorer decile but the bottom 40% of income earners.
>
> Redistribution through income taxes and cash benefits does not necessarily harm growth.
>
> Inequality has a negative impact on growth through the channel of human capital: the wider is income inequality, the lower is the chance that low-income households invest in education.
>
> (2015, 60)

Piketty is not content with merely laying out the structure of income inequality in the world; he also offers policy recommendations that he claims could go some way toward solving the problem, or at least preventing it from getting worse. He regards taxation policy as the most appropriate instrument, even though there are political hurdles that Piketty is well aware of. He reiterates that in the US the dramatic decrease in income inequality that occurred in the middle of the twentieth century was due in large measure to the imposition of practically confiscatory tax rates on high incomes. On average, between 1932 and 1980, the top rate was 81 percent (Piketty 2014, 507). However, such extraordinary rates are very unlikely to return in the US, and Piketty might have downplayed the unfairness of those high marginal rates, which by the 1970s only applied to artists and athletes—corporate executives had found ingenuous ways of avoiding them. (This is not to say that a modest tax increase on the highest earners would be undesirable, but even a modest increase is politically difficult to achieve in the present political climate and for the foreseeable future.) Even in France where the political culture is less hostile to taxation, President Hollande's electoral promise made in 2012 to raise the tax rate on salaries over a €1 million to 75 percent proved to be politically costly and, after several false starts, had to be rolled back in 2015. [14] What Piketty favors instead is a *global* tax on capital, which could be gradually implemented and could start at 0.1 percent of the value of assets (deposits, stocks, bonds, real estate, etc.) below a certain threshold and could be set at a progressively higher rate above that threshold. The purpose, however, would not be to generate large revenues by itself but rather (1) to achieve greater transparency by requiring all owners of capital to report what they own or transfer among all their bank accounts worldwide, and thus to do away with tax heavens (hence the tax has to be *global*);[15] and (2) to prevent the worsening of wealth inequalities based purely on the passive ownership of capital and to encourage the wealthy to work more productively (confiscatory rates on very large bequests could accomplish that goal). Piketty (2014, 515) acknowledges that this proposal is unlikely to be implemented in the near future, but insists that a debate must start on how to achieve the two objectives mentioned above. It would be even more unrealistic, however, for a single or only a handful of countries to move in that direction given the competitive climate that prevails in a globalized economic system. In addition to this more controversial recommendation, Piketty (313) joins the already large chorus of commentators who push for investment in education; especially in the case of the US, he recommends increased investment in public universities, which are more accessible than private universities but which in recent years have been the targets of shortsighted cuts in states' budgets.[16]

In his *Capital and Ideology*, Piketty went beyond formulating policy recommendations aimed at achieving a fairer income distribution by offering a more ambitious plan for reorganizing current institutions on the basis of a new way of understanding power relations—in other words, a new ideology. He describes it as "participatory socialism" (Piketty 2020, 3). In doing so, he is consistent with the commitment he has demonstrated over the years to the socialist cause,[17] but I would argue that this might be a rhetorical misstep. Piketty's socialism is decidedly more democratic if not anarchistic than Marxist, but the use of this term conveys connotations that are bound to provoke knee-jerk reactions in many places, and especially in North America. The road not chosen would have been to emphasize the strong parallels that can be drawn between his proposed ideology and John Rawls' "property owning democracy." Admittedly, Rawls was uncharacteristically succinct about this proposal even though he presented it as the optimal application of his principles of justice (2001, 135); it consists of institutions that "work to disperse the ownership of wealth and capital, and thus to prevent a small part of society from controlling the economy, and indirectly, political life as well" (139). Piketty's own concrete proposals could have been instrumental in fleshing out this concept, but he stopped short of doing so explicitly.[18] One could also mention another parallel with a non-Marxist reformist approach to which Piketty does acknowledge his intellectual debt but, again, without choosing to situate his work firmly within it, namely, the French solidarist tradition theorized by the philosopher Alfred Fouillée and popularized by Léon Bourgeois in the late nineteenth and early twentieth centuries. There are also some unexplored parallels with the Italian "civil economy" tradition (see Bruni 2012; Bruni and Zamagni 2016). Be it as it may, the proposals he advances in this book complement but also considerably widen the reach of those contained in his first book. They can be grouped in two categories: redistributive policies and what can best be described as *predistributive* institutional arrangements and policy reforms. The redistributive policies are mainly focused on the taxation of wealth and do not deviate much from those already proposed in *Capital in the Twenty-First Century*. But the second type consists of more innovative suggestions intended to empower members of the least advantaged groups in ways that could make them less dependent on traditional welfare state programs. They include measures such as providing seats for employees on the boards of large corporations (as is the practice in Germany and Sweden); instituting a basic capital endowment—what Piketty (2020, 983) calls a "universal inheritance" made available to all citizens at age twenty-five—that would ensure that owning wealth, as opposed to merely earning a salary, is not the exclusive privilege of the upper middle class; and various investments in, and reforms of, the education system (e.g., "training budgets" for those who choose a path other than high education). I offer no objection to any of these proposals considered singly, some of which I defend further on in this book. I want to raise two concerns, however, The first is that while it is welcome, Piketty's embrace of predistributive policies is still rather timid in comparison to his heavy emphasis of the use of taxes on wealth. Second, I perceive Piketty's interest in these measures as being merely instances of how to pave the way for a systemic transformation of extant institutions and practices that he claims should eventually take place on a global scale, even if, I concede, he is the first one to acknowledge that implementing his vision on an empowered citizenry would face serious challenges. The vision could help build a rampart against reactionary populism, but it could also be said that reactionary populism is already too entrenched in many increasingly unstable democracies to allow for these progressive transformations to proceed all at once. Economic inequalities are at the root of the current political malaise in the US, Brazil, and much of Europe, but those who are most affected by these economic conditions typically refuse to see in the mitigation of these inequalities the solution to their anger at "the elites" and alienation from "the system." Calls for more "participation" falls on deaf ears when an increasing segment of the citizenry is bent on *denying* their perceived cultural/ethnic enemies the right to participate in political affairs. I would suggest that the approach that is needed is not a top-down plan to replace a corrupt "capitalist system" by a more virtuous one on a planetary scale, but slow and steady progress at the local level, continued investments in civil society organizations, urban renaissance, and so on. The end goals may be similar—I am thinking, in particular, of reforms such as empowering employees in their workplaces or improving the quality of primary and secondary schools, especially in rural or declining industrial regions—but Piketty's utopian outlook for a global paradigm shift may just be another example of what Gerald Gaus (2016) aptly called "the tyranny of the ideal." This illusion is arguably what the French solidarists or the Italian champions of a "civil economy" have managed to avoid by putting more faith in combining law as a general framework and the capacity of civil society or local governments to do the ground work.[19] (Piketty would, no doubt, reply that tinkering at the margins is futile, but I do not share his optimism about the feasibility of a grand political plan and would suggest that diligently working on increasing the scale of the "margins" through channels that are not necessarily state-centered is a more productive approach, an idea I elaborate upon in subsequent chapters.)

Critical Assessments of Piketty's Analysis

Piketty's *Capital in the Twenty-First Century* has generated a massive amount of reviews and commentaries, not all of them positive. The positive responses emphasize the timeliness and importance of a thorough examination of the causes and effects of rising inequalities.[20] Nothing that happened since 2014 suggests that economic inequalities are any less important in the 2020s; indeed, they seem to have worsened in some parts of the world (e.g., Brazil, India) without significantly improving anywhere. Piketty's broad historical perspective is also generally praised. Several commentators (e.g., Milanovic 2017; de Nardi et al. 2017; Hodgson 2021, 241–244) have praised Piketty for insisting that while vast income inequalities are obviously a serious issue in a democracy, the root of the problem must be traced back to inequalities in the ownership of *wealth*. Piketty did not say anything dramatically new if one cares to look back at what Thomas Paine, Karl Marx, or Henry George have written on the subject of wealth, but he can be credited for putting this problem back on the policy agenda in a more empirical manner.[21]

More pointed criticisms have been directed at the three obvious aspects of his contributions: (1) the data he has assembled, (2) the theoretical apparatus he deploys, and (3) his policy recommendations. I elaborate on these three focal points in what follows without, however, pretending to offer a comprehensive assessment of all the questions raised by the dozens of reviewers who have challenged Piketty's arguments and conclusions.

Critical discussions of Piketty's data have focused on two questions: whether fiscal data are the best sources of information on inequality; and whether Piketty committed some methodological errors in measuring these data. Branko Milanovic (2017), reviewing the original French edition of Piketty's book, praised him for departing from the conventional practice of using household survey data to measure inequality, using fiscal data instead. This innovation allowed Piketty to reveal more clearly the concentration of wealth at the top of the scale. Milanovic, however, faults him for using such data alone, because fiscal data have some built-in limitations. Taxable income is not the same thing as actual income—for example, "until 1987, interest on government bonds does not appear on US tax returns because it was not subject to taxation" (Milanovic 2017 15). Household survey data also provide better information on the actual disposable income of lower- and middle-income groups. Somewhat more damaging are allegations by Chris Giles and Fernando Giugliano (2014), published in the *Financial Times*, that there are errors in Piketty's data: "simple fat-finger errors of transcription, suboptimal averaging techniques; multiple unexplained adjustments to the numbers; data entries with no sourcing, unexplained use of different time periods and inconsistent use of source data."[22] When the data are "cleaned," Piketty's conclusions appear to be much less robust, and in the case of the UK, there would seem to be a little increase in inequality since 1980.[23] In his reply to critics, Piketty (2014) concedes that some of his data, especially with respect to wealth measurement, are "less systematic than for income"; he also admits that his time series could be improved. But he adds that a paper prepared by Emmanuel Saez and Gabriel Zuckman (2014) about inequality in the US since 1913 using much more systematic data confirms his own diagnosis. Piketty also defends his use of estate tax data from Britain, which Giles considers to be very inappropriate for measuring wealth or income inequalities; Piketty argues that the alternative and perhaps more accurate survey data that Giles recommends would not have allowed him to go back as far in time as he did. However, this does not fully dispel all the charges that Giles and Giugliano had put forward.

A small part of the problem lies in Piketty's choice of using spreadsheets to present and parse his data. While appropriate for the sort of descriptive approach that he follows, that instrument does not allow an outside reviewer (such as Giles) to reconstruct all the steps (e.g., weighting of averages) that led to the reported numbers. This does not mean, however, that the data are completely unreliable. On balance, it seems that Piketty's account of past trends must be taken very seriously, even if in some regards it should be interpreted cautiously with due regard for probably unavoidable inaccuracies.

More damaging to Piketty's thesis are criticisms directed at the theoretical apparatus he deploys to offer prognostications about the prospects of capitalism for the rest of the twenty-first century. At issue is Piketty's controversial $r > g$ formula. Matthew Rognlie's (2014, 2015) technical analysis of Piketty's model has done much to undermine its validify.[24] Rognlie (2014) targeted an oddity in Piketty's use of the elasticity of substitution between capital and labor. As mentioned above, Piketty takes it for granted that this parameter has a value of 1 or above, resulting in an increasing value for r in the long run. Rognlie points out that when Piketty refers the consensus exemplified in the Cobb–Douglas production function that the elasticity of substitution can be assumed to be 1, he neglects to specify that in this case elasticity refers to the *gross* production function, that is, one in which the value of capital is *not* net of depreciation. But Piketty uses only net concepts; the elasticity in a *net* production function is necessarily lower than in a gross production function.[25] Therefore, it seems that Piketty overestimated the elasticity of substitution between capital and labor.

In his subsequent paper, Rognlie (2015) provides a broader context for this critique. First, he offers an analysis of the evolution of the net and gross capital share of the private (i.e., excluding government) domestic value added for the G7 countries between 1950 and 2010.[26] The net share displays a U-shaped pattern comparable to the trend identified by Piketty (2014). However, whereas Piketty's data point to a trough occurring around 1950, Rognlie suggests that there was a downward trend from 1950 to about 1980 and an upward trend since then; the values reached in the first decade of the twenty-first century match those of the early 1950s. Thus, he asks: "To what extent, then, is the current high share of capital income a truly novel phenomenon?" (Rognlie 2015, 10). Interestingly, when the net share is disaggregated into the housing sector and the rest of the economy, it appears that the share of nonhousing capital in 2010 remains *below* the level reached in the 1950s. The crucial role of housing in shifting the capital share upward deserves attention. Insofar as home ownership is not typically limited to the super-rich, the rise of the share of capital in the national accounts of the G7 countries does not speak to a dramatic divide between rich rentiers and middle-income earners even if, of course, access to home ownership is not accessible to many households at the bottom of the income ladder. Unintentionally, perhaps, in drawing our attention to the importance of the housing (which at times he also calls "structures") sector, Rognlie underscores a weakness in mainstream neoclassical theory, namely, its neglect for the difference that exists between land and other forms of productive capital.

Second, Rognlie constructs a few models designed to better trace the contribution of various sectors to capital income. Unfortunately, these models are tested only with data from the US. The results are nevertheless quite challenging in light of Piketty's own findings. In addition to the crucial role played by housing, he finds that "the volatile capital share elsewhere in the economy is driven principally by pure profits" (Rognlie 2015, 19), possibly reflecting a strengthening of monopoly profits. The key term here is "volatile:" it is not justifiable to expect that they will continue to increase. He also finds that, regardless of whether one sets the elasticity of substitution at 1, below 1, or above 1, that "increased savings will result in a *decline*, rather than an increase, in the net capital share, contradicting the mechanism proposed by Piketty (2014)" (Rognlie 2015, 31). He concludes that, at least as far as the US is concerned, there is no compelling reason to believe that capital will inexorably continue to get a larger share of national income. If so, the problem of economic inequality originates in discrepancies in the labor market between high and low earners. While this is not radically different from Piketty's findings, the policy conclusion one can draw from this is that rather than taxing wealth, priority ought to be given to programs that could help those at the bottom of the pay scale to improve their situation. Interestingly, Piketty (2015c, 1) seems to concede this point, adding that the "rise in labor income inequality in recent decades [in the United States] has evidently little to do with $r - g$, and is clearly a very important historical development." He adds that the $r - g$ relationship is not in itself the principal cause of trends in inequality; it merely accentuates the effects of external shocks that are the real causes of changing historical patterns. Finally, with respect to the elasticity of substitution, Piketty (5) notes that this parameter is more essential in a simple one-good model of capital accumulation, but more realistic multisector models show that inequality results from a complex mixture of influences that lead to "uncertainty regarding the future evolution of inequality, as illustrated by the example of housing and oil prices." As he concludes, this may call for more "democratic transparency" but leaves us somewhat in the dark about the future of capitalism.[27] And in his *Capital and Ideology*, he drops the formula altogether, preferring an approach that is less analytic; instead of relying on measurable causal economic variables, he attributes a greater role to the influence of ideas on the development of the structures that account for economic inequalities.

To add a final note on the debatable weaknesses of Piketty's approach, I concur with Daron Acemoglu and James Robinson (2015), who take issue with Piketty's Marxian penchant for making predictions based on supposed "laws" of capitalism (such as the one I just discussed above), as if particular circumstances, and the rich panoply of institutions that shape the conduct of economic and political affairs in the many different societies that are linked in the global economy, counted for little in the end. It is the complexity of the institutional makeup of societies such as Switzerland and Uzbekistan, or South Africa and Sweden, that explains why economic inequalities in these countries have the characteristics and effects that they do even if, in some sense, they share some "capitalist" features. Admittedly, Piketty himself moved a long way from the mechanistic and "overdetermined" explanations he offered in *Capitalism in the Twenty-First Century* when he wrote *Capital and Ideology*. In this latter work, he displays a far greater appreciation for the complex interplay of historical traditions and cultural, political, and economic theories, beliefs, and controversies. But one could argue that he still floats at a rather high level of systemic currents and tendencies rather than descending to the messy realities of actual institutions and political circumstances. And if the "laws of capitalism" have given way to the thesis that the ideology of "proprietarianism," that is, the legitimization or even "sacralization" of private ownership, has successfully undermined any and all alternative conceptions of a good society, it still conveys a sense that universal tendencies that create inequalities must be remedied by equally momentous societal transformations.[28]

Finally, the critical reactions to Piketty's policy recommendations are mostly concerned with his plea for a global tax on wealth, which he forcefully presented in his *Capitalism in the Twenty-First Century* (2014, chapter 15). My comments on this point here are brief because I return to the issue of taxation as a remedy to inequalities in Chapter 6. Suffice to say that critics have pondered on this proposal from at least two angles: its potential effects on innovation, and the impracticability of a global tax regime.

Inequalities in a Globalized World

Much of the previous discussion has been focused on inequalities in developed countries. We also have to look at inequalities among countries, as well as domestic inequalities within developing countries and the new "emerging economies." Piketty (2020) himself has acknowledged that *Capital in the Twenty-First Century* was too narrowly focused on a few affluent countries; in his more recent *Capital and Ideology*, he presents data (from "previously closed sources") on many more countries, including "Brazil, India, South Africa, Tunisia, Lebanon, Korea, Taiwan, Poland, Hungary, and to a lesser extent, China and Russia" (14). Are poorer nations left behind by globalization? If inequalities are a problem in North America or Europe, how do they compare with inequalities in Brazil or India? Are the rich getting richer and the poor getting poorer all over the world?

Beginning with the latter question, the good news is that poverty in absolute terms is gradually being eradicated. On a global scale, the immense majority of people are still quite poor. In 2014, only one-quarter of 1 percent of the world's population were worth US$1 million or more. However, abject poverty is receding fast: "From 1999 to 2012 about 840 million people got out of extreme poverty (defined as less than US$ 1.90 a day in income or consumption at purchasing power parities),[29] including 800 million in Asia, while extreme poverty still increased in Sub-Saharan Africa" (van der Linden and Reis 2018, 11). There are many reasons why this is occurring, but, at least on this count, globalization and open markets have had positive effects, thus giving its supporters, among economists (e.g., Bhagwati 2007; Bhagwati and Panagariya 2013), reasons to cheer. On the other hand, the spread between the poorest and the richest is not narrowing because of the rise of a new global class of billionaires but also because of a rising urban middle class, and one must keep in mind that subjective welfare is a complex mix of real purchasing power and perception of one's status vis-à-vis others. As new communication technologies spread even in remote rural areas (e.g., the wide usage of cell phones), the significance of relative incomes probably becomes more salient.

The question of relative differences *among* countries cannot be answered in a simple way. Some emerging economies, notably Brazil, China, and India, are spectacularly closing the gap between the poor "South" and the rich "North."[30] In fact, the rise of China as an economic and global geostrategic political and military power has become a much-discussed topic in the Asia Pacific region as well as in the US, which is increasingly preoccupied with this evolution. Other countries are not progressing at the same pace, and some are regressing. The tragic inflow of refugees and migrants into Europe and the US is explainable by the growing gap between not only "failed states" (Afghanistan, Syria, or Libya) but even moderately successful economies and the most advanced ones; the per capita income of poorer countries adjacent to richer neighbors has *decreased* when compared to the latter—this is the case notably for Morocco vs. Spain, Macedonia vs. Greece, or Mexico vs. the US, at least over the period of 1950–2007 (Milanovic 2011).[31] These differences are now a matter of common knowledge for practically everyone, and even though the human cost of migration is high, it has become the preferred option for a growing number of desperate people but also for many others who often are well educated and seek better opportunities in a world where information travels very fast. In principle, and especially from the standpoint of libertarian economists (e.g., Block 1998), a large influx of migrants could be beneficial to the host country, especially if, as is the case in Europe, demographic trends are sloping down. However, rigidities in the labor market, the sheer number of migrants, the fact that they are undocumented, together with sociocultural and political obstacles have so far prevented these potential advantages to be fully realized. The more appropriate answer is to foster economic growth within the countries of origin, but this is not sufficient. What also needs to be addressed is the growing inequality *within* most countries, including those that are on a path toward growth. (More and more migrants are best described as upwardly mobile individuals who are not among the poorest but find too few opportunities for their talents, while entrenched—and often corrupt—elites reap much of the benefits of economic growth.)

While not new, of course, the problem of inequality within each country seems to be worsening and, at any rate, is receiving far more attention than in the past. From the previous discussion, one might have concluded that income disparities in the US are inordinately high. But Russia and China show comparable Gini indices. The pre-tax Gini index in Brazil is around 0.53 (most of South America stands at about 0.5), and in South Africa it is around 0.65 (unfortunately, figures for many other Sub-Saharan African countries are not available). The case of China is particularly instructive. In the early 1980s, China's Gini index was less than 0.3; it had jumped to 0.45 in 2005 (Milanovic 2011, 79). To make matters worse, the growth has taken place very unevenly across the different regions and provinces. Most of the coastal provinces have performed above average. This is where we can find the largest and most affluent cities, such as Shanghai or Beijing, where middle-class households experience a high standard of living. But the situation is quite different in the rest of China, and five provinces (Gansu, Anhui, Guizhou, Guangxi, and Yunnan) are left far behind: "The poorest province, Guizhou, went from being half as rich as the China average to only a third" (Milanovic 2011, 80).[32] Because of strict controls over where Chinese people are allowed to live and work, many individuals are trapped in poverty. This is not to say that the immense transformations that have occurred in China and in other emerging economies throughout the world (including, more recently, several African countries) are negligible. Clearly, millions of people are now stepping out of poverty and accessing goods and services that previous generations could only dream of. And it is simply not true that all the benefits of economic growth have been grabbed by a new class of super-rich profiteers. But a vast mass of people have made so little progress that it speaking of increasing inequalities on a global scale is not too far off the mark. Nobel laureate Professor Eric Maskin is puzzled by this trend and, in particular, by what he fears is the worsening fate of workers with no skill. Low wages paid to skilled workers in developing countries attract international investments, and slowly but surely these workers are getting better-off, but farmers with no marketable skill are left behind even as the average income for the country as a whole increases (Maskin 2014). The solution to this as to many other socio-economic challenges is to invest more in education and skill training.

But Gini coefficients are not always the best instrument for comparing poverty levels, and the available data are not always current. Piketty prefers to use comparisons based the share of the total income that goes to the top decile. In 2018, Sub-Saharan Africa, India, and Brazil were above the 50 percent mark, while the Middle East regions surpassed 60 percent. Piketty (2020, 653) brings to light the fact that this region stands as "the pinnacle of global inequality." There is a long list of historical and geopolitical facts that account for this troubling reality. There are, of course, some differences among the countries in this complex region, but the end result is that "the wealth in these states is very highly concentrated, both within the native population and between natives and foreigner workers (who make up 90 percent of the population of Qatar, the Emirates, and Kuwait and 40 percent of the population of Saudi Arabia, Oman, and Bahrain)." Piketty cannot be blamed for avowing that there exists no easy solution to this situation, but his vaguely stated hope that the adoption in Western democracies of not only a more egalitarian ideology but one that also proposes "postnational solutions" (655) will eventually create ripple effects throughout the rest of the world is not very credible. Again, Piketty paints with a very broad brush that leaves too many details unaccounted for even if I am the first one to admit that what could be done in practice as far as the Middle East is concerned is not something that has been explained with any more clarity by anyone!

More Qualitative Dimensions of Welfare

As Serge-Christophe Kolm (2009, 274) notes, "The issue of inequality is very closely related to other very important social phenomena such as poverty, polarization, segmentation, clusters, class or caste structure, exclusion, isolation, eliticism, envy, status, and so on." In countries such as Japan where social hierarchies are still deeply entrenched, even a further lowering of the Gini coefficient would not have the same effect as it would in countries where social relationships are less rigid. Such inequalities play a key role in public debates, but they are more difficult to quantify than differences in wealth or income. To put it another way, the satisfaction of preferences is not reducible to differences in income levels because one may have preference for nonmaterial, essentially social conditions, such as being treated as equals (at least in democratic societies where this is the norm).

Economists for the most part are content to let sociologists and philosophers study such issues. (Indeed, I return to the subject of social equality when I discuss "relational egalitarianism" in the context of my survey of philosophical approaches to the subject of inequalities in Chapter 5.) But there is at least one notable exception: the economist Geoffrey Brennan, in collaboration with the philosopher Philip Pettit (Brennan and Pettit 2004), has used economic reasoning to propose an original analysis of an important dimension of social relations. What they call *the economy of esteem* is a system whereby esteem is allocated among individuals, and by esteem they mean both "the positive asset of approbation and the negative liability of disapprobation" (Brennan and Pettit 2004, 3). I briefly comment on their exploration of, again, what had become unchartered territory for economists.

Although esteem is something that influences people in a wide variety of settings, it plays a particularly crucial role in civil society, that is, the networks and institutions that are not reducible to the market economy or to the state. Material gains motivate people in the market, and power is an essential aspect of politics, but in many other situations, people respond to informal cues that tell them whether their conduct is worthy of esteem, or disesteem, as the case may be. Nether money nor coercion is involved, and yet being admired by, or merely gaining the respect of, others is often sufficient to inspire people to do a great many things, some of which can be very costly in terms of effort, time commitment, and so on. Examples can be drawn from the worlds of sport, the arts, and science; volunteering or otherwise contributing to community organizations, or spontaneously helping friends or strangers facing difficult circumstances, are other ways of getting recognition for one's character or virtuous disposition. This is not to say that esteem never plays a part in more obviously economic or political activities, just as money is sometimes key to political success or power to business dealings, but it still makes sense to speak of relatively distinct spheres of human activities where different motivations prevail, and often when criteria that are reasonable in one sphere are applied in another, the effects of such overlaps are dysfunctional. Just as it is reprehensible to buy votes, or to use political favors to achieve a monopoly, it would not make sense to try to get a car for free by merely telling the dealer how much one admires his or her salesmanship (even if such statement is sincere)!

It is quite clear that there is a demand for esteem: scientific researchers and academics aspire to be admired by their peers; teachers wish to be recognized by their students as mentors; volunteers want people around them to get a better opinion of the causes they advocate, and so on. Saintly characters may perhaps remain indifferent to praise or blame in the pursuit of their callings, but few people can go through life without wishing to be recognized for their talents, moral qualities, or other valued attribute, and only sociopaths can ignore blame or reprobation from people whose opinion they care for. Generally speaking, such expressions of esteem are socially beneficial, but it must be admitted that there are circumstances in which esteem brings about undesirable results, such as teenagers trying to impress fellow gang members, or hateful racists rising through the ranks of the Ku Klux Klan. To speak of "an economy of esteem," one still has to show that there is also a supply of esteem and that, at least under certain circumstances, one can observe transactions that entail deserved mutual gains in the degree to which the parties value each other's merits. That is far more challenging, as Brenan and Pettit (2004) are the first to acknowledge. At first sight, there is an incongruity here. It is unproblematic to plan to increase the supply of some sellable good or service. And a buyer can incite a reluctant seller to sell by offering to pay a higher price. But one cannot *genuinely* decide to provide others with more admiration or esteem simply by wanting to do so. Inversely, those who seek to appear more honest, generous, or otherwise more upstanding than they truly are will appear foolish or worse. (Prefacing a comment by the phrase "to be honest with you" is often an unconscious signal that one is about to tell a fib!) And trade deals that entail promises of greater *sincere* mutual admiration are equally absurd (of course, fake public displays of admiration can be exchanged or purchased, but what one gains in such deals is not esteem per se but material or social advantages that an insincere display of admiration allows one to get; or if, indeed, a third party is induced to think more highly of the person being dishonestly praised, that esteem is not really experienced as esteem by the person toward whom it is directed).

Valid as these objections may be, Brenan and Pettit argue that there are ways around them, so that the formulation of a theoretical model of an economy of esteem remains feasible. For example, while it is indeed counterproductive to deliberately try to generate esteem for one's moral qualities, it is far less so when it comes to the display of skills and talents. A virtuoso who seeks attention by consistently playing the most difficult pieces in the classical music repertoire may be considered to be something of a "show off" but will still be admired for his or her virtuosity. And the same goes for the display of similar skills in other fields (science, sports, etc.). Besides, much of what happens in the economy of esteem is either hidden or virtual but still effective. A junior academic who undertakes research projects comparable to those who have earned a more senior colleague praise will earn deserved credit even though the esteem thus gained was, in at least some measure, deliberately sought-after. A piano teacher who devotes much time and effort to train a talented pupil who goes on to become famous is, in a way, trading in esteem considerations: the esteem of the teacher for his or her student's nascent talent will be (more than) repaid by the fame that can be derived from having nurtured a fast-rising "star," and the devotion of the pupil for his or her master will be (more than) repaid by a brilliant career. But these considerations are never made explicit—indeed if they were, the relationship between the parties would sour. (In this respect, the economy of esteem is comparable to the gift economy: "pure" gifts are not very common, but that fact that the giver expects a gift in return at some point in the future, and the fact that the person for whom the gift is intended knows that, is never expressly conveyed.) It is also obvious that most people in a work-related environment will stop paying even deserved attention to the performance of others if the latter never reciprocate (assuming that the attention-giver is himself or herself doing a good or excellent job). And people are not likely to persevere doing something valuable in principle, if no one ever notices. It is also acceptable to speak of a "competition for esteem." In circumstances where esteem goes to those who perform at a higher-than-average level (e.g., Olympic sports), getting to the top is obviously a competitive endeavor. In a society where most people are honest and generally tell the truth, being respected for one's outstanding honesty requires more effort than in a dysfunctional environment where dishonesty prevails.

To sum up, all the concepts that are required for the formulation of models of something akin to an "economy" of esteem are present, even if they sometimes appear to deviate from the ordinary definitions that apply to a market economy. As Brenan and Pettit (2004, 4) remark, "There is something truly strange and wonderful about the way the economy of esteem works." To convey these peculiarities, they speak of an economy guided by an "intangible hand" (Brennan and Pettit 2004, 246), as contrasted with the better-known "invisible hand" that guides the market economy, or the "iron hand" that the state uses to enforce its regulations. A detailed examination of the operations of this parallel economy would take me too far astray.[33] But the reason why I took care to underline its often-neglected significance is that it is relevant in some crucial ways to the question of economic inequality. First of all, the "intangible hand" can occasionally rectify or smooth out some of the unfair consequences of the workings of the invisible hand. Income inequality can be more bearable, or even nearly inconsequential, if those who suffer from them happen to enjoy the social and psychic rewards that are derived from being admired by a large public, or simply by a smaller group of outstanding peers. Researchers at the peak of their careers in many fields of scientific inquiry earn considerably less than business executives or prominent lawyers who might have been their college roommates in their youth. But the esteem of their peers, the prestige they may earn from their discoveries, and the satisfaction of training the next generation of researchers at the "cutting edge" of science are often more than enough to compensate for such income gaps. Admittedly, this may sound a little naïve in the light of recent changes in intellectual property rights that make it possible for researchers in some fields, such as genomics or robotics, to earn considerable dividends; but most entrepreneurial researchers continue to research and publish after they have become quite well-off, and there still are several fields that continue to attract some of the very best minds even though opportunities for entrepreneurial ventures are much less common, for example, theoretical physics, not to mention the humanities and social sciences. The same can be said of most novelists, "bloggers," amateur athletes, members of the clergy, or professionals working for nonprofits. Technological changes in communication technologies will probably provide even more opportunities for such alternative ways of achieving "success" than they already do. It should be noted, however, that they also provide opportunities for engaging in socially reprehensible activities for which some individuals, for example, hackers, are admired by their more or less rebellious, if not criminally inclined, peers. (Brennan and Pettit see there the handiwork of the intangible "backhand.")

However, there is something to which Brennan and Pettit pay almost no attention, which is that the economy of esteem can *itself* generate inequalities. Such inequalities often complicate or worsen plain and simple economic inequalities. This is not obvious at first. As Carina Fourie (2015, 89) notes, "Advocating equality of esteem seems absurd." Not everyone can be equally meritorious, talented, or worthy of esteem in some other way. We admire people for their exceptional moral qualities, for the outstanding services they render to their community, or for their skilled performances in their fields of excellence. Inversely, it is perfectly normal to express one's disapprobation of uncivil acts or ill-conceived plans. If someone choses to be a fool, no praise is due. Nevertheless, Fourie (2015, 90) urges us to "neither condemn inequalities of esteem nor dismiss them as morally irrelevant." There are many reasons for this. Esteem is the cement that binds various social hierarchies; there are hierarchies in sports, the arts, education, and so on. All hierarchies, however, generate potentially unjust forms of social, economic, or political discrimination. For example, it is evident that the best athletes in their fields deserve more recognition than the merely average ones. But one can ask why male athletes or professional sport players are generally better known and better paid than female athletes. More generally, it can be said that there are groups that may include high-performing individuals, but because they lack some admired characteristics—characteristics that could be based on culture or wealth—they seldom get recognition. It is not (objectively measurable) merit alone that determines whether some individuals or groups are more esteemed than others. There is much talk nowadays about a new aristocracy based on educational achievements in the US. Graduates from prestigious private universities stand a better chance to be recruited for the best-paying entry jobs and/or to be rapidly promoted in many sectors of the economy, but can it really be said that a young applicant with a master's degree in economics from Harvard or Stanford is more competent and better trained than someone who holds a degree from a less prestigious state university? It is more than likely that such a student would have received a comparable training and would have been evaluated by professors who share the same academic standards as their colleagues at Harvard or Stanford (from which institutions they might themselves have graduated)? As the children of the very rich are more and more commonly expected to attend the best private universities, the social prestige of these schools is further enhanced at the expense of the (less-and-less-well-funded) institutions of higher learning where students from more modest middle-class background receive their education. And being at the top of one's field does not give one the right to be disrespectful toward others. When differences in status are used to make some people feel inferior, inequalities that are justifiable on some level can easily turn into ones that are unfair, socially dysfunctional, and psychologically harmful. Fourie (2015, 96) proposes two fundamental criteria for distinguishing between acceptable and unacceptable inequalities of esteem:

> Inequalities are morally unacceptable when they violate respect. Inequalities of esteem, even without violations of esteem, could still be problematic because they can reasonably make people feel inferior or undermine civic friendship, or both.

As far as possible, political, economic, and social institutions should follow informal norms, but formal rules may be necessary to guard against possible excesses of this sort. A democratic society cannot function well when some citizens feel so disempowered and marginalized that they cease to vote or participate in other ways. And policies could be developed to ensure that the competition for esteem is fairly open to all talents. This is especially important in areas where the economy of esteem and the market economy overlap: the rules in place should not "add salt to injuries" in situations where disadvantaged individuals or groups are prevented from accessing crucial economic resources and are loathed for that very reason (historically it has often been said of minorities facing barriers to employment that they are "lazy" or lacking in some other moral quality, the proof being that they are not working!). The subject of overlap also should remind us that while it is true that the hidden economy of esteem has for too long been neglected, and that inequality of esteem need to be taken into account, one should not lose sight of the fact that as long as the basic needs are not met, such considerations are arguably secondary (Barclay 2007).

Beyond the literature on relational equality, there are interesting discussions of the relationship between economic inequalities and a host of social or environmental issues. Too many in fact to be all reviewed here. I can only briefly outline a few such perplexing questions. The first is the by-now-more-closely-scrutinized relationship between inequality and health (Preston 1975; Deaton 2003; Wilkinson and Pickett 2006; Pickett et al. 2006; Deaton 2013). In their meta-study of 168 studies in 155 articles, Wilkinson and Pickett (2006) found that there is a large degree of support for the hypothesis that income distribution and population health are correlated. But correlation is not causation. Richard Wilkinson and Kate Pickett's (2009) much more sweeping thesis that inequality is the *cause* of not only poor health but also a long list of social ills, from drug abuse to levels of violence, is open to question. It is not hard to believe that income inequality plays a part in these social problems, but they are far too complex to be reduced to a single explanation. In spite of rising relative inequality, we have observed a reduction in violence: over the last few decades, crime rates have gone down in all developed countries and, taking a far more encompassing historical view, Steven Pinker (2011) claims that we now live in a much less violent age than our ancestors. And as Nobel Prize recipient Angus Deaton (2013, 101–125) reminds us, infant and child mortality has decreased all over the world.

But Deaton's contribution is most crucial on the question of the direction of the causal linkage between economic growth or income level, on the one hand, and health outcomes, on the other. One cannot completely rule out the hypothesis that income inequalities have some impact on health. For example, in North America, lower-income people are more likely to smoke and eat fast food, but—at least as far as smoking is concerned—the more direct causal link is probably education rather than income per se. Indeed, the picture is far more complex than it appears. As Deaton (2003, 150) puts it, the "stories about income inequality affecting health are stronger than the evidence." He returned at length to this theme in his *The Great Escape*, which is written for the general public. In a nutshell, Deaton argues that there is a variable that explains *both* economic growth and the reduction of mortality over time and space. And that variable is the development of knowledge that, as far as health outcomes are concerned, resulted in new, often cheaply implemented, public health measures, for example, better sanitation as well as new medical technologies. Of course, technological innovation is *also* and in a parallel way a major cause of economic growth. There still are significant differences across countries with respect to mortality, but insofar as medical knowledge is readily available, institutional dysfunctions and lack of political will to implement the not-necessarily-very-costly measures required to address these problems carry much of the explanatory burden. This is not to say that economic growth has no effect on health outcomes. For one thing, high levels of income create a demand for new technologies and medical research, and the ability to pay for new and sometimes quite expensive treatments. But then again, some of these treatments are not life-saving ones and satisfy relatively small groups of patients in advanced economies (e.g., sports medicine). Perhaps it is the case that causation runs in the reverse direction. David Weil (2015, 109–111), however, reports that few studies show a significant influence of health on income growth, and where that link can be established, it is rather weak.

Conclusion

Inequalities affect the lives of almost all human beings in their relations with others who own more resources, enjoy a higher social status, or are more politically powerful. Not all these inequalities are best understood through the lenses of economic models and statistics. But economists have made a decisive contribution to our understanding of the scope of the differences that separate individuals and groups in their access to the means of satisfying their material needs as well as some other less tangible ones, such as esteem. In order to answer the question of how to measure economic inequalities of income, wealth, and other determinants of well-being (e.g., health), economists have formulated synthetic indices that are convenient for comparing income distribution across societies, the Gini index being the best-known example. But as was pointed out, these indices tell only part of the story.[34] Inequalities are not an abstract problem; they must be analyzed in a historical context. One of the reasons why Piketty's work attracted as much attention as it did is precisely that it offers a rather fine-grained picture of different sorts of economic inequalities in multiple contexts over long periods of time. But the main reason is, of course, that his works have brought to light the extent to which the gap between very high-income earners and the rest of society has worsened in recent decades.

Good quantitative data are indispensable. However, it is not inequality per se that matters but rather the real or perceived imbalances in power that it brings about. When economic inequalities are discussed mainly in relation to the problem of poverty, most middle-class and professional people—the sort of voters that political leaders care most about—feel relatively untouched by it. The media have historically paid only sporadic attention to poverty. The decades of the 1960s in the US is a telling example. The decade opened with the rise of the civil rights movement, which to a large extent helps to explain President Lyndon Johnson declaring a "war on poverty" in 1964. But expectations were high and could not be fulfilled. Consequently, serious urban riots exploded by the close of the decade. Far from helping to sustain an interest in poverty, these events, among other factors, helped to usher in a more conservative political mood. Several other liberal democracies experienced similar trends. In Canada, for example, Prime Minister Pierre E. Trudeau's "Just Society" initiative was launched in 1968, but faded away in the 1970s in the face of growing economic difficulties. But today the problem of economic inequalities is posed in terms of the stagnating income of the middle classes, declining prospects for college graduates, and the concentration of wealth in the hands of the already powerful. This is likely to have a more lasting effect. The impatience of a growing number of radicalized voters and the rise of populist movements pose a real threat to social stability and democratic institutions. But has the problem become so urgent that it requires immediate policy intervention and a major shift in the allocation of public funds? In the face of the dramatic upheaval caused by the Covid-19 pandemic, the answer is obviously positive both as a matter of fact and as a moral imperative. But this is a very contingent event. What will be the answer when the world gradually returns more or less to the *status quo ante*? In the next chapter, I turn to the arguments advanced by more or less libertarian economists and classical liberal philosophers to the effect that the best solution to the problem of middle-class dissatisfaction and global inequalities is to spur economic growth by removing obstacles to entrepreneurial initiatives. These theorists sometimes invoke the notion of equality of opportunity, but their egalitarian critics interpret that idea very differently. Their views are critically discussed in Chapter 4.

Notes

1 Although the so-called Bayes' rule was proposed by Thomas Bayes in the eighteenth century, it is only during the last two decades or so that statisticians have paid much attention to it. Bayesian probability theory rests on a different epistemological footing than conventional (i.e., "frequentist") mathematical statistics. But the Bayesian subjectivist approach is rapidly gaining ground in the natural and social sciences, forcing econometricians and other users of statistics to revise their models. A very readable introduction to Bayesian reasoning can be found in Sober (2008, chapter 1); see also Howson and Urbach (2006).

2 This point was advanced by A. B. Atkinson in a manuscript written in 1973, which was finally published in 2008 (see Atkinson 2008). In the meantime, several authors had come to the same conclusion, but one or two decades later!

3 For a defense of the Pigou–Dalton principle, see Adler (2013).

4 Piketty (2014, 243) observes that the Gini coefficient does not differentiate between inequality with respect to income from labor or capital.

5 See also Boudreaux and Perry (2013).

6 'Canadians under 35 See Net-Worth Climb, But Toronto Is a Big Exception', *Better Dwelling*, https://betterdwelling.com/canadians-under-35-see-net-worth-climb-but-toronto-is-a-big-exception. See also *Statistics Canada*, www150.statcan.gc.ca/t1/tbl1/en/tv.action?pid=1110004901. It is noteworthy, however, that this trend is much less pronounced for those under the age of thirty-five; in fact, the median net worth for the under-thirty-five age group in the Toronto metropolitan area has declined for the same period.

7 This assumption, which they describe as "poor theory," is sharply criticized by Per Krusell and Anthony Smith (2015, 746).

8 It is often argued that because of technological progress and economic growth, even individuals with modest incomes by today's standards live at least as well as rich aristocrats did 200 years ago. There is some truth to this, but using various devices to

accomplish what was then done by servants may still be more stressful. We still have to wait for the advent of affordable domestic robots capable of executing almost any kind of verbal commands to truly surpass the standards of living of rich nineteenth-century rentiers.

9 In the French case, the assets of industrialists who were charged with having collaborated with the Nazis during the war were nationalized by the state, as has happened with the Renault car manufacturing company.

10 While Piketty wishes to paint a different picture of the distribution of wealth over the long term, he fully acknowledges the significance of Kuznets' pioneering work and credits him (as well as Anthony Atkinson) for having initiated a new field of research (Piketty 2014, 11, 2015b).

11 "To put inequality in democratic America in some historical perspective, it is useful to compare it to authoritarian Rome at its peak. On average, the 500 richest Roman senators had roughly 10,000 times the wealth of the average person in the empire, who was typically a landless farmer or slave. The median wealth of the richest 500 Americans ($2.6 billion in 2015) was about 58,000 times that of the median person in society. If we set aside homes and focus only on financial resources, the top 500 in the United States are easily more than 100,000 times richer than the median American" (Winters 2017, 162).

12 On stagnating wages at the bottom of the scale in the US, see the Congressional Research Service's "Real Wages Trends, 1979 to 2019," https://crsreports.congress.gov.

13 Piketty (2014, 447–452) ingenuously uses the American private universities endowment funds as a proxy for comparing the rate of return on different amounts of invested capital; he found out that Harvard is doing markedly better than any other private university; but the interesting point is that not only Harvard but all private universities with very large endowments benefit from economies of scale insofar as their management fees represent only a small percentage of their total earnings, which is not the case for smaller institutions. The larger the invested capital is, the larger is the net return.

14 Piketty, who is generally sympathetic to the French Socialist Party, opposed the tax raise for two reasons: (1) it was only levied on salaries and bonuses, but not on capital gains and dividends; and (2) it was combined with other tax increases that hit low- and middle-income earners during a recession, thereby predictably making things worse for the unemployed.

15 The paradox is that at the moment, the world as a whole is in debt (to Mars? Piketty [2014, 509] ironizes) because while liabilities are well recorded, assets are often unreported.

16 In a 2015 interview, Piketty singles out this lack of investment in public universities as one of the major causes of inequality in the United States
www.francetvinfo.fr/economie/impots/impots/thomas-piketty-en-periode-de-recession-augmenter-les-impots-comme-la-fait-hollande-c-est-catastrophique_820267.html.

17 His most recent book, titled *Time for Socialism: Dispatches from a World on Fire, 2016–2021* (2021), consists of reprinted columns he wrote for the newspaper *Le Monde.*

18 The strong similarities between Rawls' entire works—and not merely his "difference principle," which is more or less the only idea that most economists, including Piketty, have picked from Rawls' writings—are convincingly underlined by Martin O'Neill (2021).

19 On the continued relevance of the French solidarist tradition, see Dobuzinskis (2010) and Kohn (2016); I discuss the civil economy tradition at greater length in my *Moral Discourse in the History of Economic Thought* (2022).

20 Among the supporters of Piketty, perhaps the most vocal has been Paul Krugman (2014). See also the collection of mostly supportive or mildly critical essays in Boushey et al. (2017).

21 For a recent example that indicates that not only income inequalities but also wealth is on the proverbial "radar" of economists, see Knoop (2020).

22 The journalist Frédéric Georges-Tudo (2015) uses some of the same "errors" to launch a more polemical attack on Piketty, describing his work as "an imposture."

23 See also Avent (2014).

24 At that time, Rognlie was a PhD student in economics at MIT.

25 For a technical explanation of this difference, see Rognlie (2015, 22). Rognlie also cites the conclusion of Robert S. Chirinko's (2008) survey of the empirical literature, according to which the best estimate of the *gross* elasticity of substitution between capital and labor is in the order of 0.52.

26 The G7 group includes Canada, France, Germany, Italy, Japan, the United Kingdom and the United States.

27 Although this afterthought mutes the significance of Piketty's thesis, which now looks more like the traditional rhetoric of economists ("on the one hand, on the other hand …") than a key to the future of capitalism, it repudiates some of his critics who have accused him of being too simplistic (e.g., Delsol 2015).

28 Piketty reasons in terms of abstract stages of historical development; just as premodern societies gave way to modern "proprietarist" market economies, another transition could usher in the age of participatory socialism in which inequalities of wealth and income would be considerably reduced.

29 Since 2011, the international community of researchers uses this cutting mark, but it used to be US$1.25 before that date.

30 That is in terms of the percentage of the world's income that these countries account for; despite its growth, however, India remains a very poor country: only 3 percent of its population earn more than what the very poorest percentile of the US population earn.

31 A lot has happened since 2007, of course; in the wake of the 2008 financial crisis, countries such as Greece and Spain have suffered negative growth, while the Mexican economy has picked up steam. Nevertheless, the gap is not really closing: in 2013, for example, the ratio of per-capita incomes for Morocco vs. Spain was still only 18 percent, up from around 13 percent in 2007 but still much lower than for the 1950s and early 1960s when it was *above* 20 percent. In 2013 the ratio for Mexico vs. the US was just under 30 percent, meaning that the average between 1985 and 2013 has been *flat* in spite of the economic progress experienced by Mexico—a progress that has been far more unstable and fluctuating than for the United States, all things considered (the most dramatic positive change for Mexico happened between the 1950s and the mid-1980s; since then the upward trend in comparison to the United States has flattened). But even as Mexico's economy manages to stay on keel, the situation in several Central American countries has worsened, and consequently, the influx of migrants into the United States continues to be a serious issue.

32 Chinese statistical reports are far from being reliable, and the situations in some rural areas may well be even worse than reported.

33 Among many thinkers who could be cited, I will point (more or less chronologically) to Alfred Fouillée in France, Herbert Croly in the US, and T. H. Marshall in the UK as having played pioneering roles in their respective countries.

34 For a discussion of the limitations of the Gini index for measuring differences among subgroups in a population (say Hispanics in the US), see Sen (1997, 149–163).

4 Equality of Opportunity I

Classical Liberal Perspectives

On the whole, the literature with which I have engaged so far has been more concerned with outcomes than with agency, for example, receiving a wage as opposed to creating a new business or acquiring new skills. The contrast between outcomes and opportunities is far from being clear-cut,[1] but it serves as a bridge to the rest of this book. Equality of welfare evaluates the position individuals reach once they have taken part for some time in the various "games" in which they compete for social and economic advantages. Welfare economics takes equality of welfare as its ultimate goal (without pretending that it can be achieved across the board). It pays a great deal of attention to the issue of compensating those who lose out in the competitive game,[2] but pays relatively little attention to the issue of agency or responsibility. Equality of opportunity is intended to equip the players with the means to do well in the games they will be playing throughout their productive lives. It leaves room for the possibility that economic agents pay at least some price for the wrong choices they make.[3]

Equality of opportunity is a rather vague concept, but it too can be divided into two approaches. One, which is the subject of this chapter, is more concerned with ensuring that economic agents are equal in the range of opportunities that a market economy offers—what in French is called "une carrière ouverte aux talents." Unfairness from that angle takes the form of arbitrary interventions that limit the choices that some individuals could have otherwise made, for example, inequality before the law, protected monopolies, heavy taxation, and so on. Suggesting an apt parallel with the concept of negative liberty or liberty as noninterference, Thomas Nagel (2002, 93) refers to this conception as "negative equality of opportunity" by which he means "the absence of barriers for competition for places in the social and economic hierarchy, so that anyone can rise to a position for which he [*sic*] is qualified." A vibrant economy generates more opportunities for advancement; thus, economic growth can be said to be, if not a necessary condition, at least a facilitating factor for promoting this sort of equality of opportunities. (If those who do well are better-off because of the economic rents they enjoy and protect at the expense of others, the end result is likely to be a stagnating economy.) The other meaning—which is more central to the next two chapters and which is more commonly used by not only

DOI: 10.4324/9781003216247-4

egalitarian philosophers and social activists but also most progressive/heterodox economists—is more concerned with *equalizing access* to existing opportunities for advancement (e.g., education, health) rather than with maximizing opportunities for entrepreneurship and amassing wealth. Indeed, promoting this sort of equality of access to resources (but not of outcomes) could conceivably impose a cost on those who prefer to take their chances in a perfectly competitive economy, that is, reduce efficiency.

Mainstream or orthodox economists (and classical "political economist" before them) have leaned more toward the first interpretation of equality of opportunity than toward the comparatively more egalitarian one. But the arguments they have used to support what Piketty calls "proprietarianism" can be divided into two sorts of discourse. One is characterized by its reliance on a rights-based moral theory that is intended to justify the ownership of (private) property and the freedom to use one's property as one prefers. It is presented as an *a priori* condition for market efficiency and the economic prosperity that is supposed to follow logically from free markets. The other is grounded in consequentialist premises. It claims that economic freedom empirically generates prosperity. Conceivably, therefore, if it could be shown empirically that a different economic regime is more efficient, then it should be adopted as the preferred way of promoting equality of opportunity (presumably something closer to the egalitarian rather than the libertarian definition of the latter). But those who defend this consequentialist thesis strongly argue that no such alternative exists or has ever existed. I hasten to add that the actual writings of the theorists I discuss hereafter often combine these lines of reasoning without explicitly acknowledging that they are analytically distinct.

In the next section, I critically examine the discourse on property rights. Then I turn to the utilitarian approach. Finally, I raise the question of the overall effects of these discourses. It has often been argued that they are at the roots of "neoliberal policies" that are responsible for the rise of income inequalities.' Whether or not this is true, the perception by the general public is that it has indeed been the case, leading to a populist reaction—or rather two sorts of populist reactions: a leftist one and a more nationalist/identarian one. In this same section, I briefly analyze the threat that populism poses to the continued relevance of applied economics. The concluding section prepares the ground for the next chapter in which I discuss philosophical egalitarian approaches to the notion of equality of opportunity and the extent to which the latter necessarily implies taking a stance against efficiency, or whether a more egalitarian yet still reasonably efficient conception of "equality of opportunity" can be worked out.

Ownership and Freedom

It is a rather trivial observation that liberty and equality are often in some sort of tension: too much inequality limits the freedom of a great many individuals and families to lead the sort of lives they should reasonably aspire to in an affluent society, but if ever a perfect allocation of income was hypothetically achieved, it could only be maintained over time by severely limiting the property rights of talented or enterprising individuals who are likely to earn more than the average by offering new goods or services for which demand would be high (Nozick 1974, 161–164; Mankiw 2013). Milton Friedman once exclaimed in a pithy way that "you cannot have a free society without private property" (cited by Bethell 1998, 9).

The origin and implications of individual property rights has been a perennial concern for philosophers and classical political economists. Neoclassical economists, for their part, contributed little to this literature; they tended to treat property rights as a datum and looked instead for "an explanation of the forces determining the price and the number of units of a good to which these rights attach" (Demsetz 1967, 347). But in writing the article from which I quote, Harold Demsetz did much to change this situation (see also Alchian and Demsetz 1973). By disaggregating property rights into "bundles" of distinct entitlements and obligations, he opened up a broad range of investigations into the many ways in which resources can be used and exchanged, from full ownership to less direct forms of contractual arrangements (e.g., leasing). I would add that institutions and cultural norms play a large role in the creation of such "bundles" and in the manner in which they are put into effect.

The first subsection below deals with various philosophical theories about the origins of, and justifications for, property rights; I then move on to questions about which economists have more to say in the following subsection, namely, the efficient but occasionally counterproductive uses to which these rights are put.

Property Rights: Origins and Justifications

Economic liberty involves the liberty to enter any market and either buy or sell available goods and services: "A market exchange reflects the reciprocal exercise of a *liberty to buy* and a *liberty to sell*, with the seller granting the former to the buyer and the buyer granting the latter to the seller" (Buchanan 1987, 7). But the prior question is, of course, how do buyers and sellers acquire the rights to the goods or services that are (more or less) freely offered? (Implicit in this question is the idea that agents can be more or less equal in their power to acquire such rights.) There are three fundamental positions in this regard. They are the natural law thesis, the evolutionary hypothesis (i.e., the hypothesis that property is a social convention that has evolved over time), and the collectivist doctrine that more or less categorically rejects the idea that individuals can claim property rights.

The Natural Position on the Assignment of Property Rights[4]

Private property is an institution that can be traced back to antiquity and, in particular, to Ancient Rome, which had developed a comprehensive legal framework regulating the ownership and transfer of land and other kinds of property. Roman property law found its final and fullest expression in the *Corpus Juris Civilis* completed in 533, but many of the rules it codified had been in existence for centuries before then. Property rights occupy an important place in Cicero's reflections on politics and morality (see his *De Officiis*). It is generally considered that the modern understanding of property rights and of their implications for political economy took shape in the late seventeenth century.[5]

According to the political philosopher C. B. Macpherson (1962), the public philosophy of capitalism, which he described as "possessive individualism," emerged in the writings of Thomas Hobbes and found a more final expression in John Locke's political theory. There are reasons to be skeptical about Hobbes' pivotal role, however. It is clear that Hobbes played a decisive role in the articulation of a radically individualistic view of interpersonal relations—in that respect, in fact, Hobbes was far ahead of his own times. No theorist of rational choice since Hobbes has been able to convey more vivid images of the calculating individual in search of ways to fulfill his or her insatiable desires[6] than can be found in the pages of *Leviathan*. And it is also clear that the fullest economic implications of the ownership of land, money, and other goods can only be realized when people act as autonomous individuals capable of discerning their own self-interest even if, in practice, they rarely, if ever, pay attention *only* to this value. Hobbes turned the table around by justifying the existence of the state in terms of the needs of the individuals who compose it instead of subordinating individuals to the greater cause served by the state. This is a necessary first step for legitimizing economic calculations that assume that economic agents can decide on their own how to dispose of their property. However, Douglas Long (2006) brings up a very forceful objection: Hobbes most often spoke of "propriety"[7] when referring to what we now call property, and this suggests that Hobbes had not yet envisioned that economic agents could divorce their plans from the norms that define why, indeed, it is "proper" to own something, or the extent to which it is proper to claim that one owns something. In that respect, Hobbes makes it clear that there can be no "propriety" in the state of nature, and once a state is instituted, no one owns anything to which the sovereign is not also entitled.[8] In Hobbes' political economy, the political sphere is still the dominant one.

The theory of property offered by Locke—in whose works "property" is usually preferred to "propriety"[9]—became iconic of the market society and migrated into modern economics (e.g., Vaughn 1980). While there is more than a kernel of truth to this interpretation, it ignores many complexities in Locke's thought and abstracts it from his historical settings, as John F. Henry (1999) aptly reminds us. Be it as it may, any discussion of property rights must begin with Locke's theory of property as a *natural* right, as something that is an intrinsic part of human nature. That is because Locke's theory of property grounds the ownership of external objects in the notion of *self*-ownership.

In the *Second Treatise*, Locke upturned the commonly accepted idea that property rights are created by law by arguing that not only do property rights precede government institutions, since they exist in the "state of nature," but that the only reason why rational individuals would consent to become political subjects is "the Preservation of their Property" (§124). In the state of nature, ownership is acquired by mixing one's labor with external objects (§27). Thus, if I pick an apple on a tree that does not (yet) belong to anyone, that apple is mine because I own myself and, therefore, my labor and its effects. And, although land is originally owned in common, I need not obtain the consent of others for doing so (§28).[10] To obtain such a unanimous consent would be practically impossible. Inversely, once I have acquired property through my labor, others have an obligation to respect my right to use it.[11]

This is intuitively quite sensible, although appropriation through labor raises many practical questions: is there also a way for me to claim ownership of the apple tree itself? Or, as Robert Nozick (1974, 174) somewhat facetiously asks, by building a fence around a territory, do I become the owner of that territory of only the fence and the land underneath it? These are not questions that Locke tried to answer because his purpose was not to justify existing property rights—which is, however, Nozick's goal (and, by extension, that of strict libertarians)—but merely to argue that law was not the original source of property right. He was prepared to admit that the exact contours of these rights would be specified by law. Locke did, nevertheless, discuss two practical problems.

Locke thought that those who acquire property through their labor bear two kinds of responsibilities. The first is not to take more than they can use before it spoils (§30). It was immoral in his view to waste what God had created for the benefit of the whole of humankind. That particular problem, however, has been solved with the invention of money (§46): since it is possible to store precious metals, which, by common agreement, can be exchanged against all other goods, there is no need to amass more perishable goods than one can consume, and more can be purchased later with the saved gold or silver. But Locke thought of another and more perplexing responsibility. The so-called Lockean proviso poses a difficult question that is still being debated today. How is it possible to acquire property legitimately when one is allowed to do so only if "there is enough and as good left in common for others" (§26)? This is a glaring example of the sort of puzzling ambiguities that one encounters throughout the *Second Treatise*. I do not intend to discuss all the many interpretations of that sibylline phrase, but I want to examine two widely divergent theses.

We owe to James Tully (1980) what is perhaps the most restrictive interpretation of the Lockean proviso. Drawing not only from chapter 5 of the *Second Treatise* but also from the *First Treatise* and the *Essay on Human Understanding*, Tully attributes to Locke the idea that property rights would be allocated by civil society in light of prevailing values and circumstances. In other words, the qualifier "enough and as good" implies that after having left the state of nature and its abundance, those who wish to acquire property could do so only in ways prescribed by laws stipulating the implications of that qualifier. A redistribution scheme transferring a fraction of what property owners earn to those unable to make a living could be one of these implications. While Locke himself did not go that far, Tully claims to have uncovered in his belief that "charity is a natural and positive duty" (Tully 1980, 132) the seeds of this potential redistributive arrangement.[12]

At the opposite end of the spectrum, Nozick has proposed an ingenious way out of the conundrum posed by the Lockean proviso. Nozick (1974, 176) suggests that there are really two ways of interpreting it. The more "stringent" one would preclude all forms of appropriation that would result not only in a loss of opportunities for others but also in their inability to continue to gain access to the resources in question. The "weaker" interpretation only requires that when someone appropriates a resource, others are not made worse-off by denying them opportunities to improve their situations; if such opportunities can be found in a market economy, then the proviso no longer applies. Insofar as private property "increases the social product by putting means of production in the hands of those who can use them most efficiently," among other indirect benefits (Nozick 1974, 177), no opportunities are lost for anyone. Indeed, everyone can potentially be made better-off.[13] Disposing of this objection was an important step in Nozick's attempt to shore up his "entitlement theory."[14] The latter affirms the existence of three principles: justice in acquisition, justice in transfer, and a principle of rectification (Nozick 1974, 150–174). The first two are summarized as follows:

1. A person who acquires a holding in accordance with the principle of justice in acquisition is entitled to that holding.
2. A person who acquires a holding in accordance with the principle of justice in transfer, from someone else entitled to the holding, is entitled to the holding.
3. No one is entitled to a holding except by (repeated) applications of (1) and (2) (Nozick 1974, 151).

The principle of rectification states that when these conditions are not met, an injustice presumably took place, which must be rectified. Information must be gathered about "what would have occurred (or a probability distribution over what might have occurred, using the expected value) if the injustice had not taken place"; then if it turns out that the "actual description of holdings" does not match any of the "descriptions yielded by the principle … one of the descriptions yielded must be realized" (Nozick 1974, 153).[15]

It should be no surprise that Nozick's entitlement theory has not met with universal agreement. Evidently, those who argue from an *a priori* position on rights (i.e., what Nozick calls "end-state principles"), such as John Rawls and his followers, rather than from Nozick's historical standpoint, are in fundamental disagreement with it. Among the great many critiques and objections raised by egalitarian liberals, one of the most perceptive responses has been articulated by Jeremy Waldron (2005). Rather than either strengthening the case for a theory of entitlement or a theory of *a priori* rights to non–property-based welfare, Waldron proposes to develop both "hand in hand" (87). In other words, a case should be made for grounding proprietary rights and the right to a social minimum. (I will come back to the latter issue in the next chapter, but it is important to underline that the problem can be approached from the standpoint of promoting liberty as well as from the perspective of minimizing unacceptable social inequalities.)

Gopal Sreenivasan's (1995) interpretation of Locke sits somewhere between Tully's charitable Locke and the Locke as apostle of laissez faire portrayed by Nozick. This interpretations depends on making a distinction between Locke's literal theory of property and what Sreenivasan presents as "Lockean property"; the latter is what can be logically inferred from Locke's principles, but was not explicitly articulated by Locke himself. Lockean property is premised on the idea that land was originally held in common by all (before it was concretely appropriated by some). It is consistent with the argument that every member of a society where private property is the foundation of the economy has a right to a share of the hypothetical average revenues that can be generated by putting the sum total of all parcels of land to productive uses. Those who have obtained ownership through their labor are obviously able to enjoy their share—and possibly much more, considering that some parcels are more fertile than others, and some people are more productive than others. But those who are left out, because in practice land is scarce, still have a valid claim to their share of the earth's bounty. The existence of a surplus should make it possible for those who own land to satisfy these claims. This could become the basis for a redistributive scheme of some sort.[16]

The last group in the family of Lockean theories who deserve attention are the left libertarians. They fully endorse the idea of self-ownership and its corollary in terms of inviolable property rights. However, they reject the notion that one could claim an exclusive right on natural resources (land, rivers, minerals, etc.). That is, possession of these resources by individuals or firms is not prohibited, but they can be taxed up to 100 percent of the value of the rent generated by these resources. The reason provided for this policy is that contrary to other goods, land and similar resources are not the products of anyone's accomplishments. For most left libertarians, resource rents are indeed the *only* legitimate source of revenues for the state in carrying any or all of its functions (which might be rather limited). For Alfred Fouillée and the early-twentieth-century French solidarists, whose association with left libertarianism, in the strictest sense, is somewhat looser, a tax on several other sorts of economic rents, including those resulting from the use of socially produced knowledge, could serve to fund a wider range of redistributive programs (see Dobuzinskis 2010).

The idea that property in land (and other natural resources, e.g., rivers) can legitimately be constrained is not new. Taxing land owners had already been recommended by several eighteenth-century thinkers, notably, the French Physiocrat François Quesnay as well as Thomas Jefferson and Tom Paine. The main protagonists of that idea in the nineteenth century were the American journalist Henry George and the French economist Léon Walras. George was a self-taught rather than a professional economist, but no less an authority on economic history than Joseph Schumpeter ([1954] 2006, 865) thought that George had succeeded in becoming "a very orthodox economist," at least as far as his treatment of anything other than land was concerned. As for Walras, he is, of course, remembered for his theory of general equilibrium that remains the cornerstone of neoclassical economics; his "social economics," as he called it, is less well known, however. Both argued that land is not a factor of production like others, that is, labor and capital. (By contrast, most contemporary economists subsume land under capital.) In his famous *Progress and Poverty* ([1879] 1935), George explains that the

> right of ownership that springs from labor excludes the possibility of any other right of ownership. If a man be rightfully entitled to the produce of his labor, then no one can be rightfully entitled to the ownership of anything which is not the produce of his labor or of the labor of someone else from whom the right has passed to him.
>
> (336)

Consequently, there are "two classes of things … and to class them together as property is to confuse all thought when we come to consider the justice of the injustice, the right or the wrong of property" (George [1879] 1935, 337). As an example of this confusion, George points to "real estate," which includes both houses (produced by human labor) and land. The essential significance of that distinction is that

> the sanction which natural justice gives to one species of property is denied to the other; that the rightfulness which attaches to individual property in the produce of labor implies the wrongfulness of individual property in land; that, whereas the recognition of the one places all men upon equal terms, securing to each the due reward of his labor, the recognition of the other is the denial of the equal rights of men, permitting those who do not labor to take the natural reward of those who do.
>
> (338)

George did not object to inequalities due to differences in effort or ingenuity. The greatest injustice in society, for him, resides in the fact that some people can become wealthy by taking advantage of their control over land when natural law actually dictates that everyone enjoys an equal right to use what nature provides.

The policy implication of these normative premises is that income should not be taxed and that total economic freedom should prevail in all areas other than the disposition of land and natural resources in general. It follows that there should be no income tax but a "single tax" on land rent. There is no need, however, for a complete confiscation of what landowners have acquired: it "is not necessary to confiscate land; it is only necessary to confiscate rent" (George [1879] 1935, 405). He argued that in this way landowners could continue to have "possession" of the land, but they could not claim all the privileges associated with ownership.

On this point, George and Walras differed. Walras, who was aware of George's work and also appealed to natural law, offered a very similar diagnosis of the causes of economic inequality. However, he recommended that the state should purchase all rural and urban lands from their owners. The process he outlined was a very gradual one that could take decades in his estimation to be completed.[17] Once owned by the state, land could be leased on a long-term basis to those who would put it to productive use. Walras was very much in agreement with George with respect to the advantages of free markets and free trade (with the exclusion of land and natural resources). Therefore, he had in mind a limited role for the state. However, Walras was a little closer to socialism than George, albeit not orthodox socialism. He argued that the phasing out of property in land would redistribute wealth and, thereby, make it easier for workers to organize cooperatives;[18] he also suggested that the state should reform its tax policies in favor of workers-owned cooperatives. The end result of these reforms would be the advent of what Walras described as a "liberal humanitarian socialism."

After an initial wave of enthusiasm that led to the formation of a Georgist movement,[19] the single tax idea faded away after World War I. Property taxes are generally not very popular with middle-class voters.[20] But in the last quarter of the twentieth century, "left libertarians," seduced by libertarian arguments about self-ownership but not willing to give up the ideal of rectifying injustices in a meaningful way, rediscovered—if not the single tax—at least the idea that "natural resources belong to everyone in some egalitarian manner" (Vallentyne 2009, 136).

If the common ownership of natural resources implies that no one should be permitted to acquire land without first obtaining the collective consent of all members of society, it is clearly impractical and perhaps even "crazy" (Vallentyne 2009, 148). There remains two feasible ways of fulfilling the Lockean proviso in an equitable manner. One is "equal share left libertarianism" (148), which is, in essence, what George proposed; in more recent years, it has been associated with the works of Hillel Steiner (e.g., Steiner 1994). This approach requires "that one leave an equally valuable per capita share of the value of natural resources for others ... Those who use or appropriate more than their per capita share owe others compensation for their excess share" (148). A more egalitarian option favored by Vallentyne and Michael Otsuka (2003) requires "that one leave enough for others to have an opportunity for well-being that is at least as good as the opportunity for well-being that one obtained in using or appropriating natural resources" (Vallentyne 2009, 149). As Otsuka (2003, 40) remarks, this principle would probably result in frequent redistribution of the value of the share of natural resources owned by the members of society.[21]

If what justifies taxing land rents is that it is unfair to allow individuals to appropriate natural resources they did not create, would it not also be justifiable to tax rents in general, whether or not their source is nature itself? Indeed, it has been objected that merely taxing land rents would not be sufficient for funding programs designed to compensate those who are disadvantaged through no fault of their own (on this interpretation of fairness and its implication for equality of opportunity, see Chapter 5). Then what about the idea of taxing rents derived from one's social status or the profits of monopolistic firms? Today, digital platforms would be the most obvious example of the latter. As for rent from social status, Philippe van Parijs (1995) has ventured that in today's less-than-full-employment economy, merely holding a job is functionally equivalent to benefiting from a rent. Social policies based on such ideas would still be left libertarian in some sense,[22] but there would be more room for taxing a wider range of income sources.

Evolutionary Approaches

The natural law perspective rests on rationalist premises that are open to question. Harold Demsetz's (2008, 127) theory rests on a more realistic premise: "The emergence of property rights [is due] to changes in circumstances whose effects were to raise the losses associated with the lack of such rights."[23] In other words, property, having proved useful, developed over time into a convention. This explanation can be traced back to David Hume and, following him, Adam Smith and other members of the Scottish Enlightenment. More recently, this evolutionary outlook has been revived by F. A. Hayek. Broadly speaking, a similar perspective is shared by the increasingly influential neoinstitutionalists who study institutions mainly as a means for reducing transaction costs (Harris et al. 2020).

Hume saw little value in Locke's contract theory as the foundation of property rights. Nevertheless, he saw great merits in the idea of private property because of the freedom that ownership entails. He used a telling metaphor to convey the idea that property was a social discovery:

> Two men pull the oars of a boat, [they] do it by an agreement or convention, though they have never given promises to each other. Nor is the rule concerning the stability of possession the less derived from human conventions, that it arises gradually, and acquires force by a slow progression, and by our repeated experience of the inconveniences of transgressing it … In like manner are languages gradually establish'd by human conventions without any promise. In like manner do gold and silver become the common manner of exchange.
>
> (*A Treatise of Human Nature*, Bk III, Part II, Section 2 [Hume 2009 , 748])

But conventions are more easily enforceable when they are backed by law. Hence the idea that property rights must be entrenched in a legal framework. This was also what Smith thought:

> The origin of natural rights is quite evident. That a person has a right to have his body free from injury, and his liberty free from infringement unless there is a proper cause, nobody doubts. But acquired rights, such as property require more explanation. Property and civil government very much depend on one and another. The preservation of property and then inequality of possession first formed it, and the state of property must always vary with the form of government.
>
> (Quoted by West 2003, 24)

However, it is important to underline that what Smith alludes to here is the role of government in *protecting* property rights. It is easier to protect legal provisions than mere conventional arrangements, but for Smith and the whole Common Law tradition,[24] the law does not create rights *ex nihilo*. The law merely institutionalizes preexisting customs. Thus, Smith was not saying that governments create property regimes; circumstances and customs vary, and so do laws, but they do not, or ought not, mirror the plans or immediate interests of the rulers.

This distinction has been elaborated at great length by Hayek (1973). Law and judge-made law, in particular, form an order that he refers to as "nomos" or the "law of liberty." It rests on rules that made society possible, and not the other way around, that is, law is not something that the legislator enacted for specific social purposes. But even though it is quite stable over time, law does not remain static. It changes as a result of judicial decisions; judges are

> expected to decide the case as one of a kind which might occur anywhere and at any time, and therefore in a manner which will satisfy the expectations of any person placed in a similar position among persons not know to him individually.
>
> (97)

Legislation, by contrast, is created for specific purposes, usually in response to demands formulated by some groups. In modern times, such policy goals have typically curtailed economic liberty by (more or less) coercive means:

> If in the course of the last one hundred years the principle that in a free society coercion is possible only to secure obedience to universal rules of just conduct has been abandoned, this was done mainly in the service of what were called 'social' aims.
>
> (141)

Admittedly, in liberal democracies, the threat posed by such actions to property rights is reduced by various safeguards, often entrenched as constitutional rules. Property is rarely declared to be an inviolable principle in itself, but property rights are protected by constitutional and other provisions intended to guarantee due process—an obligation that ultimately derives its force from the idea of natural rights. The irony here is that as abstract and universal law (Hayek's *nomos*) is being displaced by targeted legislation, we are led back to the idea that, ultimately, property rights are best justified by an appeal to (Lockean) natural law, even though there really is nothing very natural about "natural" law. To avoid that contradiction, Hayek insisted, especially toward the end of his life,[25] that a market economy and the legal and political institutions that sustain a regime of liberty can be shown to be desirable because they, in fact, are the only way to achieve prosperity for a growing population. In other words, social evolution has produced the conditions for human flourishing in the form of the "Great Society." To weaken its (classically) liberal institutional foundations in the name of egalitarianism is self-defeating. In a parallel manner, but on the basis of a more empirical historical narrative, and adding multiple layers of cultural analysis, the economist Deirdre McCloskey has insistently argued that it was a very unique set of circumstances that allowed the emergence in Western Europe of beliefs and values from which flowed social practices—primarily those of merchants and their "bourgeois" culture—that spurred economic growth. The subtitle of the third volume of her "bourgeois trilogy" (McCloskey 2006, 2010, 2016) nicely sums up her thesis: *Bourgeois Equality: How Ideas, Not Capital or Institutions, Enriched the World* (2016). This is a very significant idea, pun intended, although it can be argued that McCloskey has not paid sufficient attention to the institutional mechanisms that have evolved to *implement* these new bourgeois values (see Weingast 2016). More controversially, McCloskey (2022) draws the epistemological conclusion that economics cannot be a positivist science but must be rooted in ethics. Even more controversially, she claims that the only ethical doctrine that is adequate for that purpose is classical liberalism. Although I do not intend to prove her wrong, insofar as I also accept the fundamental premises of classical liberalism, including the indispensability of robust property rights, the rest of this book suggests that her argument is overstated. Liberalism is a complex tradition within which there exist many currents that have also made crucial contributions to our understanding of the state–society nexus and which illuminate the central question I am concerned with, namely, how can economic growth and societal wealth (in both material and artistic/scientific/cultural sense) be achieved in a fair and equitable manner.

Counterarguments and Refutations

Two sorts of moral or ideological criticisms of property rights have been raised, mostly by socialist thinkers. The first can be traced back all the way to the Roman tribunes Tiberius and Gaius Gracchus (first century BC) and extend through the writings of Jean-Jacques Rousseau[26] and many others. It questions the unfair distribution of property and the resulting inequalities, not only in material resources but also in power and status. The remedy to these inequalities, according to this first school of thought, is to be sought in a more equal distribution of property rights, often associated with the idea of workers' self-management. The second, more radical school of thought, typified by orthodox

Marxism, denies that property rights are legitimate and seeks to replace them with some form of collective ownership and control. Space lacks here to analyze these currents of thought in all their complexities. Consequently, I zero in on the two most prominent representatives of these currents: Joseph Proudhon (1809–65) and Karl Marx (1818–83).

Proudhon

Although famous for having declared that "property is theft," Joseph Proudhon, who loved polemics, was not opposed to the concept of individual property. Far from it, in fact, in the second edition (1841) of his famous pamphlet "What Is Property?" he remarked that his original declaration was unfortunate: "*What is property?* I may not … answer, *It is theft*, without the certainty of being misunderstood." And misunderstood he certainly has been. What he objected to was its unequal distribution. In this inequality, he saw the greatest obstacle to the achievement of freedom, and freedom was for him the highest value.[27] As he explained (Proudhon 1868, 46 my translation),

> It did not suffice for me to have noticed the egoistic principle of property to abandon the institution [of property]; I say only that there is there a matter to be resolved. I believe that property, until now little understood or even not understood at all, is still to be organized.

The way in which Proudhon intended to organize property was definitely utopian, albeit not as naïvely as in the utopian fantasies spun by Charles Fourier or Robert Owen. What he envisioned was a gradual, nonviolent process in which the producers come together to form cooperatives or, as he called them, "mutualist" firms. These were supposed to be associations of independent workers who would retain ownership of their tools or owned in common and managed that which could not be individually parceled out. The Mondragon federation of workers cooperatives in the Basque region of Spain is a contemporary example of this idea in practice.

Proudhon was an anarchist. His goal was to replace the state with federated cooperatives. In other words, for him, political reforms would come as the consequence of socioeconomic transformations in civil society. First, a new system of production and distribution would emerge, and then the political institutions would be altered to reflect this new state of affairs. There would be no political revolution but a gradual evolution; in no circumstance did he recommend substituting state ownership for private (or shared) property. His was a libertarian socialist vision that preserved the liberating potentials of property, but precluded a class of *rentiers* from taking undue advantages of it.

More or less inspired by Proudhon, a tradition of "market socialism" has pursued the ideal of social justice without abandoning the model of a market economy. This tradition is still very much alive today even if it lacks a political base capable of bringing about its realization. In other words, it remains an intellectual exercise. Its central theme is that social justice and an end to economic exploitation can be achieved by transferring the control of firms to the workers themselves, but these firms would compete in a free market. Economic freedom would not disappear because individuals could possibly choose to work independently, but salaried work would be integrated within cooperative structures, empowering the employees of such firms by placing them on an equal footing. Within such firms, economic freedom would in a sense give way to democratic freedom. State control over the internal and external activities of these cooperatives would presumably be rather limited; otherwise, market socialism would morph into centrally planned socialism. But the state could still play an active role in encouraging the creation of cooperatives and, eventually, their supplanting of conventional, capitalist-owned firms. (Advocates of market socialism are not always clear about how, nor do they completely agree on the extent to which cooperatives would displace firms owned or managed by economic agents other than the employees themselves.) Although this line of thinking has generally been pursued by sociologists and other social scientists (a good example is the French "solidary economy" school of thought, e.g., Vienney 1994), a few respected economists have made decisive contributions to this paradigm, notably, Samuel Bowles (Bowles and Gintis 1998), John Roemer (Roemer and Arneson 1996), Yunker (2001), and Ted Burczak (2006).

Marx

Marx ironized about Proudhon's works; he attacked utopian socialists in his *Poverty of Philosophy* (1847), an obvious pun on Proudhon's *Philosophy of Misery*.[28] For Marx, private property of the means of production stands in the way of human emancipation. It is irremediably oppressive. Marx developed his critique along two axes that chronologically also correspond to two stages of his life and thought. The first is philosophical; it revolves around the somewhat elusive notion of "alienation." The second is more practical; it is centered on the concept of "exploitation" whereby the owners of the means of production unduly appropriate the "surplus value" generated by the workers they employ. These concepts are well known and, therefore, need not be explained in detail. But it must be stressed that the (labor-based) "surplus value" is not a concrete, measurable amount of wealth appropriated by the capitalist, but an *abstract* concept that makes sense only within the disputable context of Marx's political economy. For this reason, it has been argued by several critics that it is a far weaker argument against private ownership of the means of production that Marx had hoped it would be.

Marx's attempt to define exploitation as the extraction of "surplus value" was arguably a mistake because, while exploitation does occur anytime, there exists an imbalance of power between wage earners and their employers, grounding it in something as immaterial and impossible to measure as "labor value" failed to achieve a decisive blow against capitalist exploitation per se. As understood by Marx, "value" is not a measurable amount of wealth appropriated by the capitalist, but an abstract concept distinct from actual prices (e.g., the wages paid to workers as the price of their time spent working and the profits retained by the capitalists, parts of which can be reinvested in the business). Admittedly led astray by David Ricardo in thinking that labor has an *intrinsic* value, but for which Ricardo never found the "invariable measure" he desperately searched for, Marx ended up acknowledging (soon after he published the first volume of *Capital*) that to prove that exploitation is inherent in the wage economy. he had to find a way to transform the abstract labor value hypothesized by his Ricardian model into empirical prices. But he never convincingly resolved this problem, with which he struggled until the end of his life (Brewer 1995; Dobuzinskis 2022).

The philosophical idea of alienation cannot be so easily dismissed. In the *Economic and Philosophical Manuscripts* of 1844, a work that still bears the mark of Hegelian philosophy, Marx argued that the capitalist industrial society alienates human beings from themselves, from each other, and from nature. In other words, the path to liberty is blocked by capitalism, which robs humans of their capacity to experience the transformation of nature through work as a personal and shared experience that gives meaning to their existence and fulfills their aspirations. It is doubtful, however, that the complete abolition of private property would solve the problem. As the experience of the Soviet Union proved, collectivization does not make work more meaningful, nor does it help people master their destinies. Regardless of this historical example, it is the very process of the division of labor and the technological innovations that go with it that is at the root of the problem. Nothing short of a return to artisanal creation and a very simple rural economy could free individuals engaged in complex webs of interdependencies they do not understand and feel estranged from. But the cost of such a regress would be unacceptable. Some measure of emancipation from the hierarchical structures that prevail in large firms can be, and is, achieved in cooperatives where employees have a say in the management of the company. As I suggested previously when assessing Piketty's *Capital and Ideology*, and as I further elaborate in the concluding chapter, I see some merits in the idea of *pre*distribution. Reforms inspired by Rawls' property-owning democracy, the Italian "civil economy" tradition, or the French "économie solidaire" could shift the focus from potentially inefficient redistribution toward more efficient forms of predistribution. If appropriately enacted, such reforms could also go a long way toward addressing alienation. It is far from clear, however, that most people today are as motivated to play an active part in the management of their places of employment on a regular basis and would be willing to invest their time and efforts in the required activities, as the proponents of these reforms believe is the case.

Are Property Rights Dispensable?

Before the 1920s, the entire debate about the practicability of dispensing with private property was centered around the issue of incentives: the critiques of socialism, and especially of Marxism, pointed out that in the absence of private property and the wage system, nobody would have an incentive to save and work, and particularly to do unpopular and unpleasant jobs, such as mining, garbage pickup, refinery work, and so on. If everyone is remunerated according to their needs, and not, for example, according to the marginal revenue product, who will then take out the garbage?

The response by Marxists was that in the socialist society that would eventually emerge after a revolution and the subsequent "dictatorship of the proletariat," labor productivity would increase so much that immensely less work would have been required to achieve the same effect. Additionally, the new socialist society would create a new psychological type: a new socialist man, selfless and altruistic, who would be eager to take the hardest jobs even for a low wage in order to help his socialist comrades (Trotsky 2006). Therefore, according to Marxists, the incentives argument was moot.

However, in 1920, Ludwig von Mises published his path-breaking paper "Economic Calculation in the Socialist Commonwealth" (Mises 1990), which completely transformed the debate on socialism and private property. This paper underlined a problem that both the critics and supporters of socialism previously overlooked. Even if we assume that the New Socialist Superman, with his supranatural ethical and epistemic capabilities, would not need incentives to work, what would he (or she) be asked to do? How will the central planner in the socialist "commonwealth" determine what the New Socialist Man will be producing, in what quantities, and by what means? Every item can be produced by numerous different combinations of labor, capital, and raw materials. In the absence of market prices for these factors, the manager of the socialist enterprise would not have any credible way of discerning which one of these innumerable combinations is the most efficient. There are good reasons to think that in a socialist system it would not be possible to tell the difference between efficient production and wasting resources on unwanted goods. In a market economy, this coordinating function is fulfilled by cost accounting, by which the revenues are compared to the monetary costs. This basic business calculus allows firms to adjust their operations to the needs and requirements of their customers and suppliers. By allowing for the comparison of costs and returns, capitalistic process rationalizes economic decision-making: it gradually filters out—by monetary rewards and losses, by profit and bankruptcy—the good from the bad business decisions. Abolishing private property in the means of production would destroy this entire rationalizing in one fell swoop. Together with private property, the market for production factors would cease to exist, said Mises, and hence we would neither have real *market* prices for the factors of production nor the ability to calculate costs. According to Mises, socialist economic planning would become a "leap in the dark" (1936, 22) and an enormous waste of resources. Socialism, thus, was literally impossible, not for moral or ethical but for purely economic reasons:

> Without economic calculation there can be no economy. Hence, in a socialist state wherein the pursuit of economic calculation is impossible, there can be … no economy whatsoever. In trivial and secondary matters

> rational conduct might still be possible, but in general it would be impossible to speak of rational production any more.
>
> (Mises 1990, 14)

So, private property rights are, according to Mises, indispensable not only because they create better incentives to work and save, but, more importantly, because without private property in the means of production, there could be no rational economic planning.

The socialist theorists of that era responded by devising alternate schemes for making socialism work and by providing different explanations of the final goals of socialist economic policy (Taylor 1929; Lange 1936; Lange and Taylor 1938). They conceded that the problem how to calculate the cost and how to collect the knowledge necessary for the economic coordination was a serious one. Oskar Lange and Abba Lerner argued that Mises was right in pointing out that the sort of calculation that would be theoretically possible would be of little practical use, and for that matter, the older socialist ideas of producing without profit and distributing income according to one's needs were untenable (Lange 1936). However, they contended that this did not mean that market prices, as they exist in a capitalist economy, were the most efficient means of allocating resources. According to Taylor (1929), market prices functioned as endogenously given "parameters" that the entrepreneurs use in their calculations of profit and loss; but if the parametric character of prices is a deciding factor, then the government's central planning body could set more useful and equitable "parameters." From a diverging ideological standpoint. Vilfredo Pareto and Enrico Barone also proved that *if* the central planner could provide reliable information on the state of technology and consumer preferences, then the central panning problem, at least theoretically, could be solved by using the complex systems of simultaneous equations (Klein 1996). Hence, according to Lange and Taylor, there was nothing wrong theoretically with socialism; as for technical and practical problems, they could be solved along the way toward the ultimate goal of building a more perfectly egalitarian society (Klein 1996). But that is, of course, a big leap of faith.

Contrary to Mises, the advocates of planning argued that private property is not necessary for prices to perform their function of the resource allocators (Bergson 1948; Lange and Taylor 1938). By using the trial-and-error method, the central planning board can fine-tune the prices and set the economy on a more efficient path. This "market socialism" would mesh a socially responsible way of allocating resources with market prices;[29] in other words, it would combine the best of capitalism and socialism, the allocative efficiency of price coordination with the "social" benefits of centrally directed economy.

Criticizing Mises' argument that even a Superman would not know how to allocate resources, that is, to determine a specific price for every item, Bergson responds:

> Once tastes and techniques are given, the values of the means of production can be determined unambiguously by imputation without the intervention

> of market process. The Board of Supermen could decide readily how to allocate resources so as to assure the optimum welfare. It would simply have to solve the equations of Pareto and Barone.
>
> (1948, 446)

But this experiment was never really fully tested, and the intractable problems faced by the Soviet Union throughout its history suggest that, on the whole, the Misesian thesis was the right one. This is not to say that property rights do not create their own dilemmas.

The Use/Abuse of Property Rights

What can be said about the implications of legitimately acquired property rights? Setting aside Marxist theorists, it is generally agreed, and vigorously proclaimed by free-market apologists, that property owners should be allowed to use what they own as they see fit, provided they cause no harm in doing so. But what does "harm" mean in this context? This is the first question that I address hereafter. Then I turn to the issue of what happens, or should happen, when these rights are abused. Obviously, fraud and similar illegal practices must be dealt with through the justice system. But more perplexing are abuses that are not quite as malevolent, such as externalities and rent-seeking, as I explain further on.

Progressive economists and egalitarian philosophers take it for granted that profound inequalities of income or wealth are harmful to the common good and must be remedied. More conservative economists, and arguably most economists in general, tend to side with classical liberal-political theorists who raise questions about the extent and nature of the harm. Typically, they either minimize the severity of the problem or claim that reducing the damage caused by inequalities, even severe ones, would risk to have unintended consequences that could create even more harm, when they do not deploy both arguments together. They do, however, maintain that, at the very least, the equality of opportunity entails that property rights are well defined and not subject to arbitrary violations.

As was mentioned in the previous chapter, the significance of the data amassed by Piketty and his colleagues has been criticized. For example, it is sometimes alleged that if one looks at consumption expenditures, the living conditions of households at the bottom of the ladder have not fallen behind as dramatically as it seems when one considers only incomes. Steven Horwitz (2021, 61–62) has claimed that the "standards of living of the average American household and the poorest American households have risen significantly in the last forty or fifty years, even as inequality might have grown." Horwitz bases this claim on two factual observations: (1) inflation, as measured by the widely used Consumer Price Index, has arguably been overestimated, and (2) as costs have come down, thanks to technological change, global trade, and so on, one has to work lesser hours at the current average wage rate to afford a variety of goods than was the case in the 1970s (using that metric, an electric typewriter then was more expansive than a basic laptop today). As long as the process of competition is fair, everyone will have a chance to take advantage of a dynamic market economy. What needs to be done is to remove obstacles, such as restrictive licensure procedures, zoning regulations, and so on (Horwitz 2021, 76), that contradict the principle of equality of opportunity and limit income mobility. A parallel argument among the critics of the politics of inequality[30] is that obstacles to growth, and not inequality of income, is what policymakers ought to be concerned with. According to James Piereson (2015, 15),

> The United States may have an inequality problem but more fundamentally it has a "growth" problem. A stagnant America ... lacking broad opportunities for advancement and achievement, would represent something new and dangerous for a nation whose ideals and institutions have been built upon a foundation of growth and prosperity.

While Horwitz may have painted an exaggeratedly optimistic picture of the reality of economic life in the US, other critics of the politics of inequality are willing to concede that if not inequalities per se, at least poverty is worrisome. The challenge is, as Watson (2015, 142) amusingly puts it,

> a strategy focused on growth may not actually bring greater social mobility: the rising tide may lift all boats but people don't necessarily get to switch boats, moving from dinghy to yacht or vice versa. At the other extreme, a strategy focused solely on social mobility may be very zero-sum, which may make it hard to put in place: people with yachts will resist being transferred to dinghies. A strategy of enlarging the dinghies—making them into rowboats, say, or even small powerboats—would reduce the precariousness of life at the bottom of the nautical distribution with only marginal discomfort at the top end from having to help finance the renovations. Finally, a strategy of torpedoing or at least sending the yachts into dry dock for radical downsizing may create problems of its own, worsening life at the top without necessarily improving it at the bottom.

This is the dilemma and hence the title of this book! Fighting inequality through ambitious redistributive policies may cause more or less severe inefficiencies. Among these inefficiencies, perhaps the one about which apologists of the market economy worry the most is the effect on incentive for entrepreneurs and creative talents (Mankiw 2013; Rauh 2015; Conard 2016; Watson 2015). What could be perceived as punitively high taxes on income, let alone wealth, will discourage entrepreneurship and even provide justifications for tax evasion,[31] thereby reducing productive investments. Contrary to Piketty, for example, Rauh (2015, 40) claims that what is striking about the richest people in the US and the rest of the world is that so many of them have risen to the top from rather modest backgrounds, and not through inheritance: "The returns to skill has exploded since the 1980s." Or, as Gregory Mankiw (2013, 32) succinctly puts it, "If the incomes of the top 1 percent were much greater than their economic contributions … then the case for increasing the top tax rate would indeed be strong." One might be a little incredulous, however, about the *exact* level of these contributions considering that it has frequently been reported that the CEOs of companies that have experienced setbacks or even severe losses often have not themselves suffered any loss in their earnings! But it is true that Piketty has very few kind words for successful entrepreneurs and pathbreakers without whose innovations growth would, no doubt, have been even more sluggish in North America or Europe. And on the whole, countries with comparatively lower taxes (the US, Canada) recruit many more foreign talents than countries with comparatively higher taxes (e.g., the Scandinavian countries, France, Argentina), although this is only one of many reasons.

Now, what about the less-than-optimal, and sometimes perverse, consequences of unchecked property rights? The economics literature on these sources of inefficiencies is vast and diverse, and debates among economists who hold different ideological views are ongoing. Negative externalities, as pointed out in Chapter 2, were first theorized by Arthur Pigou. They result from decisions by economic agents who fail to take into account the negative effects of their activities on other agents and/or the community at large; the classical example is environmental pollution. Again, as I pointed out previously (see Chapter 2), the polar extremes on this problem are the position taken by proponents of strict regulation, on the one hand, and those who wish to follow Ronald Coase's recommendation to let the parties negotiate a way out of their conflicts; Pigou's advocacy of the use of targeted taxes falling somewhere in the middle, constituting an early example of what is nowadays referred to as a "nudging" approach. Since I have already discussed this issue and underlined, in particular, the limits of Coasean bargaining for dealing with problems characterized by high transaction costs, I now turn to the question of what to do about economic rents.

Economic rents flow to the owners of resources that have increased in price for reasons that typically have little or nothing to do with the owners' role in the market, and everything to do with increased demand for these resources by agents other than the owners who have plans to put these to some productive use. I have already dealt with the controversy surrounding the passive enjoyment of such rents, as it were. As I mentioned, the Georgists see in land rents, in particular, the source of severe inequalities throughout the economy and recommend taxing land rents maximally. More conservative economists are not quite as concerned as Georgists with passive rent-taking (i.e., "being at the right place at the right time"), but are much more critical of rent-seeking. When categories of economic agents (e.g., farmers, monopolists, noncompetitive firms, government employees, trade unions) lobby the government to obtain subsidies or the enactment of regulations that protect them from having to compete with more efficient producers or consolidate privileges they might have informally benefited from, they can reap the advantages of making one's place the right place to be in and forever, as it were. This results in what Richard E. Wagner (2016) calls "an entangled political economy." Libertarians are fond of responding to critics of capitalism that it is not the market process itself that brings about unfair conditions, but "crony capitalism" (Munger and Villareal-Diaz 2019; Holcombe 2021). As Gordon Tullock (1967) argued, not only are the outcomes of lobbying the cause of inefficiencies but rent-*seeking*—that is, active and persistent lobbying—itself diverts resources from more productive uses.

An entangled political economy—an economy in which organized interests take advantage of their insider status—works against the ideal of equality of opportunities.[32] This thesis was developed by Mikayla Novak (2018), who challenges the commonly held opinion that the solution to economic inequalities always involves imposing restrictions on the operations of unchecked markets through taxation or regulation. She does not quarrel with the idea that some people will be more successful in taking advantage of the opportunities they discover—these are "good" inequalities—but she also shows that in a number of instances "bad" inequalities actually result from government interventions. Even if we set aside the most egregious sort of racist or xenophobic discrimination imposed by governments in the US or elsewhere in a more or less distant past (e.g., racial segregation, selective immigration policies, or somewhat less overt forms of discrimination such as "red lining," which for decades prevented African American families from applying for government-insured mortgages), there still are plenty of examples of policies that harm disadvantaged individuals in a less overt fashion by generating rents for affluent individuals, and siphon resources in ways that are welfare-reducing. Increasing taxes, as recommended by Piketty, incentivizes well-off people to seek tax loopholes and creates rents for accountants and financial advisors; well-intended spending programs may miss their targets because of insufficient information available to the policymakers and turn out to be costly to administer, thereby creating rents for public sector employees and consultants; zoning rules tend to make housing less affordable, and so on. Is there a way out of this conundrum? Novak suggests following the path toward "economic constitutionalism" opened by James Buchanan.

James Buchanan and Roger Congleton (1998, vi) found severe flaws in majoritarian democracy: "If left unconstrained, majority coalitions will promote the interests of their own members at the expense of other persons." They recognize that in the US and other liberal democracies, there are constitutional limits to the reach of majoritarian politics. But they also argue that existing constitutional rules do not go far enough to protect property rights and economic freedom. They recommend building new rules on the "principle of generality," according to which

> political actions apply to all persons independently of membership in a dominant coalition or an effective interest group. The generality principle is violated to the extent that political action is overtly discriminatory in the sense that the effects, positive or negative, depend on personalized

> identification. The generality norm finds its post-Enlightenment philosophical foundation in Kant's normative precept for a personalized ethics and its institutional embodiment in the idealized rule of law that does, indeed, set out widely agreed upon criteria for the evaluation of legal structures.
>
> (xi)

This principle would be efficient in eliminating rent-seeking and promoting equality of entrepreneurial opportunities (e.g., by banning regulations that limit new entrants in any existing market). But could it go too far? This is what Alexandra Oprea (2019) has shown to be the case, using a game theoretic model. Her idea is that

> generality-constrained democratic politics does not necessarily outperform the unconstrained version. By modeling two-party majoritarian democracy as a type of trust game, one can identify circumstances where generality-constrained democracy results in less efficient outcomes than the unconstrained version. At the same time, generality constraints can reduce incentives for political participation and collective action by ordinary citizens in ways that may erode democratic institutions such as popular elections and political parties. This paper therefore urges caution and further investigation before implementing such constitutional constraints.
>
> (227)[33]

This is a prudent approach. Unconstrained majoritarianism is obviously dangerous and can veer into demagoguery and authoritarianism. But tying a democracy in a constitutional straitjacket could produce all sorts of unexpected consequences. There is a certain irony in the fact that theorists who are fond of alluding to Hayek's admonition about the danger of an excessive faith in rationalist solutions to complex problems are themselves prone to falling into the same trap!

To sum up, there is a philosophical tradition that is founded on the assumption that constraints imposed on economic freedom in the name of reversing income inequalities perversely create other unfair inequalities. More or less strictly libertarian economists not only agree with this normative outlook but also add that restricting the scope of property rights tends to produce inefficient outcomes. Is here an empirical case for this thesis?

Economic Liberty and Economic Development

As is evident from the previous section, much has been written about the relationship between economic liberty and economic growth or development. This ought to be a testable hypothesis, but there is no consensus on a number of crucial issues: in what sense is the causal arrow pointing (see Haber et al. 2008), how strong is the relationship, and is it more or less noticeably affected by other factors (i.e., historical, cultural, technological, political)? Indeed, if anything, the range of factors *other* than the obvious physical factors, such as land, labor, and capital, which have been shown to have an effect on economic growth, has considerably widened. Economic liberty is one of the most important of such factors, but it is not the only one. Nevertheless, a number of studies zero in on that particular factor.

The Simpler Claim

Economists have provided overwhelming evidence that well-defined property rights enforced by an independent judiciary, together with the absence of cumbersome obstacles to entrepreneurship and similar factors, are closely correlated with economic growth and prosperity. Remaining at this general level of analysis, one can point to countries such as China or Vietnam that have experienced strong economic growth since the last decade of the twentieth century when they made a successful transition from rigidly planned and controlled economies to something closer to capitalism. The exact nature of the systems these countries have put in place, however, is still puzzling. There remain a large number of nationalized industries in China and Vietnam, and the Communist Party hierarchy still has the power to interfere with every aspect of economic life even though, especially in China, the ruling elites have decided to allow markets to operate rather freely. As these economies evolve and become more and more dependent on domestic consumption rather than exports, the inefficiencies and uncertainties attributable to, for example, a less-than-impartial judiciary and still-poorly-enforced intellectual property rights could prove detrimental to China's long-term prospects. But the rapid spread of a strong entrepreneurial culture (Ernst & Young 2011) should prove instrumental in overcoming these obstacles. Similarly, the recent economic success of India is due in no small measure to the fact that the restrictive economic policies of earlier decades have been shelved. Comparable observations can be made about a growing number of countries in Latin America (e.g., Brazil, Chile) or Africa (e.g., Ghana, Mozambique, Rwanda).

The transition from communism to capitalism in Central and Eastern Europe provides somewhat a more complex picture although, on the whole, it supports the same hypothesis. The situation there is more complex because not all countries in the region have been equally successful. The Baltic States, Poland, Czechoslovakia (now the Czech Republic and Slovakia), and Slovenia, in particular, prospered after they left the Soviet Bloc (or Yugoslavia in the case of Slovenia) and generally moved toward free markets with extraordinary enthusiasm.[34] In spite of some errors—such as the paradoxical tendency to plan the privatization process in a bureaucratic manner—the results were remarkable. The exceptions are Russia and Ukraine. These institutional reforms have been only partial, and political clientelism has skewed the privatization process in favor of "oligarchs"; corruption is ubiquitous, largely because the legal systems in Russia and Ukraine lack judicial independence.[35] This discourages foreign investment. Although Russia can take advantage of its vast oil and gas resources that account for almost all the gains achieved under Vladimir Putin's leadership, its long-term economic prospects as a consequence of the war in Ukraine are more uncertain than is the case with other countries counted in the so-called BRIC (Brazil, Russia, India, and China) group of emerging countries.

But what exactly lies behind this broad-brush picture of what could be called "good governance"[36] in relation to economic growth? This is a more complicated question. There exists a vast literature concerned with the empirical measurement of the presumed effects of a whole range of factors, including the size of government, taxes, the legal system, corruption, access to credit, and labor market flexibility, on variables such as growth of GDP, GDP per capita, and so on.[37] Databases are available from the World Bank (see its Governance Matters Index), the Policy Risk Services Group (see its *International Country Risk Guide*), the Freedom House (see its Gastil's Index of Civil Liberties), the Fraser Institute (see its *Economic Freedoms of the World* series), the Heritage Foundation (see its Index of Economic Freedom), and several other think tanks.

Although there are some discrepancies between these indexes,[38] there is general agreement about which countries stand at the top and which remain at the bottom of the rankings. The highest ranked countries include Singapore, New Zealand, Switzerland, Australia, Canada, and the US (the Fraser Institute's Economic of the World Index has downgraded the US from third place in 2000 to nineteenth in 2010, but it had climbed back to sixth place in 2019).[39] Similarly, the bottom-ranked countries (not counting planned economies such as Cuba or North Korea) include Angola, the Democratic Republic of the Congo, Zimbabwe, Venezuela, and Burma/Myanmar. More significantly, there is an apparent correlation between economic prosperity and these rankings. Let us look at two datapoints separated by just under a decade provided by the Fraser Institute's *Economic Freedom of the World* reports; they show that the advantage enjoyed by countries ranking the highest on the index has significantly increased:

- Nations in the top quartile of economic freedom had an average per-capita GDP of $37,691 in 2010, compared to $5,188 for bottom-quartile nations in 2010 current international dollars.
- In the top quartile, the average income of the poorest 10 percent was $11,382, compared to $1,209 in the bottom in 2010 current international dollars. Interestingly, the average income of the poorest 10 percent in the more economically free nations is more than twice the average income in the least free nations (Gwartney et al. 2012, vi).
- Nations in the top quartile of economic freedom had an average per-capita GDP of $50,619 in 2019, compared to $5,911 for nations in the bottom quartile (PPP constant 2017, international$).
- In the top quartile, the average income of the poorest 10 percent was $14,400, compared to $1,549 in the bottom quartile (PPP constant 2017, international$). Interestingly, the average income of the poorest 10 percent

in the most economically free nations is more than twice the average per-capita income in the least free nations (Gwartney et al. 2021, vii).

Different indexes can yield somewhat different results. But Gerald Scully and Daniel Slottje (1991, 137), using nine indexes of their own design, conclude that "both RGDP [real gross domestic product] and growth are statistically significantly related to the nine indexes and the relationship is a negative one"; they add that the "consistency of the results across all the rank indexes suggests compelling evidence for a basic hypothesis that freedom is essential for economic development" (37–138). But we may want to ask whether incremental changes over relatively short periods matter at all, or whether what matters most is the absolute level reached as a result of historical and systemic determinants. Niclas Berggren (2003, 198–199) cites a roughly equivalent number of sources on both sides of this question. The reason is probably that we are dealing here with overlapping processes: one that unfolds in the long run and brings about profound transformations, that is, the building of the institutions and practices that sustain economic freedom and long-term prosperity, and another more short-term series of interacting factors that explain yearly changes in the rate of economic growth. Improvements in the degree of economic freedom can be one of these factors, but, at least temporarily, marginal changes can be outweighed by a myriad of other factors, some of which may pull the growth rate in another direction. The financial crisis of 2008 and its aftermath is a case in point. Faced with the potentially catastrophic collapse of some key sectors of their economies (e.g., banks, the automobile industry), many countries, beginning with the US, intervened in ways that caused a drop in their rankings on several freedom indexes, but at least in the case of the US, that drop was temporary. Another limitation was outlined by Morris Altman (2008), who found that economic freedom is a necessary condition for achieving reasonably high levels of real per-capita income, but, beyond a certain threshold, marginal effects are no longer very significant. Moreover, indexes such as the Fraser Institute's "Economic Freedom of the World" lump together too many variables, masking the influence of the most significant one, namely, secure private property rights.[40]

So far, I have focused on the relationship between economic freedom and the GDP, but what about substituting the more general concept of "quality of life" for the GDP? There is a vast literature on this topic that, on the whole, suggests that there is a positive correlation between economic freedom and some combinations of variables pertaining to the quality of life (Nikolaev 2014; Graafland and Compen 2012; Graafland and Lous 2018; Feldman 2017; Graafland 2020). For example, Boris Nikolaev (2014) reports positive correlations between economic freedom and thirteen out of eighteen dimensions of "the quality of life" (e.g., self-reported health, educational achievement, rooms per person, social networks, but negative correlations were reported for five dimensions, including leisure time, job security, and air quality) in thirty-four OECD countries; these relations can be plotted on easily interpretable graphs. But because "quality of life" remains a very subjective concept, these studies must be taken with the proverbial grain of salt insofar as people are likely to weigh the different dimensions, and leisure time in particular, in their own ways. Indeed I now turn to a discussion of these complexities.

A Not-So-Simple Case

A few caveats are in order. The first is that while successful in light of the evidence provided above, the strategy of promoting growth through the liberalization of domestic and global markets also deepens inequality. Using a large dataset covering 115 countries over the period 1970–2014, Mahyudin Ahmad (2017) has shown empirically that this is the case; Ahmad adds, however, that the inequality-increasing effect of liberalization policies is somewhat dampened in democratic regimes. This would seem to be a good argument for redistribution. But would not redistribution negatively affect growth? Ostry et al. (2019, 105) have found that this is not the case: "On average, across countries and over time, the things that governments have typically done to redistribute do not seem to have led to bad growth outcomes," unless redistribution is already high (in the twenty-fifth percentile), in which case further redistribution is "harmful."

The second caveat is that not all property rights are similarly conducive to economic efficiency. An accelerating trend toward the extension of (intellectual) property rights in new areas has negative effects on innovation and, consequently, growth and economic well-being (e.g., Buchanan and Yoon 2000; Boyle 2008; Heller 2008). The problem is that "too much ownership creates deadlock" (Heller 2008, xiv). Michael Heller provides dozens of telling examples of this dilemma, from biomedical research, which can be hampered by patents on gene sequences, to the broadband spectrum, to the music industry where intellectual property rights create severe transaction costs. Admittedly, this is a "moving target" in the sense that this domain is constantly evolving, and some of Heller's examples are already invalidated by ongoing legislative amendments in many jurisdictions and international negotiations. Technological evolution also keeps on shuffling the cards, as it were; for example, the relationship between open-source/Libré software and proprietary software seems to have moved from an antagonistic to a more complementary interaction (Andersen-Gott et al. 2012). But the point remains that when it comes to property rights, the old Aristotelian adage "one can have too much of a good thing" is a truth that economists should keep in mind. Of course, Marxist and other advocates of critical political economy cannot be faulted on this point, but their skepticism about property rights goes too far in the other direction, as was explained above. "Austrian" economists and libertarians, on the other hand, are also well aware of the problem and tend to be very critical of the very notion of intellectual property rights; they would prefer to get rid of them altogether, but this is probably a lost cause: it is unlikely that the rent-seekers who prevailed in this domain will easily give up their gains.

Another caveat concerns causality. The studies mentioned so far assume that the causal arrow runs from economic freedom to growth and well-being. There are, however, contrary views. Could it be that growth and prosperity facilitate the emergence of economic freedom? Adam Przeworski (2004a, 2004b) points out that contemporary dictatorial regimes happen, for the most part, to be located in poor or relatively poor countries; democracies are more diverse in this respect, but the richest countries are all democracies. Now is it because low per-capita GDP is conducive to the establishment of dictatorships, or is it that the institutions that exist under a dictatorship discourage growth? Przeworski argues that in the absence of data that simply do not exist about how the same countries fared under either democracy or dictatorship, there is no definitive answer to that question. A vast historical perspective, such as the one proposed by Douglass North et al. (2009), is a way to get around that difficulty. Historical comparisons over very long periods reveal some interesting patterns because modern democracies have emerged out of conditions that were neither very liberal nor very democratic. But beginning in the eighteenth century in Britain and France, the slow and gradual transition from traditional authoritarian conditions to more open ones (e.g., open competition for access to government positions and competitive markets in which all can participate) corresponds, to a large extent, to the period when growth also began to pick up. The US never experienced feudalism, so right from the beginning, it has been founded upon at least comparatively open institutions. Thus, it is hard to resist the conclusion that these more open conditions are the result of some virtuous circle linking political and economic freedom; the open political and economic systems (elections, party competition, markets) are mutually reinforcing (North et al. 2009, 111). This is a chicken-and-egg problem. Political freedom does not cause economic freedom, nor does economic freedom cause political freedom. They are meshed. Working with more contemporary references, Milton Friedman (1962) and, more recently, Dani Rodrick (2000) have also argued that the economic and political aspects of a citizen's freedom are mutually reinforcing. In other words, even though the causal linkages seem to work in both directions, they produce a sort of virtuous circle (see also Vivarelli 2000; Lawson and Clark 2010).

However, a closer look at the situation makes it clear that once a certain threshold has been reached, the relationship between economic freedom, civil liberties, and political efficacy (i.e., the capacity of citizens to use democratic institutions to achieve the changes they wish to bring about) becomes more complex. Under certain conditions, they tend to work at cross purposes—the economic freedom of the few can compromise the political freedom of the many. As the argument goes, unfettered markets lead to a concentration of wealth in the hands of a small elite that can use it for its own political advantages. Even in the absence of outright corruption, this imbalance of power poses a threat to democracy. Many commentators point to the US where (1) there is, indeed, a significant concentration of wealth at the top, and (2) where there are few restrictions on electoral spending, especially in the wake of the 2010

US Supreme Court case *Citizens United v. Federal Electoral Commission*, a decision that established the principle that corporations and unions are protected by the First Amendment and, therefore, cannot be barred from spending freely on "electioneering communications."[41] The amount spent by presidential candidates in 2008 was approximately $1.7 billion, close to $6 billion in 2012 and an astonishing $14 billion in 2020. Congressional elections have also become more and more expensive. The US is rather exceptional because there exist much stricter limits on electoral spending in most other liberal democracies, but these limits also have their own perverse effects, driving illegal money into the coffers of political parties. When such vast sums are spent, it is hard to resist the conclusion that the political debate is skewed in favor of views and interests that may be at odds with the "public interest." Admittedly, the "public interest" in pluralist societies is itself increasingly a myth, but such pluralistic interests are increasingly hierarchically structured, allowing moneyed interests to play a disproportionately large role.

Of course, this is not a new phenomenon. In the US, for example, the situation was arguably even more unbalanced in the last decades of the nineteenth century (the "gilded age" of powerful tycoons and "robber barons"). On the other hand, the "rich" are not always a unified force: there are sectoral, regional, cultural, and other differences that prevent the subversion of the interests of the majority by a unified class of "capitalists." But it remains that we have known since Aristotle that political freedom supposes equal access to the political arena where issues of concern to the *public*, as opposed to private interests, can be discussed among citizens who are able to recognize each other as equals. That ideal does not preclude actual differences of wealth and status, but implies that legal and other protections must be set in place to prevent abuses of power. In insisting on that original republican ideal, we would only be returning to Adam Smith's views on the need to insulate politics from the machination of commercial interests who he suspected were always ready to subvert political power to advance their own cause (Smith [1776] 1981, Book I, chapter XI, Part 3). Rent-seeking, however, is not the apanage of only one class. Combating inequalities should not become a pretext for the continued expansion of state powers over all aspects of the economy, thereby further "entangling" an already deeply "entangled political economy" (Wagner 2016), which perversely redistributes economic resources toward professionals whose expertise is to navigate this complex terrain (usually on behalf of already privileged clients).

Conclusion: Responsible Liberty

Building on the theoretical foundation laid down by philosophers such as Locke or Hume, economists have argued that secure property rights and institutions that do not discourage entrepreneurial innovation are a necessary condition for prosperity. That is, respect for contractual obligations, mechanisms for their enforcement, and freedom to use one's resources as one believes is appropriate for achieving one's goals are essential for the conduct of economic affairs. But, with the exceptions of strict libertarians, economists are prepared to admit that property rights can occasionally be modified or restricted in ways that reflect constraints imposed by externalities, transactions costs, cultural and customary practices, and a host of other considerations that other social scientists are typically inclined to pay far more attention to. If anything, the renewed interest in economic freedom has been prompted in large measure by this debate. It has been greatly facilitated by recent advances in the empirical measurement of the correlation between a number of identifiable factors such as the level of taxation, the intrusiveness of regulations, monetary policy, openness to trade, and so on, on the one hand, and economic performance, on the other.

Important as economic freedom is for economic growth, there are limits beyond which it enters in conflict with other considerations (e.g., should financial resources be the prevalent means of gaining access to policymakers?). Each one of us has a responsibility to provide for our needs and of those whom we care, and ought to have the freedom to use our property as we see fit, but within reasonable limits reflecting obligations we have toward others and toward the natural environment. How the line should be drawn is not for economists to decide. These are questions that ought to be settled through a process of deliberation within a framework that more or less achieves the requirements of what Rawls (1993, lecture VI) called "public reason" (but see also Sen 2009; Gauss 2011).[42] Such arguments necessarily draw from a wider range of considerations than those discussed hereto. Indeed, the orthodox or (more or less overtly) conservative economists' preferred definition of equality of opportunity as fair opportunity to take advantage of the unlimited prospects for advancement generated by the market process is only one of several possible interpretations of this rather nebulous notion. These other interpretations, their origins, implications, and compatibility (or lack thereof) with economic efficiency are examined in the next chapter.

Notes

1 For example, Thomas Piketty's *Capital and Ideology*, which was discussed in the previous chapter, addresses a wide range of issues that go well beyond equality of welfare in a narrow sense.

2 See the discussion of the Kaldor–Hicks criterion in Chapter 2.

3 "The distinction between morally acceptable and unacceptable inequality is perhaps the most important philosophical egalitarian thought of the last 40 years" (Roemer and Trannoy 2015).

4 I borrow this phrase from Hans-Herman Hoppe (1989, 10).

5 For a contrary and very unorthodox view about the history, and indeed prehistory, of (multiple forms of) property rights, see Graeber and Wengrow (2021).

6 It is worth noting that Hobbes did *not* deny that men and women could be equal in the state of nature: "There is not always that difference of strength, or prudence between the man and the women," although such a difference can be established once a Commonwealth has been formed (see Hobbes' *Leviathan* [2008}, 137).

7 For instance: "By particular Contracts each single man may have his own Right, and Propriety, so as one may say *This is mine*, the other, *That is his*" (Hobbes, *De Cive*, chapter VI). In Long (2006), however, it is asserted that Hobbes *never* uses "property," which is a typographical error, as the author himself assured me.

8 "He [i.e., 'any man'] hath no propriety in which the Chief Ruler (whose Commands are the Lawes, whose will contains the will of each man, and who, by every single person, is constituted the Supreme Judge) hath not a Right" (Hobbes, *De Cive*, chapter VI).

9 Usually but not always, for example, in in paragraph 36 of *The Secong Treatises on Government*, Locke wrote

> I dare boldly assert that the same rule of propriety—viz that every man should have as much as he could make use of, would hold still in the world, without straitening anybody, since there is land enough in the world to suffice double the inhabitants, had not the invention of money, and the tacit agreement of men to put a value on it, introduced (by consent) larger possessions and a right to them; which, how it has done, I shall by and by show more at large.
>
> (Locke 2003, 115)

10 Locke needed to make that point to counter Filmer's argument that original communism would have rendered a social contract impossible.

11 Locke set up the problem of justifying individual property rights as a choice between upholding such rights and leaving unclaimed the resources of the world. But this is a fictional narrative. In practice, there are many past and present examples of "commons" being held and managed by small communities, such as Alpine meadows in Switzerland, or the irrigation canals in L'Horta de Vanencia (Spain), as Elinor Ostrom (1990) has shown. Ostrom's seminal work launched a research program carried out by the Indiana University Workshop on Political Theory and Policy Analysis.

12 Tully refers here to an often-cited passage in the *First Treatise*:

> As Justice gives every Man a Title to the product of his honest industry so Charity gives every Man a Title to so much out of another's Plenty, as will keep him from extream [*sic*] want, where he has no means to subsist otherwise.
>
> (Locke 2003, 30)

But Locke also asserted that able-bodied individuals capable of doing productive work are not entitled to charity (Sreenivasan 1995, 103); this is a caveat that Tully glosses over.

13 C. B. Macpherson (1962) proposed a variant of this argument: Citing textual evidence from Locke, he argues that those left without property can be employed by the property owners; they are worse-off because the wage relationship is an unequal one, but they are not left without any means of subsistence.

14 Actually, in chapter 6 of *Anarchy, State end Utopia* (1974), Nozick deals with two possible objections to his "entitlement theory": the Lockean proviso and Rawls' theory of justice as fairness. The latter, including Nozick's comments, is dealt with in the next chapter.

15 Nozick, however, says little more about this thorny issue; for a more complete discussion of what rectification might entail, see Simmons (1995). The French philosopher Alfred Fouillée also built an elaborate theory of "reparative justice" that could

complement Nozick's notion of rectification; on Fouillée, see Dobuzinskis (2010). However, Edward Feser (2005) offers a radical libertarian position that rectification is never appropriate because "there is no such thing as an unjust initial acquisition."

16 Sreenivasan (1995, 117) suggests that "this function could manifestly be discharged only by a civil state." But that is arguably an overstatement; it is possible to envision that the redistribution that follows from a proper interpretation of Lockean property could, at least in part, be carried out through voluntary initiatives, thereby fulfilling the duty of charity that (Tully's) Locke insisted upon.

17 Walras (1987, 496) envisioned a three-step process: (1) "the state, without changing anything fundamental about the land tax, gives it the form of a co-ownership of land"; (2) "then, provided with its share, the state purchases back from the land owners their part and pays them by means of bonds on its debt"; finally, (3) "the state acts as a lessor for the land it owns by then in relation to rent consumers or entrepreneurs." Walras noted that at the beginning of this process, which could take decades, the interest on the debt would exceed revenues from rents, but eventually rents would exceed the value of the bonds.

18 Walras was only one in a long series of liberal/progressive economists who have supported the idea of workers-owned or -controlled cooperatives, from Mill to Pigou ([1952] 2002, 205–206) to Joseph Stiglitz (2009).

19 George, trying to capitalize on the success of his writings, ran for mayor of New York City in 1886, but failed to get elected.

20 On the fate of Georgism and how it could be revived in the twenty-first century, see Dobuzinskis (2020).

21 If this turned out to be insufficient to provide for the needs of the disabled, Otsuka (2003, chapter 2) recommends that rather than resorting to a universal income tax, "the able-bodied who have been properly convicted of performing justifiable criminal acts" should alone be taxed. (Ordinary citizens could still make voluntary contributions.)

22 From a libertarian standpoint, individuals should not be expected *a priori* to contribute to the common good. They could be coerced to do so only if it can be shown that a fraction of their holdings is due to factors other than their efforts or talents; this could be the result of deliberately planned social arrangements or inadvertently occurring events or circumstances that happen to benefit some individuals disproportionally. Having the good luck or having had access to good schools and quality education is probably the most telling example.

23 The quote is from a response by Demsetz to a critique of his earlier (1967) article. Interestingly, in that article, Demsetz relies extensively on historical evidence that as the fur trade became a more and more competitive enterprise in the eighteenth century in what is now Quebec and Ontario, resulting, in fact, in overhunting, Indigenous communities began to assert property rights about specifying hunting/trapping territories. But these rights were claimed by individual families (competing among each other) rather than by the Indigenous communities as a collectivity.

24 Some parallels can be found in the continental traditions, such as Montesquieu's theory of law.

25 See Hayek.

26

> In a celebrated passage of his *Discourse on Inequality* (1755), Rousseau (2012, 91) wrote: The first man who, having enclosed a piece of ground, bethought himself of saying *This is mine*, and found people simple enough to believe him,

was the real founder of civil society. From how many crimes, wars and murders, from how many horrors and misfortunes might not any one have saved mankind, by pulling up the stakes, or filling up the ditch, and crying to his fellows, 'Beware of listening to this impostor; you are undone if you once forget that the fruits of the earth belong to us all, and the earth itself to nobody.'

27

Proudhon was highly critical of collectivism, as he put it in his *Philosophie de la misère* (1846): Communism reproduces, but in a reverse manner, all the contradictions of political economy. Its secret consists in substituting collective man to the individual in every social function: production, consumption, education, the family. And since this new evolution neither conciliates nor resolves anything, it fatally ends up into iniquity and misery, just like preceding turn of ideas.

(cited in Canto-Sperber 2004, 96)

28 In his critique of Proudhon's analysis of value in this work, however, Marx unintentionally revealed that Proudhon was ahead of him in his grasp of economic realities. Proudhon never subscribed to the labor theory of value, and he understood that value results from no other source than scarcity; Proudhon considered that both the producer and the consumer freely enter the market as individuals capable of making choices for themselves under conditions of scarcity. Marx faulted Proudhon for not having grasped Ricardo's analysis, but, in retrospect, that criticism falls flat.

29 It is important to understand that this pre–World War II "market socialism" had nothing to do with what more contemporary theorists (e.g., John Roemer, Ted Burczak) call market socialism, that is, an economic system in which *real* markets exist but where workers nevertheless have some (or even a high) degree of control over the firms in which they work; see further below in this chapter.

30 See the various contributions to the following edited volumes: Church, Miller, and Taylor (2015) and Manish and Miller (2021); see also Conard (2016) as well as reports and publication by think tanks such as the Heritage Foundation, The Cato Institute, or the Fraser Institute.

31 On the problem of tax evasion, see Argentiero et al. (2021).

32 Although it must be conceded that the sort of entanglements Wagner denounces, while also realistically insisting that they cannot be easily "disentangled," are typically inefficient, there are examples of more virtuous types of entanglements, such as the creation of the internet or "Operation Warp Speed," which produces a vaccine against the COVID-19 virus. (Operation Warp Speed involved coordinated efforts between the US Department of Defense, the US Department of Health and Human Services, and various other government agencies, on the one hand, and large pharmaceutical companies such as Pfizer, Moderna, and Johnson & Johnson, on the other.)

33 The demonstration hinges on Oprea's negative assessment of Buchanan and Congleton's (1998, chapter 2) formal model, which she claims oversimplifies politics. Their model is a quasi-prisoner's dilemma presented in normal form. Oprea (2019) suggests that a more appropriate model would be a trust game in an extensive (i.e., sequential) form. In this game, the players have the option of anticipating where they will be after two rounds and of trusting each other to alternatively take advantage of the maximum payoffs, instead of defecting after one round; she claims that this model, which has been extensively tested empirically, better captures the logic of pollical games. It is more likely to yield an equilibrium that is pareto-superior to

what Buchanan and Congleton claims should happen in an unconstrained majoritarian democracy. Moreover, she argues (243) that a constitutionally entrenched generality principle "would simultaneously reduce turnout in elections and erode the ability of political parties to perform key democratic functions."

34 Poland rose in the Fraser Institute's "Economic Freedom of the World" index from 101st place in 1985 to 74th in 2000 and 40th place in 2009, but fell back to 75th in 2019.

35 Russia was in 113th place in the Fraser Institute's "Economic Freedom of the World" index in 2000 and rose to 95th place in 2010 and 89th place in 2018, but falling back to 100th in 2019; the corresponding rankings for Ukraine are 119th, 107th, 131st, and 129th. It is difficult to make much sense of these fluctuations, which reflects in part the unreliability of some of the data. What is clear, however, is that whatever effort Russia made under Dmitry Medvedev to liberalize its economy, they have had little effect in the long run. With regard to Ukraine, sufficient data on the effects of President Vlodomyr Zelensky's announced reform are still not available from the Fraser Institute.

36 Beginning in the 1990s, good governance has been promoted vigorously by the IMF, the World Bank, and the OECD. However, the sometimes excessively rigid and demanding manner in which this concept has sometimes been implemented has led in more recent years to the more modest notion of "good enough governance"; see Grindle (2007).

37 A small sample of that literature includes Altman (2007), Carlsson and Lundström (2002), Chong and Calderon (1997), Ayal and Karras (1998), Barro (1997), and Knack and Keefer (1995).

38 For example, a comparison between the Heritage Foundation and Fraser Institute rankings reveals the following differences:

	Fraser Institute (2019 data from the 2021 report)	*Heritage Foundation (2022)*
UK	12th	24th
The Netherlands	19th	8th
Germany	22nd	16th
France	53rd	52nd

The relative rankings, however, are almost identical, and both place Japan in the twentieth position.

39 About a decade ago, Honk Kong was ranked at the top and still was at the top in the Fraser Institute report (2021). But the Fraser Institute stated that the 2021 report was based on 2019 data and that the repressive measures implemented by China since then will cause a severe downgrading of Honk Kong; the Heritage Foundation index no longer lists Honk Kong.

40 In a rebuttal, Joshua Hall and Robert Lawson (2008) fault Altman for basing his conclusions on an inadequate methodology that relies on univariate regressions to study complex phenomena better suited for multivariate approaches. They acknowledge that some variables may indeed have a more direct effect on growth than others, but note that no consensus exists on exactly which ones account for most of

the variance. As for the effects of changes in the Economic Freedom of the World (EFW) index, they explain that the

> correlation between income and change in the EFW index is negative simply because it is poor countries that are reforming the most. Rich countries are already market economies and have little reforming to do. There is simply no theoretical reason that the change in EFW index should be highly correlated with the current level of income.
>
> (3)

(But Altman could reply that this is nitpicking on their part: while the negative correlation might be in doubt, the point he is precisely trying to make is that past a certain threshold, economic freedom becomes less relevant.) Finally, with respect to the threshold effect, or nonlinearity of the functional relationship between economic freedom and growth, they admit that this *could* be the case, but insist that Altman has not provided a sufficiently sophisticated analysis to prove his point.

41 The interests of corporations and their executives who form a large fraction of the mythical "1 percent" richest individuals in the US (successful entrepreneurs such as Bill Gates are, in fact, exceptionally rare) have become more intertwined than was the case in the 1950s or 1960s—the era of the grey "organization men" for whom corporations were a bureaucracy in which they had an assigned role—as a result of two developments: (1) the move toward granting executives compensation packages that include stock options and other rewards that far exceed salaries that themselves have become more inflated; and (2) sizable tax cuts that allow executives to keep a much larger share of their earnings.

42 Such debates take place within constraints imposed by constitutional rules or well-established legal conventions, although they can (but more rarely) result in changes to these rules themselves. Several countries have entrenched clauses protecting property rights in their constitutions, most notably the US (Fifth and Fourteenth Amendments) but also the Czech Republic, France, Germany, and Ireland. The first protocol of the European Convention on Human Rights also protects property rights. Commonwealth countries whose constitutions are largely based on conventions and ordinary statutes rely more on the Common Law and jurisprudence to achieve the same effect (interestingly, the written part of the Canadian constitution—the Canadian Charter of Rights and Freedoms—does *not* include an explicit guarantee of property rights). More or less theoretical political debates and practical policy issues are centered on the question of how to reconcile such protection with the provision of common goods. Article 43 of the Irish Constitution, after acknowledging the "natural right, antecedent to positive law, to the private ownership of external goods," explicitly acknowledges the dilemma by stating:

> 2.1 The State recognises, however, that the exercise of the rights mentioned in the foregoing provisions of this Article ought, in civil society, to be regulated by the principles of social justice.
>
> 2.2 The State, accordingly, may as occasion requires delimit by law the exercise of the said rights with a view to reconciling their exercise with the exigencies of the common good.

5 Equality of Opportunity II

Egalitarian Perspectives

While the economists' discourse on growth and efficiency is undeniably influential, it is not the only source of ideas flowing into the current debate on socioeconomic inequalities. Political philosophy and the social sciences are the main sources of these alternative views. Taking a detour through these disciplines should yield the criteria for evaluating the ethical appropriateness of the theories discussed in the previous chapter. But it also reveals that all these discourses occasionally overlap. Some prominent economists are themselves philosophers in their own right who bring economic ideas to the table; inversely, concepts first proposed by political philosophers have found their way into the economists' discourse, such as John Rawls' "difference principle", which was inspired by the game-theoretic concept of maximin.

This chapter is concerned mostly with the egalitarian interpretations of the notion of equality of opportunity. It reverses the prioritizing of efficiency over equity, which is more or less implicit in most of the works discussed in the previous chapter. The contrast does not stem from a complete denial of the merits of equality of opportunity on one side and its unqualified acceptance on the other, but rather from the fact that the egalitarian thinkers to whom I now turn insist that opportunities are not created equally for all. Therefore, simply asserting that everyone should be given an equal *formal* chance to take advantage of opportunities generated by economic growth does not pass muster. There might be all sorts of reasons (gender, racial discrimination, family circumstances, bad health, lack of skills, etc.) why some individuals cannot fairly compete. So, Rawls' *Theory of Justice*, first published in 1971,[1] is the obligatory reference point for all subsequent literature. I do not intend to look back much further into the origins of contemporary controversies.

I distinguish between ideal and nonideal theories or approaches. The former include works that present a coherent set of values meant to be, if not universally valid, at least appropriate for an entire community or regime type, such as liberal democracies. The latter are more pluralistic and open-ended; they consist of criteria and guidelines that can be adapted to particular societal or individual circumstances and do not aim for a transcendent goal. Not uncoincidentally, they are more realistic in diagnosing concrete inequalities. Reducing *inequalities*

DOI: 10.4324/9781003216247-5

from that standpoint matters more than achieving some approximation of equality. I argue that the latter paradigm is preferable, starting by comparing these theories as fairly as possible. I also draw some comparisons with theories that are explicitly nonegalitarian, albeit not indifferent to injustices, that is, theories that seek to evaluate the market process in the light of values that are meant either to trump or merely to coexist with the fair distribution of resources, such as liberty, cooperation, merit, and so on. None of these values, I argue, can reasonably be invoked to justify absolute poverty or immutable status differences.

Ideal Theories

Contemporary egalitarian theorists stay away from the kind of radical equality of conditions that Plato envisioned for the "guardians" of his ideal city (albeit not for the polis as a whole) or Marx's utopian communism.[2] But there are thoroughly debated plans for limiting inequalities to what can justifiably be accepted in a free and democratic society. Even though the theorists in question (e.g., John Rawls, Ronald Dworkin, G. A. Cohen, among others) all leave room for contingent adaptations to circumstances and differences among historical or cultural contexts, they argue that a just society must be characterized by an ideal combination of norms, values, and institutional rules. In spite of their differences on other issues, they agree on at least one point: inequalities must be justified in terms of a coherent set of criteria that flow from an adherence to shared goals and values. In saying so, I am aware that even the "nonideal" theories I intend to contrast with these "ideal" theories can themselves loosely be characterized as such because the complete opposite of this description would result in utter moral chaos. So, it is only a matter of degree. But the "ideal" theories that are the subject of this section are far more insistent on the unity of the evaluative criteria they advance than the "nonideal" ones. Rawls' theory of justice as fairness fits this description.

Rawls

A detailed examination of Rawls' far-reaching theory of justice as fairness is not needed here. I focus on three key points:

- the Rawlsian principles of justice as fairness, of course, but also …
- the philosophical premises and methodological tools deployed to justify them (and some of the most salient critiques directed at this demonstration);
- the questions evoked more or less indirectly by Rawls' choices, such as whether we need an ideal theory, whether fairness is the right angle for approaching the problem of inequalities, and the respective importance of rational theorizing and political deliberations in working toward a resolution of that problem.

Rawls' theory of justice as fairness went through several revisions that can be traced through his writings (1993, [1971] 1999, 2001). But many themes and ideas have remained untouched. His goal was more far-reaching than merely offering a solution to economic inequalities, although this concern certainly occupies a central place in his plan for a just society. That concern is indeed manifest in the third-ranked principle among the principles of justice he enumerated. They are:

> (a) Each person has the same indefeasible claim to a fully adequate scheme of equal basic liberties, which scheme is compatible with the same scheme of liberties for all; and
> (b) Social and economic inequalities are to satisfy two conditions: first, they are to be attached to offices and positions open to all under conditions of fair equality of opportunity; and second, they are to be to the greatest benefit of the least-advantaged members of society (the difference principle).
>
> (Rawls 2001, 42–43)

Two remarks are in order here. The first is that these principles are lexically ordered, meaning that the first one must be met before the other ones come into play or, to be more specific, the "difference principle" cannot be pursued at the cost of violating the "equal basic liberties" to which everyone is entitled. These basic liberties, however, do *not* include economic liberties (i.e., the unfettered use of private property). Thus, for example, legislation imposing taxes on the wealthy to finance programs intended to support the least advantaged would be legitimate, but not legislation banning criticism of the goal of these programs or engaging in reasonable opposition to their implementation.

The second point is that these principles are not meant to govern every aspect of political life or the functioning of civil society at large, but only the political conditions under which "primary goods" are allocated. These primary goods include:

> (i) The basic rights and liberties: freedom of thought and liberty of conscience, and the rest. These rights and liberties are essential institutional conditions required for the adequate development and full and informed exercise of the two moral powers (in the two fundamental cases).
> (ii) Freedom of movement and free choice of occupation against a background of diverse opportunities, which opportunities allow the pursuit of a variety of ends and give effect to decisions to revise and alter them.
> (iii) Powers and prerogatives of offices and positions of authority and responsibility.
> (iv) Income and wealth, understood as all-purpose means (having an exchange value generally needed to achieve a wide range of ends whatever they may be).

(v) The social bases of self-respect, understood as those aspects of basic institutions normally essential if citizens are to have a lively sense of their worth as persons and to be able to advance their ends with self-confidence.

(Rawls 2001, 58–59)

This is a comprehensive list of practically everything the object of public debates, although it conspicuously leaves out property rights. This comprehensiveness, however, is also a weakness insofar as Rawls failed to fully explain how these primary goods should be indexed. If, as seems likely, they cannot all be given equal weight under all circumstances, which ones should be prioritized? The first principle evidently is instrumental in prioritizing the "goods" listed under (i) above. But the problem remains open for the rest. A possible retort is that it is not up to philosophers to dictate to the members of a political community how they should arrange their affairs in minute details. But if so, why should they attribute more significance to these primary goods than to other considerations (e.g., ecological sustainability)? This brings me to the next question: what is the justification for the principles and the goods to which they are relevant?

Rawls started from a clear but somewhat unconvincing answer to that question, but then muddied the water by trying to make his theory more consistent with societal complexity. His first strategy was to follow a two-pronged approach. First, he used the device of the "original position" from which the principles are logically deduced; and second, he moved on to the problem of showing how this whole theoretical framework can be made congruent with the "moral psychology" of rational individuals, regardless of how they were discovered. As is well known, the original position consists of an imagined situation in which representative individuals (possibly representing their entire household) are placed behind a "veil of ignorance": that hides from them information that might prevent them from being impartial in selecting the principles of justice that ought to apply to the society in which they would be living once the veil is lifted. Since, for instance, they do not know whether they start from a privileged status, they would presumably not choose a societal arrangement in which only a small elite of affluent people have access to most of the resources, and everyone else would be obligated to serve their whims and needs! As rational individuals, presumably, they would choose to articulate something like the first principle.

Rawls also assumes that rational individuals in the original position would be risk-averse. Hence, they would find merits in the maximin principle that is used in game theory to minimize uncertainty and, therefore, come up with the difference principle (i.e., the least advantaged end up with the maximum of the minimum they can get). Note also that, from the standpoint of economics, the difference principle acknowledges the value of incentives since it can be used to justify income inequalities between well-educated individuals performing tasks that are highly beneficial to all (e.g., surgeons working in hospitals that provide emergency care to all) and individuals who are less well positioned (e.g., low-skilled service workers). But it also means that, as Nozick objected (1974, 213–216), talented individuals do not fully own their talents since it is not unquestionably established that differences in talents are sufficient to justify income differentials.

What reasons would citizens of a democratic society have for accepting conclusions reached by their hypothetical representatives placed behind a veil of ignorance? Why would the principle of justice be considered "worthy of a citizen's devoted allegiance" (Rawls 1993, 174; see also [1971] 1999, 415)? Rawls gave his first answer to this problem in Part III of *A Theory of Justice*. But he later distanced himself from it as he went through what he described as a transition from "metaphysical to political liberalism" (1985). It is tempting to interpret this change, which I elaborate upon below, as a response to the critiques raised by many reviewers of *A Theory of Justice*, and most notably by communitarian thinkers (e.g., Gewirth 1982; Sandel [1982] 1998; Walzer 1983), to the effect that the rational subject posited by Rawls is strangely divorced from the sociopolitical contexts within which claims of human rights and civil liberties are considered meaningful. But Rawls never acknowledged that he was responding to such criticisms and insisted that he became dissatisfied with his attempted reconciliation of "the right" with "the good" in Part III. That is, he came to view his initial treatment of the problem as depending too much on an abstract, *a priori* notion of moral goodness.

The key to his change of perspective is the concept of an "overlapping consensus." Rawls conceded that the "fact of pluralism" (1993, 63) works against the assumption that the citizens of contemporary democracies could all unproblematically share a comprehensive moral doctrine. People have different religious, cultural, or philosophical beliefs, and it would be illiberal to impose on them a comprehensive philosophical outlook on the "good life." But he argued that a consensus can be reached by engaging in a reasonable discussion about specifically *political* questions pertaining to the legitimation of constitutional arrangements and other basic structures of a society in which justice as fairness serves as a guiding principle of cooperation. The members of a pluralistic society can identify in their respective comprehensive doctrines the overlapping beliefs upon which this consensus can be established. It follows that Rawls' political liberalism is relevant only to the remediation of economic inequalities in constitutional democracies where there exists a venerable democratic tradition.[3] This probably excludes most formerly communist societies (on Poland, see Radkiewicz and Jarmakowski-Kostrzanowsk 2021).

I stated previously that Rawls' turn to "political liberalism" muddied the waters, as it were. What I mean is that it is far from clear that the overlapping consensus and deliberations informed by what he called "public reason" (see Lecture VI in Rawls 1993) would result in the adoption and legitimation of *exactly* the same principles that he initially defended as being rational. Even if it can be optimistically supposed that these processes would result in the acceptance of, and allegiance to, essential civil liberties and fair (i.e., not merely formal) equality of opportunity in the allocation of public offices, their definition could range over a wide range of possibilities. As for the difference principle, it is even less clear that it would be adopted by consensus or even a large majority. One reason, which I discuss a little further below, is that the citizens of liberal democracies can also be supposed to be committed to other values such as individual responsibility and just desert. Another reason is that his "political" liberalism is rather oddly apolitical. Democratic politics is not about reaching a consensus; it is about winning the support of majorities, which can evolve over time and be peacefully replaced by new ones. Admittedly, a consensus is needed in constitutional politics, and this admission may rescue an approximation of the first principle. But there is no reason that outside of the original position, where citizens are not cloaked by the veil of ignorance, anything close to a consensus could be reached on the difference principle. For one thing, since I am mostly concerned about the economic angle on the question of inequalities, this principle seems to be potentially very costly to implement. It goes well beyond the commonly accepted notion of "social insurance" since it is in essence a scheme to insure everyone against practically all risks: not just illness or unemployment but any dimension of social life that may create a "disadvantage."

I see no reason to challenge Rawls' definition of justice as being essentially concerned with fairness—the fair allocation of primary goods. That is not only because fairness is consistent with most moral theories and religious doctrines but also because it has been empirically established by behavioral economics that economic agents expect to be treated fairly; indeed, fairness has deep evolutionary roots (Kahneman et al. 1986; Binmore 2005; Gintis 2009; Hetzer and Sornette 2013; Dobuzinskis 2022). But fairness is a rather vague notion that is constantly being redefined by governments and civil society when dealing with changing circumstances (e.g., public health during a pandemic). By contrast, Rawls' ideal theory aims for a very high goal: not just an aspirational ideal but a blueprint for institutional design. Admittedly, many of these institutions already exist in liberal democracies, and it is sensible to require that these institutions (e.g., the legal and judicial system) live up to their mission. But Rawls also recommends more profound changes, such as a transition to property-owning democracy (Rawls 2001, 135–138).[4]

Could there be a consensus on this reform? Possibly, as Tong Zhichao (2015) argues, it actually harkens back to a deeply rooted pre–New Deal reformist American tradition (see also Jackson 2012). But the notion that fairness is all of one piece—so to speak, that the citizens of pluralist, but increasingly polarized, societies must be guided by a coherent set of principles, that they must be concerned with the allocation of a specific bundle of goods—is unconvincing. Although feminist critics (Abbey 2013) have claimed that comprehensive and far-reaching as Rawls' theory may appear to be, it leaves many questions concerning the place of women in the economy and the private sphere unanswered. Rawls was aware of the need to distinguish between the purposes and need for an "ideal theory" as well as a complementary nonideal one to address questions to which the former cannot be expected to provide answers.

After asking whether the abstract principles of justice "provide any guidance for instances of injustice," Rawls ([1971] 1999, 216) explains that this requires

> to split the theory of justice into two parts. The first or ideal part assumes strict compliance and works out the principles that characterize a well-ordered society under favorable circumstances. It develops the conception of a perfectly just basic structure and the corresponding duties and obligations of persons under the fixed constraints of human life. My main concern is with this part of the theory. Nonideal theory, the second part, is worked out after an ideal conception of justice has been chosen; only then do the parties ask which principles to adopt under less happy conditions. This division of the theory has, as I have indicated, two rather different subparts. One consists of the principles for governing adjustments to natural limitations and historical contingencies, and the other of principles for meeting injustice.[5]

The notion of responsibility provides a logical hinge between these two facets. After all, positing that autonomous individuals are free to set their own goals and choose the means of achieving them ought to be central to the principles of justice that define a liberal political community. But their actions for which they should, in large part, be held responsible will necessarily be the main cause of the "historical contingencies" a nonideal theory should be concerned with. However, Rawls has been criticized for not going far enough in his definition of what responsibility entails. He accepted that free and autonomous individuals ought to be held responsible for their fate, but only to a *limited* extent. Individuals should have the freedom to choose their own goals in life, including their choice of occupations (Rawls 1999, 240). But society has an obligation to ensure that they are given the resources they need to achieve them; their responsibility, then, only concerns the use they make of these opportunities (Arneson 2008). I now turn to theories, starting with Ronal Dworkin's advocacy of "equality of resources," that posit a greater degree of responsibility of individuals for their own conditions. This comes a little closer to the beliefs shared by many, if not most, economists about the advantages of competition, risk-taking, entrepreneurship, or investment in human capital.[6]

Dworkin

In comparison to Rawls', Ronald Dworkin's theory of distributive justice is more respectful of property rights and seeks to interfere minimally with market processes while still aiming for a fair allocation of resources. This does not mean, however, that he joined Nozick on the side of complete laissez faire. Nor, for that matter, did he side with Pigou's utilitarianism;[7] indeed, as I explain below, he rejected equality of welfare altogether.

His reflections on equality—first proposed in two articles republished in his book, *Sovereign Virtue: The Theory and Practice of Equality* (2000)[8]—unfold in two steps. The first consists of a refutation of what he calls "equality of welfare," which can be compared to what Amartya Sen describes as "welfarism," but is arguably even more far-reaching. Dworkin (2000, 13) admits that, in practice, equality of welfare boils down to equality of income (or, at least, aims in that direction). But for Dworkin, "welfare" theoretically consists of anything, no matter how absurdly subjective it may seem, that counts as satisfaction of the desire to have a pleasant life. This raises the problem of "expensive tastes" (48). If some people could convincingly pretend that a life without champagne, plovers' eggs (a delicacy in the nineteenth century now banned from sale in the UK), or other luxurious goods would be not only a little disappointing but truly miserable, then, according to Dworkin's interpretation of the principle of equality of welfare, society ought to provide those persons with the means to satisfy their expensive tastes, just as society owes to everyone else the means to feed themselves as they see fit but, presumably, at a lower cost. However, societal resources are finite, and meeting everyone's expectations of a comfortable life, exactly as they imagine it, is impractical, thereby depriving everyone, even those whose expectations are not outlandish. And even if we could assume for the sake of argument that there really exist people with sincere expensive tastes—as opposed to merely trying to rig the system in their selfish favor—acquiring the information needed to identify such individuals or households would be very costly and probably impossible.

This is not to say that no one is ever morally entitled to special considerations. Far more than Rawls, Dworkin was very attentive to the needs of disabled people who often require more of certain resources (e.g., professional care) than others. Disabled individuals did *not* generally choose their physical or mental handicap.[9] Expensive tastes, by contrast, are deliberately chosen even if one should probably take into account the social environment; for example, some members of aristocratic families may genuinely believe that they have no choice but to engage in very expensive activities, send their children to elite schools, and so on, just to keep up with the standards of their class. The obvious conclusion, therefore, is that people should be held *responsible for their choices*. In a free and just society, no one should be prevented from choosing to lead the kind of life they prefer, but they ought not to expect society to grant all their wishes. Indeed, to do so would violate a fundamental principle of justice, namely, that everyone deserves "equal concern and respect"; the corollary of this principle is that a pollical community is morally obligated to treat its members' "fates as equally important and respect their individual responsibilities for their own lives" (Dworkin 2011, 330). I also want to add that in explaining why he agrees with Dworkin by summarily dismissing equality of welfare because it implies the feasibility of interpersonal comparisons of utility, the economist Hal Varian (1985) articulates a position held by most of his colleagues (as he himself asserts).[10]

Dworkin went on from there to formulating an alternative that he called equality of resources. To demonstrate the advantages of adopting this perspective, namely, that it is more sensitive to choice, Dworkin worked out his own state of nature analogy. Dworkin's thought experiment is somewhat more realistic than Rawls' original position insofar as it does not require depriving the representative agents of as much relevant information about their own selves and the institutions (including markets and money) within which they will have to operate in the "real world."[11]

Dworkin starts with a barebone model of a market where there is no production or trade. He asks us to picture shipwrecked "immigrants" on a desert island. Their problem is how to allocate the available resources in a fair manner—meaning, more specifically, that when all is done, no one has reasons to envy someone else's basket of goods. Note in passing that not only is "envy-freeness" intuitively fair and conducive to social peace, but, as Joseph Heath (2004, 315) notes, it is a way of getting around the problem of gathering unavailable information about exactly which resources people need to reach their own goals.

In a manner reminiscent of Léon Walras' method for explaining how a market equilibrium can be reached, Dworkin posits that the "immigrants" will set up an auction after having assigned to each an equal number of clamshells that serve as a currency. So far, so good: after bidding competitively for what they want, the islanders have acquired what they want at the price they were prepared to pay.[12] They can start working on their life projects.

And then things get more complicated. As Dworkin (2000, 73) admits, "If [the "immigrants"] are left alone, once the auction is completed, to produce and trade as they wish, then the envy test will shortly fail." But there is no justification for attempting to maintain the *status quo ante* for two reasons. The first is that doing so would result in economic inefficiencies. But the more compelling reason is ethical: treating every member of society with equal respect entails treating them as responsible individuals who should be allowed to take risks and bear the consequences. Therefore, they cannot expect to be compensated for losses resulting from what Dworkin calls "option luck" (73), that is, choices freely made under circumstances that are not foisted on them.

Nonetheless, circumstances do matter. Losses, injuries, and so on, attributable to "brute luck," that is, events or circumstances over which individuals have little or no control, may justifiably be compensated. Although, here again, there should be room for choice, the mechanism Dworkin proposed is an insurance scheme. It is, of course, inspired by the model of a market economy since, in real life, consumers can contract with private insurance companies to protect themselves against a wide range of risks. But Dworkin's insurance market, a second step in his imagined auction, is "hypothetical." It is obviously so because the auction is hypothetical, but it is also hypothetical in a more substantive way insofar as the "immigrants" are given the option to purchase coverage against some risks that private insurers may not actually cover (e.g., underemployment), and/or because the defects of the private insurance market (e.g., bias against people with preexisting health conditions) are rectified. In other words, he does not simply argue that the state can abdicate its social responsibilities by simply turning to private insurers.

Therefore, the state can legitimately tax its citizens, since taxes are the equivalent of premiums for publicly funded insurance programs (e.g., health insurance). To design an appropriate tax regime, the state must resort to an averaging procedure; the averaging procedure ensures that those who could not afford to pay for the sort of expensive coverage they need (e.g., people who are severely handicapped by birth) are protected. It would be generally accepted by the taxpayers as long as, for the average person, "the expected welfare of insuring would be higher than he expected welfare of not doing so" (Dworkin 2000, 100). Being set at this reasonable level, the tax system should not work against people who are talented and ambitious, but, at the same time, would be advantageous to those who have few talents or are handicapped in some other ways. But ambitious individuals who fail should not, as a matter of right, expect society to rescue them from their mistakes.

Lest I create the impression that Dworkin has not given sufficient attention to many of the possible implications and possible counterarguments, I wish to add that both *Sovereign Virtue* and *Justice for Hedgehogs* provide a wealth of details and take the readers through carefully argued scenarios, which cannot be analyzed here. I do want to underline, however, that Dworkin took very seriously the objection that pursuing egalitarian goals necessarily means sacrificing liberty. Dworkin (2000, chapter 3) offers insightful comments on why liberty, properly understood as the freedom to set personal goals and use one's resources with a minimum of restrictions, and a fair distribution of resources protecting individuals against brute luck are complementary objectives if one seeks to treat people with "equal concern and respect."

Yet, in spite of Dworkin's deft treatment of the subject, critics have raised myriads of objections, some of which merit our attention here.[13] First, let's consider criticisms targeting Dworkin's use of an auction as the starting point of his thought experiment. As Joseph Heath (2004) remarks, the egalitarian logic of Dworkin's theory rests entirely on the assumption that the shipwrecked islanders agree to grant each other the same initial wealth endowment. The auction merely ensures that the bundles of goods they end up with are pareto-efficient. Combining the ideas of equality and efficiency (or envy-freeness) is a prudent proposition because both are relevant to his project. In particular, it solves the "expensive tastes" problem since those who want to spend most of their initial endowment on champagne have only themselves to blame if they have less of everything else! But these hypothetical procedures are separate; unfortunately, Dworkin paid little attention to how an agreement on an equal share of clamshells is reached in the first place.

Admittedly, this issue is clarified in *Justice for Hedgehogs*, where he explains (2011, chapter 9) why dignity is the cornerstone of ethics, that is, the foundation for all political values such as equality or liberty. But that means that his auction thought experiment is not the initial step in his defense of equality of resources. Moreover, technical questions can be raised about the implicit assumptions built into Dworkin's auction. The Walrasian model he seems to have in mind, which was fully formalized by Gérard Debreu (1959), is that of a perfectly competitive market with perfect information. But, as Lars Lindblom (2015) remarks, in such a model, "option luck" has no place. The model presupposes certainty and, therefore, "no choices under risk when there is complete certainty" (2). From that angle, a minimum income program would seem to be a simpler and better instrument for reaching Dworkin's goal of combining efficiency and equity. There are other flaws in his market analogy, such as his ad hoc manner for dealing with externalities, which seems to grant unwarranted discretion to his hypothetical auctioneer (e.g., 2000, 156). The point is not that Dworkin was unaware of the problem posed by externalities, but rather that his choice of a neoclassical market model provides no solid ground for dealing with these problems (Heath 2004, 330–331).

Let me now turn to criticisms that zero in on more fundamental aspects of Dworkin's theory, beginning with his use of an insurance scheme to preserve a fair distribution in a competitive market economy. It is an ingenious device that seems to reconcile responsibility and fairness. Indeed, this is probably why the early proponents of the welfare state have used the concept of "social insurance" as a selling argument. But several otherwise sympathetic critics (e.g., Roemer 1985, 2012; van der Veen 2002) have raised intriguing questions. In a nutshell, it is well known that when making decisions about their future well-being, most people are less than fully rational. They could be misled into undervaluing the amount of coverage they need to cope with the challenges they will face over the course of their lives, including the fact that their skill sets may not be worth much. The averaging procedure recommended by Dworkin may not compensate for these biases. In the end, therefore, envy-freeness will not prove to be resilient.

The economist Marc Fleurbaey (2008, 2012; Fleurbaey and Maniquet 2018) has proposed a different way of defending egalitarianism while also taking individual responsibility seriously. But he does away with the problematic envy test. His contribution, which is rooted in the "optimal taxation" tradition of economic research,[14] consists in providing a method for calculating taxes as a means of achieving a fair distribution of resources. Fairness here entails being "responsibility-sensitive" while at the same time acknowledging that inequalities are caused by factors for which individuals cannot be held responsible (family background, etc.).[15] He calls it an "egalitarian equivalent" transfer. This is not quite as simple to summarize[16] as Dworkin's auction with a hypothetical insurance market, and its practical relevance is less obvious. But it is intriguing and must be taken seriously because it illustrates the fruitfulness of the sort of dialogue between economists and political theorists that this book seeks to stimulate. An outcome of this debate is the already substantial and growing economics literature on fairness, which is beginning to match in significance the philosophical literature on fairness.

Fleurbaey's core idea consists in comparing a person's welfare to what would be the case in a counterfactual situation. The latter is a reference point in which the remaining differences are ones for which individuals can be held responsible (they reflect differences in their respective preferences). The formal definition is as follows:

> Define a reference type of circumstances and give priority (leximin) to individuals whose current level of well-being would be obtained with the least resources if their circumstances were of the reference type (and their responsibility characteristics unchanged).
>
> (Fleurbaey 2008, 63)

For example, if the goal is to equalize all agents with respect to the socio-economic and other reasons that make some people more work-averse than others—for example, parents (and usually mothers) of young children might be work-averse because they would prefer to spend more time caring for their children (and perhaps also aging parents)—the reference world can be one in which employed/salaried work does not exist. The question then becomes one of making individuals *indifferent* between their actual earnings and getting a lump-sum payment to make up for the lack of salaried income. For example, Jane, who would like the opportunity to devote herself to caring for her family full time but cannot afford to do so and works part time for $2,000 a month, might be indifferent between her actual situation and not working plus receiving a lump sum of $500 per month. John, on the other hand, finds satisfaction in a full-time job he is qualified for and earns $5,000 a month; he would trade his life for one in the counterfactual world only if he was to receive a lump sum of $1,200. In this scenario, Jane is disadvantaged vis-à-vis John and is entitled to a subsidy. The transfers would produce a situation in which both would end up being indifferent between their adjusted actual earnings and receiving the *same* hypothetical lump sum somewhere between $500 and $1,000 in a world where they would not have to work for a living.[17] The counterfactual world could be formulated in a number of other possible ways to discount circumstances that create unequal opportunities (e.g., job quality, health).

This approach is very original and has the advantage of not necessitating the use of interpersonal comparisons of utility (it only uses intrapersonal comparisons), something which is still controversial among economists. However, how it could be practically implemented is far from clear. There would evidently be an immense challenge in gathering the required information, although surveys could be designed for that purpose.[18] But if one is willing to move some distance away from the specifics of Fleurbaey analysis and focus more broadly on the transfer mechanism he sketched out, one could view it as offering a framework for the design of a negative income tax, a topic I discuss in greater length in the next chapter.

Fleurbaey's reflections offer a convenient transition to a discussion of "luck egalitarian" theories more generally. These are theories that have their origins in Dworkin's pioneering works, but take his paradigm in somewhat different directions Thus, in what follows, I address two sorts of criticisms: (1) those offered by thinkers who share many of Dworkin's foundational premises but offer alternative interpretations of what they imply, and (2) criticisms of the whole paradigm, even if some of them are seemingly targeted at Dworkin.

Luck Egalitarianism

All luck egalitarians, such as Richard Arneson, G. A. (Jerry) Cohen, Thomas Nagel, John Roemer, or Larry Temkin, share the non-Rawlsian premise that individuals should bear some responsibility for their fate (hence the phrase "responsibility-sensitive" egalitarianism) and only need to be compensated for their "brute luck." But they disagree on how egalitarian the end result ought to be and how to reach it. Here I treat only the most salient issues at stake.[19]

Cohen was self-declared Marxist at ease using the language of analytical philosophy[20] and was fully conversant with the normative economics literature. He is definitely the most egalitarian among those discussed in this chapter. Not surprisingly, he reproached both Rawls and Dworkin for not going far enough in defending equality and conceding too much to the prevailing liberal ethos. This is particularly evident in Cohen's analysis of the import of Rawls' principles of justice. As a liberal, Rawls argued that the principles of justice as fairness are meant only to assist in building the institutional structure of a well-ordered society. Outside of the public domain, autonomous individuals ought to be free to arrange their own affairs as they see fit provided they abide by the rules set out by these institutions. In his very first article on political justice, Rawls had already clarified that he was not interested in justice "as a virtue of particular actions or persons" (1958, 165; see also 1999, 6). But Cohen (2000, 2008) objected to this limiting perspective. He argued that we should think of justice as a commitment to equality that is relevant to all aspects of everyday life, as a guide to making personal decisions in the marketplace and other contexts, including gender relations and families; in fact, Cohen explicitly used the feminist injunction "the personal is political" (2008, 116–118) to illustrate what he meant.

It would, indeed, be desirable if employer–employee negotiations were conducted in a spirit of justice, and a variety of means could perhaps be used to encourage this evolution, including, for example, legislation mandating the public disclosure of gender gaps in salaries. But it can also be objected that Cohen is going too far. Two issues are relevant here. The first is that it is unrealistic to expect that everyone will take it upon themselves to make their social environment more just. What about free riders? The second is that this vision unjustifiably singles out fair equality when several other values would be plausibly, at least, as important, such as compassion, humility, prudence, and so on. In some instances, these values may conflict with the pursuit of equality in social relations; for example, at least up to a point, it is not immoral to favor one's children over strangers.

Cohen also distanced himself from Dworkin. He shared with Dworkin the conviction that option luck should be distinguished from brute luck and that only disadvantages resulting from the latter create a legitimate claim on society. To wit, Cohen stated (1989, 916) that "the right reading of egalitarianism ... is to eliminate *involuntary disadvantage*." But he disagreed with Dworkin on the question of whether resources constitute the appropriate "currency" of egalitarian justice. If there is a way to resolve the problem posed by "expensive tastes," Cohen argued that there would be no need to completely abandon the welfarist approach. And he estimated that Richard Arneson's notion of "equal opportunity for welfare" offered that solution. However, he suggested (916) that this theory should be revised by substituting welfare with the more encompassing concept of "advantage." Before elaborating on this point, however, I must explain what Arneson means by equal opportunity for welfare.

Arneson (1989) shares Dworkin's conviction that responsibility sets limits to how far public policies should go in trying to establish fairer institutions and living conditions. Gamblers who lose at the casino are not morally entitled to full compensation for their irrational choices even if they end up among the "worse-offs." (In practice, social services dispensing income assistance are not always in a position to make that distinction, but it matters in terms of *justifying* the disbursement of scarce resources: it is only because it can rationally be demonstrated that the gambler is not a typical case and that most of the worse-offs are *not* responsible for their fate that social assistance is legitimate.) But he disagrees with Dworkin that focusing on resources is the best approach to the problem.

Arneson (1989, 88) provides a very insightful methodological tool for comparing the various egalitarian theories currently being debated. It consists in a 2×2 table. The rows distinguish between a straight (S) allocation and a more indirect allocation in terms of opportunities (O); the columns distinguish between an allocation of welfare (W), that is, outcomes that bring about a certain level of satisfaction, and an allocation of resources (R). Arneson does not fill out all the cells in the table, but I suggest that the SW cell corresponds to classical welfare economics; the SR evokes Rawls' idea of a fair distribution of primary goods as a means toward guaranteeing a decent standard of living; the OR cell matches Dworkin's theory, as Arneson explicitly implies; and the OW matches Arneson's own recommended approach. The direct allocation of welfare-enhancing goods and services runs into the already discussed problem of "expensive tastes." Rawls' theory does not deal adequately—at least not without further qualifications and adjustments—with individual differences in needs (e.g., disabled people will be less well served by programs targeted toward low-income households in general). Dworkin's equality of resources approach is marred by the "slavery of the talented" problem.

What is at stake here is the question of whether talents, that is, natural skills and character dispositions, which are often the result of socialization, are included in the resources to be equalized. If they are not, then it is difficult to imagine that sufficient progress toward social justice will be accomplished. But if they are, then we run into what Dworkin (2000, 90) recognizes as a serious challenge: the productive uses of their time by the talented will be in high demand and, therefore, the talented will be faced with the dilemma of either acquiring full control over that resource, at the cost of having less to spend on other resources in the initial auction, or be forced to devote a lot of their time to producing goods for the benefit of others. This is why Dworkin did not include talents in the initial auction, but used the separate tool of the hypothetical insurance to deal with the problem. That is to say, the untalented can insure themselves against the consequences of this disadvantage.

However, as pointed out already, it is likely that they will be underinsured. Arneson argues that the OW combination does not suffer from any of these flaws. In essence, it is a variant of the equality of welfare that factors in individual choices; it implies that "each [person] must face an array of options that is equivalent to every other person's in terms of the prospects for preference satisfaction it offers" (1989, 85). Another difference between Arneson and Dworkin is that Arneson understands responsibility as responsibility for those things that are under a person's control, that is, only options that are not predetermined by that person's previous *voluntary* actions affecting his or her concrete circumstances should be equalized, whereas Dworkin holds people responsible for their choice of preferences, since the bundle of resources they start with reflects their preferences. But preferences are not obviously voluntarily selected.

What does this all mean in practice? Arneson is not clear about how his scheme could be operationalized. He admits that

> in the real world, with imperfect information available to citizens and policymakers, and imperfect willingness on the part of citizens and officials to carry out conscientiously whatever norm is chosen, the practical implications of these conflicting principles may be hard to discern, and may not diverge much in practise. Familiar information-gathering and information-using problems will make us unwilling to authorize government agencies to determine people's distributive shares on the basis of their preference satisfaction prospects, which will often be unknowable for all practical purposes.
>
> (1989, 87)[21]

As I mentioned above, Cohen agreed with Arneson's critique of Dworkin, but would have preferred to replace "welfare," which he considered to be too narrow, with the more encompassing notion of "advantage." It includes welfare but also the resources for attaining what could be deemed "a desirable state of the person" (Cohen 1993, 28). He suggests that the notion of "midfare" better captures his meaning (and, one can presume, could become the metric of advantage):

> Midfare is constituted of states of the person produced by goods, states in virtue of which utility levels take the value they do. It is "posterior" to "having goods" and "prior" to "having utility."

In other words, it is not limited to the satisfaction immediately provided by chosen goods; it takes into account the sense of being able to put these goods to some use that fits within the individuals' broader goals in life. For example, one gets satisfaction (utility) from food, but having access to food also makes people confident in their ability to get on with their lives. And continuing with the semantic distinctions, Cohen indicated that he preferred "access" to opportunity because, while opportunity evokes the options that are available in the market, justice must not be constrained by what markets can provide. In his words (2004, 17), the market is "a brute luck machine."[22]

This brief survey provides a general idea of the direction in which egalitarian theorists moved as they grew more dissatisfied with the general tenets of Rawls' theory. Provided, of course, that the distinction between "brute" and "option" luck has any purchase on practice, which is not always obvious (see Voigt 2007), the idea of holding people responsible for their choices, at least to some extent, and to differentiate between bad luck and deliberate risk-taking is in line with common sense. It resonates strongly with most people for whom compensating the victims of unfair circumstances seems like the right thing to do.[23] But this is not to say that luck egalitarianism has not been met with trenchant criticisms. To some extent, these criticisms overlap with critical perspectives on the specific theories discussed so far, but it is also necessary to consider the points of view that address the very premises of the paradigm.

We could start with the question of whether making people pay *ex post* for their decisions is fair. *Ex ante* (i.e., before actually doing anything), someone may decide to take up smoking against the advice of friends and family; life insurance policies typically specify that by making such a choice, clients forfeit payment to their chosen beneficiaries in the event of their death. But is it ethical to say that because people ought to be responsible for their choices, smokers who end up with lung cancer are not entitled to health care? It seems exaggeratedly harsh; indeed, this is why it is called the "harshness objection" in the literature on justice (Voigt 2007; Albertson and Nielsen 2020). The asymmetry of information is crucial here. Several decades ago, people taking up smoking might initially have approached it merely out of curiosity or peer pressure as immature, uninformed teenagers. They would have been unaware of how addictive nicotine is and why they might have great difficulty quitting when they wished to quit later. (Indeed, this is the sort of argument that the plaintiff successfully used against the tobacco companies in the landmark US Supreme Court case *Cipollone v. Liggett* [1992].) Or smokers could argue that their *ex ante* option luck has turned into brute luck because it eventually became clear that they were genetically predisposed to cancer, something which is out of their control. Or they could argue on consequentialist grounds that denying them treatment (by making it prohibitively expensive) would deprive society of their unique talents, make it necessary for their dependents to draw on public resources, and so on, thereby negating the supposed collective benefit of holding people responsible for their action, which is to not overly burden innocent third parties.

Another commonly cited example is the accident victim who happens to be an uninsured car driver not wearing a seatbelt, or a motorcyclist without a helmet. Should this careless person be left to die on the side of the road? Advocates of luck egalitarianism are troubled by this sort of question and have responded in several ways that reflect different conceptualizations of option luck. Both Voigt (2007) and Albertsen and Nielsen (2020) provide very tightly argued analyses of all these nuances. Suffice it to say that while the harshness objection cannot be ignored, it has not dealt a fatal blow to luck egalitarianism. What is required from its advocate is a more concerted effort to clarify their goals and consider adding meaningful qualifications, such as recognizing that people are not fully rational and can make forgivable mistakes in evaluating the risks they take, instead of pretending that the brute-versus-option luck distinction provides precise and infallible answers to the problem of how to promote distributive justice. From my pragmatic standpoint, and in line with the arguments against ideal theory I present further below, the most appropriate response is to recognize that luck egalitarianism should leave room for *other* moral values than responsibility. For example, if the consequences of option luck are catastrophic and end up depriving imprudent people or their dependents of the most basic needs and their chance of survival, then compassion, and perhaps even a duty to intervene to save the lives of persons in danger, must overrule considerations of responsibility or contractual obligations. This is what Albertsen and Nielsen (2020, 429) describe as the "pluralist strategy," which they attribute to Cohen (2008), Shlomi Segall (2010), or Larry Temkin (2011). From a broadly pragmatist standpoint, the pluralist perspective makes sense.

Feminist critics (Folbre 1994; Armitage 2006; Kim 2010) acknowledge that Ronald Dworkin and luck egalitarians, in general, count gender-based biases and concrete obstacles among the manifestations of brute luck that disadvantage women. They support policies that would eliminate the gender pay gap from which employed women continue to suffer in various degrees in all countries (it is lower in the EU than in the US, but the average in 2019 for the EU was still 14.1 percent[24]). Indeed, they could hardly be called "egalitarians" if they did not. But feminist critics argue that this stance fails to address the *structural causes* of gender-based inequalities. Simply treating the symptoms is not enough. A related issue concerns the tendency of luck egalitarians to focus on economic inequalities. They do not focus exclusively on income inequalities. But they show a greater degree of concern for earning discrepancies than for other forms of inequalities. Feminist critics, by contrast, have always insisted that the unacceptable inequalities include not only the ones that prevail in the marketplace, serious as they may be, but also those that exist in the private sphere, the family in particular. To address the latter, what is required is not only policy reforms but a *cultural* transformation for addressing structural injustice based on gender, ethnicity, language, and so on. The deeply entrenched roots of sexism or racism are not just a matter of bad luck. (At the very least, one could fault the luck egalitarians for their rhetorical use of a phrase by which they often mean more than mere chance.) And the opposite of bad luck, namely choice, is not always experienced by some women or other members of oppressed groups as being unconstrained and purely voluntary. There are many choices that women make that cause them to be disadvantaged but for which they ought not always be held responsible, for example, choosing part-time work because child care is unavailable or unaffordable, and so on. I return to this problem later in the context of examining "nonideal" approaches when discussing the "relational" conception of equality and the notions of a "caring economy."

Some critics have focused on the ideological connotations of luck egalitarianism. The contention is that luck egalitarianism is not truly progressive—as egalitarianism is purportedly intended to be—because it can be interpreted as another manifestation of the rise of neoliberalism. For the very same reason that some find luck egalitarianism appealing, namely, that it is "responsibility-sensitive," others object to its alleged concessions to the logic of the market. David Miller (2014) faults Cohen for having mistakenly believed that luck egalitarianism offers a way to justify or repurpose the old Marxist principle "from each according to his abilities, to each according to his needs." Cohen was right to argue that the "needs" component of this principle implies the freedom to make meaningful choices; not everyone needs the same things (e.g., what a paraplegic person needs and wants to choose on a menu of options will look very different from what an "average" individual will choose). But, according to Miller, luck egalitarianism does not fit the bill because it places no restriction on choices that could affect *other* people in ways that are not compatible with the nurturing of the sort of equal-to-equal interpersonal relations that should prevail in a truly socialist community of the type Cohen advocated.

Other critics have been blunter. Chris Armstrong (2006) accuses luck egalitarian theorists of playing into the hands of the "neoliberal" ideologues bent on winding down the welfare state.[25] Or, as the saying goes: with friends like this, who needs enemies! Armstrong situates Dworkin's insurance scheme in the broader rhetorical context of "risk management" and the privatization of social services, including health. For such critics, market mechanisms cannot be harnessed to achieve egalitarian goals. The economists' retort would be to point out that an ideological blindness to opportunity costs can only be counterproductive in the long run and that one does not have to be a "market fundamentalist" to be concerned about efficiency and trade-offs.

Ironically, at the other end of the ideological spectrum, classical liberals—the label that so-called neoliberals prefer to apply to themselves—are just as critical of Dworkin, whose egalitarianism they find unconvincing. James Otteson (2019, 26), for example, writes that "the distinction between option luck and brute luck, which initially seems promising, turns out not to be dispositive in relatively routine, everyday cases." More specifically, Otteson claims that (1) not only is it very challenging to sort out option luck from brute luck, but not all the effects of what can be deemed to be brute luck need to be compensated; (2) even if one grants that compensation is due, implementing a compensatory scheme is bound to run into serious epistemological obstacles (the relevant information is not easily available, or may be impossible to obtain); and (3) even if these obstacles could be overcome, the cost of compensating all those who feel disappointed by the outcomes of a market economy could well prove to be unaffordable.

This offers a good starting point for a conversation about the limitations of luck egalitarianism. Unfortunately, the specific arguments Otteson develops are unconvincing for two reasons. The first is that the hypothetical cases he offers to buttress his arguments are not obviously relevant. One of them consists of a coffee shop owner who suffers a loss from the arrival of a competing coffee shop on his street; Otteson asks whether the owner should receive compensation for his declining profit since he did not choose to face competition. But the luck egalitarians never claimed that this sort of bad luck counts; they have in mind disadvantages that have more profound impacts, such as suffering from poor health as a result of low income, environmental pollutants, and so on. The second reason is that Otteson's rhetorical use of the term "disappointment," instead of disadvantage or injustice, transparently implies that compensation is not owed since merely being disappointed usually does not evoke in most people more than a mild form of sympathy, not a desire to financially sacrifice to help the victim of such circumstances.

As for the costs of relief programs triggered by a concern for injustices caused by brute luck, this is an empirical question. If low levels of education, poor health, and so on negatively affect productivity, rectifying the causes of these problems might well turn out to be economically efficient. But Otteson's larger point about the information deficit that well-intended policymakers will inevitably encounter is well taken.[26] Neither separating option luck from brute luck nor designing appropriate responses are easy tasks; they may result in "government failures."

In brief, luck egalitarianism is more commonsensical than Rawls' theory insofar as most taxpayers are more likely to support programs justified in terms of the effects of plain "brute luck" than by the peremptory injunction to always prioritize the needs of the "least advantaged." But it is not immune to justifiable criticisms. I would like to add, however, that the Covid-19 pandemic has vividly illustrated the relevance and force of the moral imperative of eliminating the effects of brute luck. There has been unquestioned support in practically all countries for massive public spending, adding up to trillions of dollars, to mitigate the economic effects and precarity brought about by the pandemic. As time went on, however, the luck egalitarian thinking of governments that moved in the direction of penalizing the nonvaccinated by choice, although it was in line with majority opinion everywhere, was met with considerable resistance (well beyond the truck convoy that besieged the Canadian Parliament in January 2022).

This brings to the fore the question of whether differentiating between option luck and brute luck can be perceived or reframed as being a form of arrogant elitism and is consequently fraught with political risks. This is another way of recasting the "harshness objection." Whether, in this instance, a more flexible or accommodating approach was feasible or could even have been successfully "sold" to the ideologically entrenched "anti-vaxxers" is a question to which I have no answer. This questioning of the relevance and applicability of the kind of theories of justice discussed so far, that is, theories that start from clear *a priori* assumptions about what is just and fair, is precisely the focus of the next section.

Nonideal Approaches

Is it feasible and, if so, desirable to build fully coherent theories of justice that offer allegedly optimal paths toward a better world? As Sen (2009, 264) sarcastically puts it, the authors of these theories all play the "beat that" game in dealing with each other's proposals, leaving their readers perplexed.[27] The theorists I now turn to argue that what ideal theories claim to accomplish is neither feasible nor desirable. In the real world, the path toward an ideal vision is fraught with serious obstacles, and in any event, we may not even need an abstract standard of justice to deal effectively and more nimbly with pressing issues. Precisely because they do not propose alternative "theories," I prefer the term "approaches" to describe their contributions. There is an already large and growing literature on the justification and applicability of these approaches, which seem to constitute the latest phase in the evolution of contemporary scholarship on inequalities. This literature makes it clear that the concept of the "nonideal" originated in different intellectual contexts and has not converged toward a single research program (which, in any event, would be rather oxymoronic).

As previously mentioned, the dichotomy between ideal and nonideal theorizing about fairness can be traced back to Rawls' theory of justice. But the insightful discussion he offered about the difficult task of designing institutions that are adapted to the problems citizens face in their social lives is nevertheless subordinate to, and constrained by, his search for overarching principles and their justification. (As Jacob T. Levy [2016, 316] aptly puts it: "Rawls understood himself to be *doing* ideal theory.") I now turn to theorists who have argued that there is no need for an ideal theory of justice and have sought to illustrate the practical significance of their nonideal approaches. I have chosen Amartya Sen and Elizabeth Anderson as exemplars in that respect to get the discussion going.

The economist Amartya Sen is doubly relevant to my purpose in this chapter. First, because he has articulated a cogent critique of Rawls' ideal theory of justice. Second, because he has proposed a nonideal alternative approach that has received considerable attention, namely, his "capabilities approach." Moreover, not only did Sen contribute to our understanding of distributive justice as a philosophical question by positioning himself in opposition to Rawls' ideal theory, but he also defended it as a better way to promote economic development. Thus, engaging with Sen on the subject of justice is also a way to tie back the previous philosophical debates to my main concern in this book—the alleged tension between efficiency and equity.

Let me start with the philosophical angle. In his *The Idea of justice* (2009), Sen acknowledges the brilliance of Rawls' works and praises him for having framed the problem of justice as resting upon the "foundational priority of fairness" (62). But he loses no time zeroing in on what he regards as its most serious flaw. Identifying "only one kind of impartial argument" about what constitutes fair principles of justice is highly problematic (10–11). The difficulty stems from the observation that debating which, if any, "transcendental" theory is the best path toward distributive justice can only occur in liberal democracies. But this creates a paradox. By definition, such regimes are pluralistic, leaving plenty of room for the expression and pursuit of different values. Public policies are in flux precisely because an agreement about how to balance these values is always fleeting.

Rawlsian theorists could immediately respond with two arguments. The first is that Rawls acknowledged the "fact of pluralism" and proposed his concept of "an overlapping consensus" to address it. And the second is that all that is needed is a consensus on *procedural rules* and not one on substantive goals; within a given constitutional order, a variety of institutional reforms and substantive policy initiatives can be pursued. But I suggest that these counterarguments fail to completely shore up the premise that an ideal theory of justice is needed. As Sen points out (2009, 10–12), there is no convincing reason to think that once the "fact of pluralism" is conceded, Rawls' principles will emerge unscathed as the ultimate "overlapping consensus." As for procedural rules, one can concede that Rawls' first principle is indeed indispensable for guaranteeing the political freedoms that define a liberal, nonauthoritarian democracy. However, the "difference principle" comes closer to articulating a substantive policy goal than a procedural rule. Some problems might appropriately be approached by prioritizing the needs of the least advantaged, while others might be more appropriately tackled by Dworkin's insurance scheme. Others might argue that a basic income is the best solution, and so on and so forth. (From a pragmatic standpoint, just as it makes little sense to constitutionally entrench the difference principle, it could turn out to be a very serious mistake to constitutionally entrench a basic income scheme before experimenting with it.) Coming back to the fundamental question of efficiency vs. equity, *mutatis mutandis*, most economists would probably argue that even if the rules of a market economy ought to be constrained to some extent to achieve a measure of equity, there is no one best way to do so.

Sen challenges the "institutional fundamentalism" (2009, 83) within which Rawls and several other contemporary philosophers seem to be trapped. Arguing that a "transcendental identification [of an ideally fair institutional arrangement] is … neither necessary nor sufficient for arriving at comparative judgments of justice" (102), he advocates a more flexible strategy for remedying inequalities: the capability approach.[28] This approach has become very influential and has been extensively discussed and criticized. Most readers who are interested in economic inequalities will already have encountered it, but let me briefly restate its essential features[29] before tuning to some relevant critiques.

Sen's starting point is that merely focusing on "primary goods" (Rawls) or resources (Dworkin) is not sufficiently pragmatic. The analyst interested in solving poverty or reducing inequalities must consider how these resources are used and the extent to which they actually enhance someone's well-being.[30] What matters is what people need for doing the things they value. Physically challenged people need more resources than normal individuals to function adequately in society, for example. Not only must basic needs be met, but, depending on the societal context in which people find themselves, various kinds of goods and services are essential for functioning as a self-respecting member of society. Hence the term "functionings" for these things (Sen 1999, 75). Not all members of society have the same degree of control over these assets. Hence the notion of "capabilities" as a set of functionings an individual can feasibly have access to, and among which they may freely choose.

This does not mean that capacities are proportional to functionings. Sen ()1999 gives the example of a person who fasts for religious reasons and has no more food in his or her set of functionings than a starving person. But the former enjoys greater capabilities than the latter because fasting is voluntary—the fasting person values their freedom to do without food when, in fact, they could have chosen to eat more, a choice that the starving person was not given a chance to exercise. It follows that equalizing capabilities rather than resources is the best strategy for achieving social justice—a responsibility that often rests with governments, although it does not always have to be so.

Two corollaries follow. The first is that freedom is constitutive of the capability approach. As Sen (1993, 33) explains, "The freedom to lead different types of life is reflected in the person's capability set." In fact, he sees two dimensions to this freedom: an instrumental one and a telic one. Freedom is a means to make one's life better, to enable people to become what they aspire to be. Functionings are chosen and can be combined in different ways. When people are unable to do so, there is a reason for intervention by policymakers. Better access to education is an obvious instrument for widening the capacity sets of large numbers of individuals and families. But freedom can also be an end itself.

The second corollary is the importance of context. Because capabilities differ from one societal setting to another, across space, cultures, and other criteria, Sen's approach has the double merit of being realistic and sensitive to crucial situational differences. These can be differences that positively matter to people and should remind policymakers or NGOs that the same "solutions" do not work equally well everywhere, but it also offers a lens for perceiving the context-dependent causes of injustices and oppression, such as the gender-based roles that often place women at a competitive disadvantage in the workplace, not to mention more serious forms of discrimination or abuse.

At least from Sen's point of view, there is no *a priori* optimal allocation of capability sets throughout society. The allocation of the material and organizational resources necessary for equalizing capabilities in order to empower individuals must be decided through democratic means. Political freedoms and the practice of democratic decision-making are an integral part of Sen's overall vision (1999, chapter 6; 2010, Part IV). He resolutely opposes the idea that economic efficiency, as defined by experts, should take priority over democratic debates. But Sen is not naïve about democracy. Years before "post-truth" became a topical subject, he had insisted that democratic debates must not be dominated by narrow interests, and democracy is more than just majoritarianism. It is natural for ordinary citizens to approach problems from where they stand, but in the end, decisions will have to be made in the light of what Sen (2009, 161) calls "transpositional objectivity." This is not achieved by relying on pure theory but through the discovery of other people's point of views, by being attentive to the needs of strangers. Sen provides no clue as to how to do this, but it would be difficult to spell out *a priori* how this eminently practical problem can be resolved.

Elizabeth Anderson (1999, 2010) acerbically criticizes luck egalitarians for insinuating that people who qualify for receiving help are losers, in some sense, or pitiable victims. By contrast, she sees in Sen's analysis, which she qualifies as "equality in the space of freedom" (1999, 316), a useful basis for developing a more emancipating perspective that she calls "relational egalitarianism." The latter addresses the problem of redistributing wealth, but is not essentially defined by it. As Anderson (314) puts it, egalitarians "should be concerned with the relationships within which … goods are distributed, not only the distribution of goods themselves." Thus, economic inequalities are not merely a question of measuring differences in welfare, but an indication that the democratic process has somehow failed its citizens.

Anderson conceives the economy as a "system of cooperation" in which every participant should be treated fairly. When/if this is not the case, they can—acting as equal citizens—decide to take measures to rectify these inequities by transforming them into more reciprocal interactions (e.g., mandating employers to pay their employees a decent wage). The main goal of relational egalitarianism, as defended not only by Anderson but also by Samuel Scheffler and Jonathan Wolff, among others,[31] is to empower individuals so that they can escape (at least the most oppressive) restraints placed on their lives by socio-economic or political hierarchies. C. Fourie et al. (2015, 1) sum up the relational egalitarian perspective as follows:

> The structure of relationships can be more or less egalitarian, more or less hierarchical. When we [by which they mean "we, relational egalitarians"] appeal to the value of equality, we mean the value primarily of egalitarian and non-hierarchical relationships, and not of distributions, which may only be instrumentally valuable in terms of how well they reflect or help to achieve egalitarian relationships.

Perfect equality of resources is not feasible, but individuals should expect to be *treated* as equals in all spheres of life (the labor market, the political sphere, the family, and so on). From that standpoint, the quality of social relations becomes the benchmark for assessing how far a society is moving toward the goal of justice. But this is a nonideal approach insofar as it does not specify exactly how a just society should be structured.

The "ethics of care" is closely related to relational egalitarianism. Although in some ways it is very ancient—there are interesting parallels with Buddhism—the contemporary origin of this moral doctrine is generally attributed to the feminist philosopher Carol Gilligan (1982). Her point of departure was a critique of the psychologist Lawrence Kohlberg's well-known scale of moral development. At the top of this scale, we find the ideal of an impartial person who evaluates moral dilemmas in light of universal principles. Gilligan challenged this view, arguing that it does not match women's experience, as women are often tied to the practice of caring for another, something which requires a close attention to circumstances and practical choices based more of an understanding of the specificity of the needs of those for whom we care (e.g., children, elderly people, neighbors) than recourse to universal principles. Indeed, the very notion of justice as an abstract ideal is questionable. As Stephanie Collins (2015, 4) explains:

> Care ethicists start by taking the experience of decision-making as crucial data for ethical and political theorising. They point out that, when deliberating about what we morally ought to do in some concrete scenario, we typically take account of the particularities and complexities of the relationships between the unique persons in the dilemma. We do not apply abstract rules or perform regimented calculi. These decision-making processes often strike us as coldly lacking in moral qualities or not quite suitable for the given situation. Rather, we consider concrete, particular others in complex webs of relationships. Because of their complexities, our relationships with particular others (and those particular others themselves) seem to be an irreducible part of moral justification and deliberation. Principles—understood as conditionals ("if X, then Y" statements) with an imperative ("do this") consequent—are at best insufficient, and at worst distortive, for proper moral justification and deliberation.

This useful overview of the core ideas of the ethics of care oversimplifies some of the questions it raises. For example, there is an ongoing debate about the extent to which the ethics of care departs radically from traditional views about justice. What I want to bring up, because it is relevant to the purpose of this book, is the impact that the ethics of care has had on feminist economics. There is by now a growing field of research centered on the notion of a "care economy" (see Donath 2000; Mahon and Robinson 2011; Dwyer 2013 and several online resources such as "The Care Economy" and "Care Work and the Economy"[32]). This is the economic sphere in which unpaid or often poorly paid works take place; it is generally undervalued and neglected by conventional economics, but is crucial for providing childcare and other essential service to all those who need assistance because of disabilities, age, illness, and so on. The recent pandemic illustrates the (literally) vital importance of this sphere and has occasioned a much-needed rethinking of its place in the economic life of any country. But the pandemic has also underlined the extent to which our "ideal" theories of justice are inadequate for dealing with new challenges.

I now want to assess some premises shared by the capability approach and relational egalitarianism, but also underline several significant differences between them. Both approaches tend to assume that the information required to move from theory to practice can be obtained, yet that is far from certain. The flip side of being context-sensitive is that contexts vary enormously and in ways that are not always knowable to analysts interested in operationalizing these approaches, or to policymakers intent on implementing them. As far as the first challenge is concerned, it should be noted that Sen and the economist Jean Drèze have produced empirical studies of the impact of various levels of capabilities on health and other aspects of well-being in India and other developing countries, showing that income differences alone are insufficient to explain variations in the data.[33]

Feminist theorists have a generally positive view of the capability approach because it encompasses many of the concerns they have about the multiplicity of situations in which gender-based inequalities can occur (Robeyns 2017, 115). While very supportive of Sen's project and recognizing that he has demonstrated a keen understanding of the challenges faced by women, Martha Nussbaum (2011, 17–45) has insisted that women's interests cannot be protected unless the vague notion of capabilities is made more explicit by requiring that they ought to be aimed at achieving ten essential objectives.[34] Failing to pay attention to some of these goals would be detrimental to women, albeit not women only—Nussbaum's vision is universalist. Now there is an ongoing debate on this point. Sen, for one, has never accepted the idea that capabilities should be limited to a specific list. His point is not that Nussbaum's concerns about, in particular, the interests of women or some other more or less marginalized groups should be neglected, but rather that human diversity is so complex that no list can be complete or definitive. Moreover, free and truly open democratic debates should bring about a resolution of the demands expressed by these groups. In other words, the role of the theorist is not to impose their views of the good, but to analyze the social processes through which human emancipation can best be achieved.

Marianne T. Hill's (2003) critique is more fundamental. While still sympathetic to Sen's approach and its emphasis on freedom, she starts from an assumption common to many feminist theorists, namely that unequal gender relations stem from *structural* inequalities. Hill faults Sen for not going beyond the individualist social choice paradigm, with which Sen is closely associated, and for not addressing the roots of social power. She shares Sen's faith in democracy, but advocates a more ambitious form of democratic transformation. But, as events in the early twenty-first century have shown, such transformations can also give rise to reactionary counter-movements for whom democratic politics are turned around to *resist* social transformations.

Indeed, with his characteristic wit, Cohen (1990, 377) suggested that even Sen's version of the capability approach requires a level of "athleticism" that is unlikely to be reached by most citizens. By he meant that if all the details of the capability approach are expected to be spelled out through democratic deliberations, its defenders overestimate the virtuousness of citizens, their commitment to freedom, and civic engagement. The same could be said to be even more true of relational egalitarians such as Samuel Scheffler, who insists that the achievement of distributive objectives must be conditional on a "deliberative constraint," which can be described as "a practice of decision-making within which all parties involved show equal respect and concern for each other's comparable interests" (Fourie et al. 2015b, 11). In other words, these approaches escape from the trap of ideal theory about the ultimate goal of justice by setting up their own ideal vision of civic engagement. I would suggest that a more pragmatic appreciation of the practical limitations of the political process, including the perverse effects of rent-seeking by less-than-disinterested groups and interests,[35] is what is truly implied by a nonideal perspective.

Several commentators have criticized the capability approach and relational egalitarianism as being paternalistic.[36] The point here is that these approaches, when pushed to the limit, imply that not everyone is fully aware of their true needs and that, consequently, policy interventions are required to provide all with the capabilities they ought to have. There is some truth to the charge that these approaches occasionally deviate from the assumption that respect for free and autonomous individuals implies that they are the only ones who know what is good for them. But I agree with Mozafar Qizilbash (2011, 28–29) that the charge of paternalism is more appropriately directed at Nussbaum than at Sen, who refrains from specifying which capabilities are essential. And while one should indeed be very wary of experts who claim to know more than they do about what people desire, it is also clear that, under certain extreme conditions, such as severe deprivation that prevent people from realizing what is owed to them, or as a result of poor choices that over time become self-reinforcing (e.g., substance abuse), "paternalistic" interventions can be justified.

From the standpoint of economic efficiency, however, there are limits beyond which this reasoning should not be pushed. The capability approach is not necessarily an invitation to unlimited government intervention in the economy. But it is not self-limiting, contrary to the responsibility-sensitive theories discussed previously. The proverbial hard-nosed economist would probably argue that, at least as far as the use of public funds is concerned, priority ought to be given to enhancing capabilities that can contribute to economic growth (e.g., better access to education, especially for girls and women in developing societies).

I have framed much of the previous discussion in terms of the difference between ideal and nonideal theory. These categories can intuitively be understood as contrasting perfection versus an acceptance of pragmatic compromises about the ends and means of moving toward higher levels of welfare, happiness, social cooperation, and so on. The ideal understood as perfection is rooted primarily in abstract moral philosophy; the more pragmatic approaches take on board a lot of what the social sciences in general, and economics in particular, have to say about concrete inequalities. In this chapter, Sen's pointed critique of Rawls' "transcendental" conception of justice has already helped us get a firmer grasp of some of the issues involved in this debate. But there is now a very sizable literature on nonideal theory, which suggests that the problem is rather more complicated than I have so far implied, so we need to take a closer look at the very notion of nonideal theory.

Laura Valentini (2012) distinguishes between three distinct meanings of ideal theory: (1) assuming full compliance with the (ideal) principles, (2) choosing an idealistic/utopian conception of justice without consideration for any feasibility constraint, and (3) proposing a clear end goal. Of course, nonideal types can be inferred: (1a) assuming less-than-full compliance, (2a) taking feasibility constraints into account, and (3a) preferring open-ended or less-than-final goals. Rawls' discussion of the nonideal side of his theory concerns mostly point (1): when designing institutions intended to implement his principles, it is prudent to ask whether everyone will fully comply with their rules (i.e., the problem of stability). This is not contentious. But the other two problems (2 & 2a, 3 & 3a) need to be considered more attentively.

With respect to feasibility constraints, it seems reasonable to assume that economists and social scientists take such constraints seriously. Keeping in mind that one of the objectives of this book is to explore avenues for initiating a dialogue between economists and moral philosophers on the subject of inequalities, I suggest that the best strategy in this regard is to start from position (2a). The controversies swirling around the positions (3) and (3a) are more puzzling. Neoclassical economists, who defined the "mainstream" of professional economics for a long time, assume that a general equilibrium is not only possible, but once reached would also be normatively defensible since it would be Pareto-optimal. It is however difficult to envision how this end point would appeal to egalitarian philosophers. As long as the two camps could not budge on this point, no productive dialogue could be established.[37]

By introducing a plurality of potential goals for economic growth and development, recent trends toward behavioral models and evolutionary economics open the door to a more fruitful engagement. To continue with the theme of the ideal being defined in terms of the ends of justice, Brian Kogelmann (2020) adds an insightful refinement by combining this theme with another traditional theme in political economy: self-interest. Kogelmann (2020) amusingly refers to the ideal theories aimed at a final goal as "East of Eden" theories and their nonideal opposites that are content with open-ended goals as "West of Babel," but for simplicity's sake, I relabel them "end goal" vs. "open-ended." Kogelmann insightfully points out that the contrast between ideal and nonideal can also be drawn along an intersecting axis: whether human beings can be trusted to act morally in most circumstances, or not (they can be expected to act as self-interested "knaves," in Hume's term). This yields a 2×2 table and four corresponding types of theories of justice:

	End goal	*Open-ended*
Ideal (moral)	I	II
Nonideal (self-interested)	III	IV

Quadrant I is illustrated by Rawls, III by Thomas Hobbes,[38] and IV is the approach Kogelmann favors. Whether Sen fits squarely within IV is not absolutely clear; in his technical contributions to the social choice method in pure economic theory, he posits self-interest, but in his writings on justice, he seems to accept something like Rawls' "sense of justice" as part of the basic psychology of the citizens of a democratic society. I also tend to think even when acting as economic agents, but especially in other societal contexts, that people are neither pure altruists nor pure egoists; "enlightened self-interest" is arguably the best way to describe this hybrid disposition. That is to say, a way of thinking about one's interest that is capable of including the interests of others when mutual advantages can be achieved either instantly or over a longer period of time during which reciprocal interactions can be built.

In other words, Kogelmann's typology should not be taken too literally, but it is an interesting way to start a discussion. It is also an appropriate tool for discussing the work of the contemporary philosopher who has offered the most sophisticated analysis of ideal vs. nonideal theories of justice, namely Gerald Gaus (2018), whom Kogelmann appropriately locates in quadrant IV. Although very sophisticated and complex, Gaus' thesis can be summed up as follows: (1) given the deep cultural and ideological differences that characterize contemporary liberal democracies, as well as the diverse psychosocial dispositions of their citizens (e.g., more or less other-oriented), the search for a unique end goal is an almost unsurmountable challenge; and (2) even if such a goal could be proposed, committing society to its pursuit is bound not only to result in disappointing failures[39] but will also along the way close off opportunities to explore second best solutions that could over time turn out to be more advantageous. The dogged pursuit of impossible projects is costly both in the literal sense but also in terms of opportunity costs. Nonideal theorists from different disciplinary backgrounds could perhaps converge toward the adoption of "second best" solutions (this is indeed the premise that runs through the next chapter).[40]

What's So Good about Egalitarianism?

Economic arguments against egalitarianism were discussed in the previous chapter, but here I want to address criticisms that are more philosophical in nature and which, for that reason, take the form of more or less direct responses to the theories discussed above. This section is organized around two themes; (1) whether simply addressing poverty is more justifiable than aiming for equality (of whatever metric one chooses), which is the position known as "prioritarianism"; and (2) whether it can be said that markets are moral (Zak 2008), by which I mean that if they are the site of socially beneficial and ethically defensible interactions, viewing them primarily as the source of objectionable inequalities is at best a truncated view of reality, and at worst a serious mistake.

Prioritarianism is not a reactionary defense of the status quo or a glorification of laissez-faire capitalism. It does not object to interventions intended to assist individuals or families who experience severe deprivation or even disadvantages of a less dramatic nature. But its main proponents (Parfit 2000; Frankfurt 2015) argue that a willingness to remedy some injustices that stem from inequalities does not *ipso facto* commit one to the ideology of egalitarianism. The problem with egalitarianism, from their standpoint, is that it posits that equality has an intrinsic value—a position they reject more (in Harry Frankfurt's case) or less (Derek Parfit) categorically.

In a much-discussed text, Parfit (2000) set out to analyze the different meanings of egalitarianism and their respective limitations as well as a "prioritarian" alternative. Parfit distinguishes between "telic" and "deontic" egalitarians. The former believe that "it is in itself bad that some people are worse-off than others" (4). They, therefore, approve of efforts aimed at (their telos) reducing, or perhaps even eliminating, the gap between the worse-off and the better-off. The latter do not think that arguments supporting equality should be based on achieving such an outcome, but on some other morally defensible value (e.g., respect for persons). But in merely analyzing the implications of these positions, Parfit identified a paradox stemming from telic egalitarianism, which he called the "levelling down objection." The point here is that egalitarians must prefer over other alternatives the one that is least costly to the worse-off, even if that may mean in some instances taking the better-off down to the level of the worse-off without in any way improving the conditions of the worse-off (as compared to making the worse-off only slightly so, but considerably improving the living conditions of the rest of society). As Michael Weber (2019, 1) notes, "The levelling down objection has convinced many to reject egalitarianism." Deontic egalitarianism does not suffer from this weakness, but it can be criticized for not offering any argument against global inequalities that cannot clearly be attributed to any obvious wrongdoings (Parfit 2000, 104–105). Parfit claims that none of these charges can be leveled against prioritarianism which seeks to do more for people who are worse-off in an *absolute* sense.

Even less supportive of egalitarianism are normative arguments—often supported by more or less conservative economists—that underline the extent to which moral values play a socially beneficial role in shaping the behavior of economic agents, structuring market transactions and keeping dysfunctional tendencies in check.[41] That is to say, justice is inherent in markets rather than an external standpoint from which to consider the potentially harmful effects of market transactions. From that standpoint, one can speak of "moral markets" (Zak 2008); because people are not motivated (only) by selfish motivations, economic transactions end up forming a "community of advantage" (Sugden 2018). It follows that heavy-handed interventions intended to promote *a priori* policy mechanisms could work against the capacity of individuals to cooperate freely in establishing mutually beneficial outcomes. These perspectives should not be confused with a pollyannaish belief that markets are flawless and injustices never occur, but they tend to put the burden of proof on those who claim that the social contract needs to be fundamentally renegotiated rather than incrementally amended. On this point, Sugden (2018, 262) explains:

> What I have in mind is less grand in scope than Rawls's theory, but similar in spirit. Within the limited domain of economics, I am looking for arrangements that will provide opportunities for individuals to realize mutual benefits. It is essential to the contractarian approach [or, in any event, the one Sugden has in mind] that each person's benefit is defined in terms of what he or she wants to achieve, rather than in terms of some unified conception of human well-being that is supposed to apply to everyone.

Albeit "similar in spirit," Sugden's vision is definitely less egalitarian. The essential idea is that when interacting in the market, each participant gives to every other one the opportunity "to satisfy normal expectations about the consequences of their interactions for them" (262).[42] The same can be said of John Tomasi's (2012) reinterpretation of Rawls, that is, his reinterpretation is far less egalitarian than the original. Tomasi faults libertarians for their inability to understand that social justice is morally desirable, but he faults egalitarians or "high liberals" for ignoring economic realities. He claims that Rawls' ends can be met by relying on market processes rather than through state intervention. Tomasi approves, in general terms, Rawls' reasoning process for arriving at his principles, but blames him (and other "high liberals") for downplaying the significance of economic liberties. While Tomasi does not reject the notion of an original position, he suggests (38) that the recommendations that the parties would adopt might not necessarily correspond exactly to what Rawls proposes. So, instead of Rawlsian justice as fairness, Tomasi recommends "free market fairness." As far as the first principle is concerned, Tomasi insists that property rights ought to be included in the basic liberties because they are indeed experienced by most individuals as a fundamental aspect of their participation in economic life. Taking his clue from the fact that Rawls recognizes the right to choose one's occupation, Tomasi (77) argues:

> If the freedom to choose an occupation is essential for the moral powers [note that this is indeed what Rawls implies], the freedom to sell, trade, and donate one's labor looks equally essential for the same reasons. After all,

> one is defined by one's workplace experience not simply by *what* profession one pursues. One is also defined by *where* one chooses to work, by the *terms* that one seeks and accepts for one's work, the *number of hours* that one devotes to one's work, and much more besides.

And as regards the difference principle, Tomasi insists that free markets generally help the most disadvantaged better than a heavily regulated economy, but this does not exclude the possibility of also establishing a basic income as protection against brute luck (2012, 230). While I have a great deal of sympathy for Tomasi's overall position—that social justice and economic liberties are not mutually incompatible and could even be self-reinforcing—I suggest that his scheme remains disappointingly short on details. Moreover, his insistence that economic liberties are necessary for the most complete achievement of "self-authorship" sets up a rather heroic ideal that neglects other considerations, such as caring for dependents.

Conclusion

It is trivial to observe that opportunities for making one's life better, or at least not be left out when others are benefiting from economic growth, are unequally distributed. Therefore, some corrective policy measures are required. Practically all economists acknowledge that fact, even though they disagree on how far these measures should go. For the most part, however, economists have deferred to philosophers when it comes to justifying the scope and contents of redistributive schemes. Over the course of the last fifty years or so, philosophers have been more than willing to respond to the challenge. A great deal of intellectual brilliance has been displayed by scholars engaged in spirited debates about what constitutes social justice, under what circumstances remedial interventions are required, and what sort of principles ought to guide the distribution of socially useful or prized values. Justice theorists have left no philosophical stone unturned, but the practical significance of their analyses is not always obvious. Not only are the concepts being debated abstract, but the ultimate recommendations that can be inferred from these theories seem to always be addressing "yesterday's problem." I must qualify this flippant remark. Of course, poverty, food deprivation, severe power imbalances among economic categories, ethnic and linguistic groups, and gender-based discrimination, to name a few, are not problems that come and go as intellectual fashions change. But the ways they are concretely posed constantly change, and the significance they take in people's lives evolves and is reframed by more or less sincere or opportunistic opinion leaders, political parties, and civil society organizations. In dealing with constantly evolving challenges, such as climate change, pandemics, migration crises, international conflicts, and so on, empirically minded researchers or policymakers may come to the conclusion that philosophical theories provide only vague signposts for selecting concrete priorities. Moreover, if and when rhetorical arguments about justice are used in the political arena, they tend to pit righteous reformers—the much maligned "elites"—against those whom Hillary Clinton injudiciously labeled "a basket of deplorables."

The deadly Covid-19 pandemic has shown that in some circumstances—circumstances that many experts fear will become less and less exceptional—prioritizing the needs of "the least advantaged" conflicts with other equally relevant considerations. Admittedly, the populations living in crowded housing conditions and those who cannot afford to work remotely on a computer are far more at risk, and health officials should make certain that these communities are included in a vaccination campaign (and receive other kinds of support). But vaccination will only work if a very high proportion of the *total* population is vaccinated for free, which incidentally implies a very significant reallocation of budgetary resources. Similarly, low-wage workers are more directly affected by the loss of employment caused by lockouts, but the scale of the problem is so large that the global economy could have collapsed with catastrophic consequences if governments had not made a massive effort to sustain employment across the board. Some countries, such as France, decided to incentivize businesses for not reducing their workforce as their sales declined; others provided financial assistance directly to a vast range of employees and small businesses. But the point is that, in this instance, utilitarianism triumphed over the maximin approach, which is not to say that it necessarily should be true in all cases.

Coming back to political polarization and the rhetorical excesses that have aggravated it, the dramatic rise of populism illustrates the unsuspected cost of taking "ideal theory" too literally. By that I mean that fairness ought not be equated with an *a priori*, moralistic understanding of what is fair in an abstract sense. Analytical philosophers are fond of supporting their arguments by cleverly concocting more or less implausible scenarios featuring fictional characters with names such as Jill and Jack, but are rarely concerned with what real people actually believe. (Neoclassical economists fall in the same trap when it comes to "rational" choice, which is why recent advances in experimental economics are like a breath of fresh air.) What matters is not how fairness is defined in these thought experiments, but what real individuals *perceive* is fair/unfair in their own circumstances, even if they may lack the tools to evaluate the extent to which their circumstances objectively place them in an advantageous or disadvantageous position in terms of their access to public goods or some other metric. This point is forcefully argued by Eric Protzer and Paul Summerville (2022) for whom social mobility, or lack thereof, is at the root of the populist reaction. Unless social mobility is diffuse and widespread, improving it at one end of the spectrum in an attempt to equalize opportunities could well prove to be politically counterproductive An investigative journalist for the *Boston Globe* obtained the following quote from a Trump voter:

> The government never helped me, but I was OK with that. I made mistakes, had some scary moments, and my wife worked at the local library to help out. I paid my bills, including my doctor bills. Now I see my tax dollars

> going to handouts for others who didn't work as hard as I did, and I can't afford my healthcare. Everyone is being taken care of but me. I feel left out, and it makes me feel that I want my country back.
>
> (cited by Protzer and Paul Summerville 2022, 39)

Now the lesson to be drawn is *not* that such sentiments (behind which one may suspect lurk implicit racist prejudices) should guide policymakers, who should then rush to abolish affirmative action programs or stop producing public goods altogether! It is rather that fairness is a powerful emotion that not only can evoke sympathy for the victims of discrimination but also can generate resentment when people across a wide swath of socioeconomic conditions, including those whose "deprivations" might be more illusory than tangible, feel that their own needs, aspirations, and values are not taken seriously by those who have the power to make material as well as symbolic decisions. Remedying negative injustices is crucial, but so is also ensuring that rewards are fairly and widely distributed intragenerationally and intergenerationally. Indeed, as Protzer and Paul Summerville (2022, 92) note, countries where social mobility is high, such as Canada or Sweden, are also countries where reactionary populist parties have made the least advance. Strong social mobility on its own may not be sufficient to put an end to populist rhetorical claims that "the system" is corrupt, but I would argue that most, if not all, of the definitions of social progress outlined so far will get a more favorable reception from the public if they are debated in a context where social mobility can be taken more or less for granted. Populism thrives on the belief that things were better for the middle class in a mythical past, past that has to be revisited by rolling back all the advances of the last few decades.

This does not mean that ideal theory is irrelevant. It should serve as a moral barrier against both political opportunism and reformist zeal. Profound reforms may be needed to deal with ongoing challenges and ensure that liberal democracies continue to serve the needs and aspirations of their citizens. But not at the cost of violating the liberal values that make it possible to debate the implications of these concerns in the first place and to build safeguards against the creation of new hierarchies in the name of expediency. (The tension inherent in remaining faithful to the democratic ideal while also calling upon technical expertise when appropriate without empowering an elite of experts beyond what is strictly required to deal with an issue is a vexing one, as john Dewey [2008] explained many decades ago and as the recent pandemic vividly illustrates.) Theorists can remind us of the true significance of concepts such as "freedom" or "equality," which in the recent past have been warped to serve the unreasonable demands of extremist advocates for ideologically shortsighted causes. Rawls' first principle still resonates as an imperative that should stand in the path of intolerant egalitarianism. But from a pragmatic standpoint, Dworkin's admonition to always demonstrate "equal respect and concern" for the well-being of all persons is a useful reminder that calls for "freedom" from norms, and rules (e.g., mask mandates) intended to protect the most vulnerable citizens (e.g., elderly persons) may violate the even more morally compelling injunction to "do no harm." Ideal theory is an indispensable instrument of reflection and analysis for ensuring that in answering insistent calls for remedying deep inequalities or even merely irksome ones, the cause of justice is ultimately served. The Rawlsian notion of "reflective equilibrium" is quite apt in this context, and it is the indispensable role of normative theorists to speak as forcefully as they can about the importance of first principles (e.g., equal respect for all members of an organized political community) and to ensure that intuitive policy ideas remain consistent with them (see, e.g., Campbell 2014).

But as I suggested immediately above, ideal theory is not a very useful source of efficient solutions to complex, multidimensional, and constantly shifting socioeconomic problems. Within the normative constraints I have just alluded to, policy agendas and/or initiatives from civil society ought to make room for a wide range of ideas and proposals. In spite of all the efforts deployed by theorists such as Rawls or Dworkin to show that there is a narrow path that logically leads from their ethical premises to their preferred method for reducing inequalities, for example, an insurance market, I hope to have shown that alternative methods should never be ruled out. And even if that means settling for "second best" solutions for achieving a specific goal, say equalizing resources, much can be gained in terms of meeting some other valued objective, say promoting pluralism. In fact, no solution is ever optimal in all respects: it may be efficient but difficult to "sell" politically; it might provide some advantages to the worst-off but do very little to improve the lots of lower-middle-class groups; and so on. The objective of the next chapter is to apply the lessons learned in this chapter to an evaluation of concrete policy measures gleaned from the applied economic literature.

Notes

1 The last edition (1999) contains some significant revisions.
2 Even Marx left some room for inequalities when he implied that in the good society, distribution of resources should be "from each according to their abilities, to each according to their needs."
3 Whether the most disadvantaged individuals or households are properly addressed, let alone prioritized, in democracies is not evident. The welfare state was originally established to support working-class males and their families; it has, of course, evolved, but typically racially based prejudices against the "underserving poor" (e.g., refugees) subsist and have become more virulent in recent years. One could also point to the homelessness crisis that afflicts North American and European countries.
4 On property-owning democracy, see Chapter 3.
5 Although *A Theory of Justice* is mostly concerned with ideal theory, in *The Law of Peoples* (1999), Rawls acknowledges that when dealing with international relations, it is necessary to more delicately balance ideal and nonideal theory.
6 Hal Varian (1985), however, suggests that economists have not given Dworkin's theory the critical attention it deserves.
7 In fact, Dworkin never mentions Pigou.

8 He returned to this theme in his last book, *Justice for Hedgehogs* (2011).

9 Someone whose handicap is the result of a preventable accident caused by a *conscious* decision to take high risks (e.g., "extreme sports") does not fit that description.

10 As I have indicated in Chapter 1, more economists today than when Varian was writing are willing to concede that interpersonal comparisons are unavoidable when a cost–benefit analysis of policy options is the appropriate tool for designing policies (e.g., a carbon tax), even though, in theory, such comparisons are problematic (but not altogether unfeasible if we take sympathy into account).

11 The markets that Dworkin describes are the sort of idealized, perfectly competitive markets that neoclassical economists have been much criticized for adopting as the foundation of their analyses.

12 Note incidentally that when the auction is completed, everyone is on the same level, contrary to Rawls' prioritizing of the needs of the least advantaged/worse-off members of society.

13 My own view, presented a little further below, is that for all its merits, Dworkin's theory runs into the difficulties that all "ideal" theories unnecessarily create for their proponents.

14 This tradition was built on the seminal work of James Mirrlees (1971, 1976).

15 Fleurbaey (2008) leaves the definition of these circumstances wide open, simply denoting them by a vector y_i for each individual i.

16 Before offering an insightful assessment of this theory, Kristi Olson (2020, chapter 7) provides an easily readable overview of Fleurbaey's works that are primarily addressed to readers with a solid background in normative economics.

17 Incidentally, Jane's case is distinct from a preference for hedonistic idleness, which would have entailed Jane expecting a higher lump sum to pleasantly occupy her free time, possibly negating her need for a subsidy in this example, but also suggesting that her low productivity is due not to an aversion to hard work but to her need for additional time to devote to nonremunerated work; inversely, if Jane loved her work so much that the only way for her to accept trading her salary for a lump sum would be a very high lump sum, this would also decrease the need for a subsidy since her well-being and her sense of fairness would depend less on material rewards.

18 The issue of implementation is touched upon, albeit still at a high level of abstraction, in Fleurbaey and Maniquet (2018).

19 For an overview and a defense of luck egalitarianism, see Carl Knight's *Luck Egalitarianism* (2009); see also Knight (2013, 2021). According to Knight (2021, 350), this paradigm "has come to be arguably the most influential theory of equality in Anglophone political philosophy." Thus, although the Rawlsian approach has not completely faded away, luck egalitarianism is more topical nowadays. But, as the rest of this chapter suggests, luck egalitarianism is itself increasingly challenged by critics who advocate a relational approach.

20 In fact, Cohen was the leading figure in the by-now-more-or-less-intellectually-defunct school of "analytical Marxism," which attempted to articulate Marx's goals using the tools of analytical philosophy and rational choice rather than the flawed concepts of Marxist economics.

21 Regardless of the empirical difficulties associated with differentiating among these distinct theories, it is interesting to note that there is evidence to the effect that "the degree of circumstances-based inequalities, rather than income inequality, could be related to aggregate economic performance and economic growth" (Fleurbaey and

Peragine 2013, 118; this assertion is based on Bourguignon et al. [2007] and World Bank [2006]).

22 For a comprehensive analysis of Cohen's critique of the impact of markets on justice, see Albertsen (2019).

23 Experimental evidence for this statement can be found in Cappelen et al. (2013); Tinghog et al. (2017).

24 www.statista.com/statistics/1203135/gender-pay-gap-in-europe-by-country/.

25 Writing at a time when the term "neoliberalism" was not quite as frequently used as it is today, Elizabeth Anderson (1999, 292) characterized luck egalitarianism as "a hybrid of capitalism and the welfare state." The passage from which this quote is drawn clearly suggests that she considered it as a step backward.

26 Note that it is not only conservative critics who raise this question. Filling this information gap could require the state to resort to intrusive measure and thereby, as the progressive egalitarian philosopher Elizabeth Anderson (1999, 26) remarks, luck egalitarianism "interferes with citizens' privacy and liberty."

27 In the cited passage, Sen has Dworkin in mind, but it is clear that he uses Dworkin as an exemplar rather than as a unique case.

28 The implicit assumption here is that what constitutes injustice is self-evident; this view, which I take to be experientially demonstrable, can be traced to Adam Smith's notion of sympathy: we spontaneously sympathize with those who have been wronged. But for a critique of the "manifest injustice" thesis, see Wolff (2015, 216–224).

29 For a more technical summary, see Dobuzinskis (2022, 135–136).

30 Sen (2009, 21–23) acknowledges his debt in this regard to the Indian jurisprudence tradition, which distinguishes between *niti*, defined as justice according to abstract rules, and *nyaya*, meaning achieving a just outcome.

31 See the contributions to Fourie et al. (2015).

32 The links are https://thecareecconomy.ca and https://research.american.edu/care workeconomy.

33 See Drèze and Sen (2002); see also Brighouse and Robeyns (2010, Part II); Gotoh (2021, chapter 3).

34 These are (Nussbaum 2011, 33–34):

1. Life. Being able to live to the end of a human life of normal length; not dying prematurely, or before one's life is so reduced as to be not worth living.
2. Bodily Health. Being able to have good health, including reproductive health; to be adequately nourished; to have adequate shelter.
3. Bodily Integrity. Being able to move freely from place to place; to be secure against violent assault, including sexual assault and domestic violence; having opportunities for sexual satisfaction and for choice in matters of reproduction.
4. Senses, Imagination, and Thought. Being able to use the senses, to imagine, think, and reason—and to do these things in a "truly human" way, a way informed and cultivated by an adequate education, including, but by no means limited to, literacy and basic mathematical and scientific training. Being able to use imagination and thought in connection with experiencing and producing works and events of one's own choice, religious, literary, musical, and so forth. Being able to use one's mind in ways protected by guarantees of freedom of expression with respect to both political and artistic speech, and freedom of

religious exercise. Being able to have pleasurable experiences and to avoid non-beneficial pain.

5. Emotions. Being able to have attachments to things and people outside ourselves; to love those who love and care for us, to grieve at their absence; in general, to love, to grieve, to experience longing, gratitude, and justified anger. Not having one's emotional development blighted by fear and anxiety. (Supporting this capability means supporting forms of human association that can be shown to be crucial in their development.)
6. Practical Reason. Being able to form a conception of the good and to engage in critical reflection about the planning of one's life. (This entails protection for the liberty of conscience and religious observance.)
7. Affiliation. Being able to live with and toward others, to recognize and show concern for other humans, to engage in various forms of social interaction; to be able to imagine the situation of another. (Protecting this capability means protecting institutions that constitute and nourish such forms of affiliation, and also protecting the freedom of assembly and political speech.) Having the social bases of self-respect and non-humiliation; being able to be treated as a dignified being whose worth is equal to that of others. This entails provisions of non-discrimination on the basis of race, sex, sexual orientation, ethnicity, caste, religion, national origin and species.
8. Other Species. Being able to live with concern for and in relation to animals, plants, and the world of nature.
9. Play. Being able to laugh, to play, to enjoy recreational activities.
10. Control over one's Environment. Political. Being able to participate effectively in political choices that govern one's life; having the right of political participation, protections of free speech and association. Material. Being able to hold property (both land and movable goods), and having property rights on an equal basis with others; having the right to seek employment on an equal basis with others; having the freedom from unwarranted search and seizure. In work, being able to work as a human, exercising practical reason and entering into meaningful relationships of mutual recognition with other workers.

35 See Dobuzinskis (2022, chapter 6).

36 Qizilbash (2011) provides a useful overview of these critiques; see also Arneson (2018, 200–204) on relational egalitarianism.

37 Although the contributions to Church et al. (2015) do not explicitly pose the problem in these terms, they clearly imply that Chicago school economists have little patience for egalitarianism!

38 One could include many other thinkers in the classical social contract tradition (e.g., Locke), and Kogelmann also locates James Buchanan's "constitutional politics" (see Buchanan and Tullock 1962) in quadrant III.

39 In the concluding section, I suggest that the rise of populist movements in contemporary democracies is a manifestation of this sort of collective frustration, if we assume that the end goal of the last two to three decades has been to build a prosperous global economy and a deeply interconnected cosmopolitan global society.

40 Colin Farrelly (2007) follows a parallel path by arguing that the most promising avenue for opening a broad-based debate among scholars and practitioners (e.g., on the subject of healthcare) is to avoid framing the issues in terms of their relevance to rigidly defined ideal ends.

41 A growing number of economists and social psychologists (Kolm [2000a; 2000b]; Bowles and Gintis [2011]; Sigmund et al. [2002]; McCloskey [2006]; Langrill and Storr [2012]), using both empirical evidence and a critical reappraisal of what Adam Smith and other classical political economists already intuited, have shown that if greed and selfishness were the sole motivations guiding economic life, markets would be grossly inefficient. For example, contracts could not be negotiated if the parties so distrust each other that they could not expect the contract would be carried out in a spirit of good faith; most contracts, moreover, are incomplete and normally the parties behave in such a way that the implicit implications of the contract are met voluntarily.

42 Elsewhere, Sugden (2015) goes beyond the "invisible hand" argument that actions motivated by self-interest involuntarily contribute to the general welfare by making a stronger claim that markets can be conceptualized as games in which the players *intentionally* decide to cooperate for mutual advantage. For a critique of this strong claim, see Fumagalli (2020). I agree with Roberto Fumagalli that the scope of intentional cooperation is thwarted by empirical realities and structural constraints. But this critique does not invalidate Sudgen's point that market transactions are not inherently predicated on selfish motivations. If so, then, to satisfy nonselfish concerns about fairness does not *ipso facto* imply an exclusive reliance on social norms that are exogenous to the sphere of market transactions.

6 Growth and (In)equality II

What to Do about Inequality?

As the literature on economic inequalities keeps on expanding, new suggestions about how to resolve the problem are added to an already long list. My fist task in this chapter is to synthesize these ideas. This task has been made simpler by Todd Knoop (2020, chapter 7) who has offered a comprehensive and coherent overview of such recommendations. Knoop sensibly categorizes the responses to the challenge of inequality as falling either under the rubric of "structural" approaches or "fiscal" policies (i.e., taxes and transfers). I follow a rather similar plan, but I want to make a clearer distinction between reforms that directly concern the current structure of the welfare state as well as alternatives to it, on the one hand, and socioeconomic reforms that are more concerned with the empowerment of individuals within a market economy. The latter should be ranked first in accordance with the normative criteria I outlined above. Thus, the next three sections are organized as follows: first, a discussion of reforms that could empower those who arguably lack the means of acting as free and autonomous citizens in a liberal democracy; then a critical examination of strategies for reforming the welfare state, which I divide into an assessment of current and alternative approaches to income transfers, on the one hand, and tax reforms, on the other hand.

I do not intend to merely offer a smorgasbord of "solutions." So, my second task is to bring to bear on the proposals gleaned from the economics and policy literatures the normative perspectives that have been critically analyzed in the previous chapters. The upshot is not a strict and definitive ranking of the proposed solutions, but an admittedly tentative one that is intended merely to initiate a conversation. Now, to recap, the normative lenses I have sketched out so far are: (1) with respect to ends, a nonideal perspective that emphasizes fairness and liberty/autonomy but admits of a plurality of values and the possibility of trade-offs among them through a process of democratic deliberation; and (2) with respect to means, a pragmatic attention to economic feasibility and practical political constraints (e.g., whether there is sufficient public support for the proposed measures). This critical evaluation bears mostly on the ideas and measures listed in each of the following sections than on the three categories themselves, although I tend to regard the structural reforms outlined in the next section as more fundamental even if some of them may be somewhat utopian.

DOI: 10.4324/9781003216247-6

Sociopolitical Reforms: Variations on the Theme of Empowerment

Economic inequalities evidently involve the distribution of income, but the roots of income disparities can be traced to a variety of factors that are sociopolitical and not narrowly economic. Remedying inequalities, therefore, means empowering people to develop the capabilities they need to lead satisfying, and perhaps even happier, lives. Reducing severe inequalities is not only justifiable in and by itself, but it can also contribute to growth and collective welfare. First among all these means is education. Next I turn to measures that concern the relative balance of power between employers and employees, namely, minimum wage laws, and at least some of the ways in which the rather utopian ideal of a "property-owning democracy" could be achieved. Finally, I raise the question—without pretending to fully resolve it—of what can be done on the international scene to deal with global inequalities.

Education

Education is empowering in many ways that reach far beyond the economic sphere, but for my purpose, I bracket out these other aspects. It unquestionably is a powerful lever for promoting economic growth as well as facilitating social mobility. Unequal access to this resource is a major cause of inequality. This is why prioritizing education is a very advisable policy, even though the effects of a massive investment in education are not going to be felt immediately. Investing in education produces very beneficial results in countries where literacy is at a low rate for much of the population. It has a direct effect on reducing poverty, especially for girls and women. The facts of the matter are more ambiguous in advanced economies where it is not primary schooling but higher education that has the most noticeable effect on earning potentials. This is not because education is any less crucial in advanced economies. Far from it, the generation and transmission of knowledge and skills have always been important, but in today's "knowledge economy," they are even more crucial. Several decades ago already, the Dutch economist Jan Tinbergen argued that rather than "a battle between labor and capital," we are now witnessing "a race between technological development and increases in schooling" (Deaton 2013, 191). The problem is rather that *in the present circumstances*, education is an inefficient engine of social mobility. On the basis of a careful examination of the data from 113 countries, Daniele Checchi (2004,101) concludes that

> for a given level of per capita income, income inequality has a U-shaped relationship with the average years of education in the population, with a turning point around 6.48 years. For all countries below this threshold, the two variables are negatively correlated, while the two become positively correlated above this threshold. Using the regional averages reported in Table 4.3 , we can say that additional education promotes inequality

in the OECD countries (and very recently also in the formerly planned economies), whereas it is beneficial with respect to inequality in the other regions of the world.

The relationship between the number of years of education and inequality is U-shaped: beyond a threshold, education becomes an aggravating factor. This pattern is a good news–bad news sort of story. The left-hand side of the curve conveys the good news that primary and secondary education in poorer regions contributes to reducing inequalities. Due attention, however, should be paid to the gender gap. Significant progress has been made in the last few decades, but there are significant regional differences. Using data that do not go beyond 1990,

> [Stephan] Klassen (2002) estimated that 0.9 percentage points of the 1.8 percentage point annual per capita growth difference between the countries in MENA and those in East Asia and the Pacific (EAP) can be attributed to higher initial gender inequality in education there as well as a slower closing of the gap vis-à-vis EAP.
>
> (Klassen and Lamanna 2009, 92)

Using data that stretch over another decade, Stephan Klassen and Francesca Lamanna (2009, 110) report that the situation has considerably improved for the MENA where the loss is about 0.7 percentage point per year but not for sub-Saharan Africa. (Closing the gender gap ought to be also a priority in the rest of the world, of course, but much progress has been made; in North America, the gap has been closed in the social sciences, at least for undergraduate degrees, but not for science and technology.)

The problem lies on the right-hand side of the curve. Of course, not everyone can or should obtain a college degree, but the curve is too steep. Simply put, higher education is a major factor in the reproduction of social hierarchies and unfair inequalities. Although much progress was made in earlier decades, the situation in the twenty-first century in many, albeit not all, advanced economies is preoccupying. As Knoop (2019: 174) notes with respect to the US,

> The children of highly educated parents also tend to be highly educated, and less-educated parents tend to have less-educated children. Any structural reform program that aims to change the nature of market income inequality has to deal with the fact that income inequality largely reflects education inequality.

For several decades, especially in the postwar era, getting a college degree was one of the surest ways to do better than one's parents, and millions of returning "GIs", and later their sons and daughters, did just that. Even in countries such as the UK or France where higher education has always benefited the elites and has worked as a mechanism for reproducing social hierarchies, progress was made in the second half of the twentieth century in terms of reducing some of these barriers. However, in most developed countries, this healthy trend seems to have slowed down considerably. In the US, for example, the "college wage premium" has decreased for recent cohorts as compared to what it was for the 1950–70 cohort, although the wage premium for graduate (advanced) degrees has increased (Ashworth and Ransom 2019, 149). And insofar as access to higher education is increasingly out of reach for lower-income families, once again, higher education serves to reinforce social and economic inequalities rather than undermining them (Checchi 2004 Lindley and Machin 2012). What has changed is that the differential in earnings separating those who hold a college degree from those who do not has widened. Thus, to return to the case of the US, while the "American Dream" was not exclusively restricted to college graduates, this is becoming the case. And insofar as university education has also become considerably more expensive as well as more competitive, high school students from underprivileged backgrounds are increasingly unlikely to obtain the credentials that would allow them to achieve social mobility. Joanne Lindley and Stephen Machin (2012) have expressed similar concerns with respect to the UK: while the number of young people gaining access to higher education has increased considerably over the years, it still remains that students who come from affluent families have a clear advantage.

The conclusion that should be drawn from these remarks is not that higher education is inherently a cause of unfair inequalities but that, at present, it is functioning better as an engine of overall economic growth than as an engine of mobility, and arguably even produces perverse effects in that regard. The problem presents itself in two ways: it stems from inequities in the cost of higher education, and it is linked to deep-seated sociocultural traditions and institutional practices. Let me begin with the first. This problem is not unique to the US, but is arguably even deeper there. It stems from the dramatic inequality between the level of resources available to students who should be planning to go to college—in affluent neighborhoods this is hardly a problem, but serious obstacles stand in the way of poorer students. For example, Joanne Lindley and Stephen Machin (2012) point out that while the number of young people in the UK gaining access to higher education has increased considerably over the years, it still remains that students who come from affluent families have a clear advantage. The UK is not unique in this regard. The problem is worse in the US where the funding of education co mes primarily from property taxes collected at the local level. Therefore, one finds good schools in prosperous suburbs and much less resource-endowed schools in poorer neighborhoods. In California, the effects of Proposition 13, which placed a ceiling on property taxes, have had a detrimental impact on the entire school system. The other facet of the funding problem concerns the dramatic increase in tuition fees. They have become exorbitant in private universities. But they were always rather high (and actually, meritorious students can obtain scholarships relatively easily). The problem is more acute for state university systems that used to be more affordable. As the debt burden of most US states has increased, funding for the vast majority of state universities and colleges has been cut and tuition fees have increased. In recent years, the situation has been aggravated by an ideological aversion for higher education in many "red states." Universities and colleges have no other option than to raise fees. Not surprisingly, a vast number of university students in the US graduate with a very substantial level of debt.

Tuition fees, however, are far from being the only problem. In some countries where access to higher education is free, there are cultural barriers that stand in the way of underprivileged students. How to remove these barriers is more challenging than the comparatively simpler issue of making higher education more affordable. Of course, the situations and depth of the crisis varies from country to country; for example, the Nordic countries have fared rather well, however, not only because tuition is free but also because the system is generally democratic. In other European contexts (e.g., France, Germany, Italy), by contrast, tuition is also free, but there are more diffuse cultural and institutional barriers that stand in the way of underprivileged students. In France, access to the elite schools ("grandes écoles") is restricted by challenging entrance examinations in which students from privileged cultural backgrounds typically perform better; in Germany (Mayer et al. 2007), and indeed most of Europe outside of the Nordic countries, the challenges are more subtle, but the unequal distribution of cultural capital is real and has a marked effect on university admission or completion of studies.

What can be done to make education the engine of social mobility it ought to be? This is a complex problem, but some remedies are rather obvious. In emerging economies where access to primary education is lagging,[1] which is still the case in much of Sub-Saharan Africa and South Asia (e.g., Bangladesh), renewed effort to promote literacy should be undertaken. In developed economies, schools in all neighborhoods should receive approximately equal funding, but arguably the largest gap concerns university systems that could be more adequately funded. And teachers and college instructors should be well paid (teachers in Finland, for example, are well compensated and socially respected). While this recommendation is a proverbial "no brainer," it is not likely to be heeded for the reason that education is competing more and more intensely with other priorities, and notably health, as the population of most advanced economies is aging. In the US, the budgetary challenge is complicated by ideological polarization: there no longer is as wide a support for public education as there existed before, and there is even a new current of anti-intellectualism that makes it more difficult for universities and colleges to plead for increased budgets, But the problem is not just a lack of resources. What is far more challenging to resolve—in at least some contexts—is the disproportion in economic rents that some arguably overrated degrees confer and the sociocultural inequalities that prevent students from a variety of more or less disadvantaged backgrounds from obtaining these highly prized degrees. It will take a cultural revolution to convince employers that degrees from the Ivy League schools in the US, Cambridge or Oxford in the UK, or Ecole Polytechnique in France are not as reliable a source of information about the aptitudes and talents of an applicant as they are deemed to be.[2] To recap, education is in principle "the silver bullet," especially from the standpoint of the capabilities approach, but, in practice, seems to work less and less well as a result of the twin challenge posed by inadequate public funding[3] and sociocultural barriers to access.

Minimum Wage

In theory, an optimal tax system—a topic I discuss in the next section—should provide resources for funding programs, the effects of which would be equivalent to moving the minimal wage closer to the real cost of living. But this principle supposes the existence of a perfect competition. If the labor market suffers from imperfections—something which is not difficult to envisage—it might be better to think of optimal taxation and minimum wage as being complementary policy instruments (Hunggerbühler and Lehmann 2009). Moreover, regardless of pure economic theory, it has proved increasingly difficult in recent decades to raise taxes or even to resist voters' demand for lowering taxes than to use regulatory tools and shift the burden of reducing inequalities to employers. A minimum wage is not a new idea, but, especially in North America, it has moved back to the top of the social policy agenda. National and subnational governments are involved,[4] but they seem to be catching up initiatives taken by cities. In the late 2010s, Seattle, Los Angeles, Cincinnati, and Vancouver, to name a few, took the lead in that respect. But the idea is not limited to North America. A great many countries, from Australia to Zambia, have legislated a minimum wage. Across the EU, minimum wages have increased significantly in the 2010s.

When Gary Becker (Becker and Becker 1997, 37) wrote in one of his columns for *Business Week* that a "higher minimum [wage] will further reduce the employment opportunities of workers with few skills," he was expressing the common wisdom among economists. "Raising minimum wage kills jobs" (e.g., Hanke 2014) is a commonly heard argument. The logic is rather impeccable. In sectors of the economy where profit margins are very thin (e.g., retail, fast food), even a small shift in labor costs can have serious negative effects on the viability of a small business enterprise or on larger firms' capacity to expand and hire more employees. But, in spite of the orthodox consensus on the perverse effects of mandated wages, the evidence on this question is somewhat murky. Among other reasons, the effects of a minimum wage depend greatly on the elasticity of the demand for labor, which varies for different categories of workers.

The debate was reignited in the early 1990s by David Card (1992a,1992b), Lawrence F. Katz and Alan B. Krueger (1992), and Card and Krueger (1994). These scholars gathered evidence from natural experiments supporting the claim that in many circumstances raising the minimum wage is likely to have, at worst, a minimal negative impact and could even result in a positive effect on employment. (Largely based on this contribution, the Canadian American economist David Card was one of three recipients of the Nobel Prize in economics in 2021.) The literature on this subject is by now so vast that I cannot pretend to examine it in detail here. The overall conclusion of comprehensive surveys of the literature or "meta-studies" (Doucoulagio and Stanley 2009; Belman and Wolfson 2014) is that raising the minimum wage does *not* invariably and inevitably reduce employment. The actual effects depend on a host of factors, including the magnitude of the increase, geographical location, types of employment, demographic factors (e.g., teenagers vs. adults[5]), and so on. One thing is clear, however. This subject is going to stay at the top of the policy agenda for some time to come considering that, at least in the US, wage reform is a more feasible form of redistribution than taxation. As inflation returns to the scene, there is increasing pressure on government and employers not to desert the working poor.

While, ever since Pigou, economists have argued in favor of protecting workers at the lower end of the scale, they are divided on the subject of minimum wages. Political philosophers or legal scholars are generally less skeptical. One commonly expressed justification is in terms of the dignity of workers (Anderson 2008; Davidov 2009, 2018). That is to say, it is an instrument against exploitation that empowers wage earners by allowing them to escape from the social stigma of extreme poverty;[6] the "othering" of the poor is not going to be solved by minimum wage legislation, especially considering that in large metropolitan centers the minimum wage still falls below the poverty line. But this policy instrument fits rather well within the emphasis on dignity and respect that "relational egalitarians" (see Chapter 5) insist must be an integral part of any program design to alleviate economic inequalities. Critics may argue, however, that minimum wages do not truly empower workers because they leave untouched the structural causes of the imbalance of power between employers and employees. I now turn to proposals that address this challenge.

"Predistribution": Asset-Based Approaches

One can either leave the rules of the market economy intact—especially with respect to how property rights are allocated and protected—and then remedy the inequalities that even reasonably well-functioning markets operating on such rules generate, or one can change the rules. Rewriting the rules would serve the purpose of allocating resources in a more equitable manner, thereby negating the need for remedying interventions.[7] The former is the politics of redistribution; the latter the politics of "*pre*distribution." This strategy is more radical in the sense that it challenges the acquisition or transfer of property rights, although the changes proposed by the advocates of redistribution range from relatively minor to more far-reaching ones. But it is also more conservative in that (1) helping people to acquire assets gives them a stake in the market economy and, thereby, helps to legitimize it, and (2) placing a lower priority on the redistribution of income could reduce the reliance on at least some fiscal or regulatory interventions that are deemed to have a negative impact on efficiency. Indeed, advocates of predistribution can be found across the whole ideological spectrum, from "red Tories" to (non-Marxist) socialists; they come from different intellectual horizons and include economists (e.g., Henry George in the past, and Samuel Bowles or Joseph Stiglitz today) and philosophers (Bruce Ackerman, Martin O'Neil, John Rawls).

Predistribution can take many forms, but the central idea is that justice is ultimately better served by tackling inequalities with respect to assets rather than income. The most generic way of describing policies aiming toward predistribution is to refer to them as asset-based approaches; this is synonymous with property-owning democracy, but potentially encompasses a broader range of policies. The most often discussed methods for reallocating assets—and, thereby, giving individuals and/or communities more control over their lives—include:

- taxing land rents (to the point of reducing land ownership to a nominal concept);
- facilitating the acquisition of property (e.g., real estate);
- codetermination (i.e., giving employees a voice in the management of corporations and encouraging the creation of cooperatives);
- providing lump-sum payments to individuals early in life;
- area-specific policies for building personal or community assets of a nonfinancial nature (e.g., health).

Land Ownership

The idea that large disparities in land ownership are one of the major causes of injustice is, of course, not new. It has sparked calls for land reform going back centuries. Land reform has been a pressing issue in Latin America for a very long time, but it is only relatively recently that significant progress has been made on that front. The problems and obstacles toward a more equitable distribution of agricultural land vary from place to place (e.g., what is relevant to South Africa is not necessarily relevant to Nepal, and so on). For this reason—and not because it is not important—I cannot give sufficient attention to this matter in the limited space I have here (but see Lipton 2009). Instead, I focus on a more abstract and, therefore, more generalizable approach concerned with inequities caused by land rents and, more generally, economic rents. This approach was pioneered by the social reformer Henry George who, in the process of advocating his ideas, also became a serious political economist. To put it succinctly, land as a factor of production is rather unique in that it generates revenue for the owner whether or not it is put to productive use. When the value of the uses to which land can (even only potentially) be put to (for producing goods or providing housing) increases exogenously, the owner can increase the actual rent being charged or simply sell the land at a profit.[8] But this "economic rent" is unearned, parasitic income at least in the sense that it is not a reward for making a higher positive contribution to the collective welfare. (Technically speaking, the economic rent that a parcel of land *A* yields amounts to the opportunity cost for the renter/lessee of moving to parcel *B*, which is the least productive of all the available parcels of lands on which a marketable good—food, housing, and so on—can be produced without incurring a loss; when demand for the goods or services that can be produced on these parcels of land goes up, so does the rent that their owners can charge, or the profit they can make by selling their property.) Owners of any plot of land in most large metropolitan centers are well aware that they have passively become asset-rich in the twenty-first century.

As mentioned in Chapter 4, Henry George argued in his *Progress and Poverty* ([1879] 1935) that the primary cause of poverty in the industrial age was increasing land rents. They redirect to landowners much of what should be owed to wage earners for their productive contribution to the general welfare. His solution was to socialize land rent by taxing it at a rate of 100 percent. Now even taking into account the interconnection between industrialization and urbanization, and the speculation that is taking place in the late nineteenth century, it is doubtful that land rents were the *primary* cause of low wages. Indeed, by the early twentieth century, wage increases were significant. But George's idea of replacing *all* taxes by a "single" tax on land value is sound from the standpoint of economic theory, because it is the only tax that does not distort incentives and is fully consistent with the ideal of economic freedom. (The same cannot be said of income taxes, sales taxes, etc.) For this reason George was a progressive libertarian, and the same can be said of his "Georgist" followers: libertarian because he pleaded for economic freedom; progressive because (1) the predistribution effected by, in a sense, dispossessing landlords and speculators served the interest of both the workers and their enterprising employers, and (2) because the revenues from the single tax could be used to fund redistributive programs, albeit probably relatively modest ones since the core functions of the state—justice, defense, the provision of public goods—would take priority.[9] This is consistent with the notion of equitable growth that undergirds most of my comments throughout this book. But I want to suggest that Georgism leans too heavily toward the side of ideal theory, which I have argued should be avoided. The fact is that after George's death in 1897, Georgism experienced a brief triumph and then, by the middle of the twentieth century, faded away. In the world of ideas, Georgism has experienced something of a renaissance in the last few decades, partly because of the explosion in the price of real estate. But the "single tax" on land rent, which was its core principle, has never been fully implemented anywhere and is not likely to be in the foreseeable future.[10] Now I should qualify this critique in two ways. First, with respect to empirical reality, Georgism has inspired the reform of municipal taxation in many places in North America and Australia, but this is obviously not sufficient for fulfilling George's hopes for a better future. Second, the idea of taxing economic rents other than land rents is a sound idea, which is being partly implemented by the EU with respect to the rents appropriated by digital platforms. In the long run, finding new ways of predistributing economic gains by shifting the burden of taxation from productive economic agents to rent-seekers and speculators is certainly something that should be pursued.

Another predistributive policy for dealing with inequalities is land ownership, but this time, based on premises that are completely opposite to Georgism, consists of measures intended to help households with modest incomes to buy their own homes. This goal is a recurring theme in British and American politics. In the US, there has been a longstanding effort to help low-income families enter the housing market. The centerpiece of this program was the Community Reinvestment Act; first passed in 1977 as an instrument to prevent discrimination in mortgage lending practices, it has been amended several times since then. These amendments, together with the regulations put in place to guide their implementation, aimed at ensuring that all mortgage lending banks were making sufficient efforts to expand homeownership (Wallison 2009). In the 1990s, Congress has repeatedly mandated the "government-sponsored enterprises" (GSEs) known as Fannie Mae (Federal National Mortgage Association) and Freddie Mac (Federal Home Loan Mortgage Corporation) to repurchase mortgages. Beginning in 1997, these agencies were under pressure to purchase subprime (riskier) mortgages, thereby encouraging lending institutions to create even more mortgages with very low loan-to-value (LTV) ratios. When President George W. Bush came into office in 2001, he went further, advocating that everyone should own a home as part of his vaunted "Ownership Society" initiative. In response, the US Department of Housing and Urban Development (HUD) pressured Fannie Mae and Freddie Mac to finance an even greater number of mortgages to people with modest incomes and to borrowers of color. While this is a laudable goal, the result was that too many mortgages were approved for people who were not able to afford them (Mian and Sufi 2014). As is well known, once securitized, the mortgages became "toxic assets," which brought about the collapse of some major investment banks and precipitated the financial crisis of 2007–08. Future attempts at helping lower income households to own their own homes should pay close attention to the risk of policy failures of this sort.

Codetermination

Minimum wages are a coercive way to raise the income of unskilled workers, but it does not necessarily mean that all salaried employees get their "fair share." Giving a voice to all employees in corporate governance would go some way toward ensuring that they are compensated fairly for their diverse contributions to the firm's profits. For example, engineers who do research and development work cannot always trust management to reward them appropriately for their inputs into the productive process. Shareholders, who typically are the only interests represented on the board of directors, have relatively short-term views on what is good for the company and may be tempted to cut labor costs as soon as profits decrease. This is a problem because nowadays most shares are owned by private equity firms that care little about the internal operations of the corporations in which they have invested. Democratizing corporate governance could counterbalance these biases.[11] An interesting and often cited example of this concept is "codetermination" in Germany. It is not a unique case in the EU where employees have some access to corporate boards in a majority of countries. But, as Hayden and Bodie 2020 173) note,

> The German system of codetermination offers the most robust protection of employee representation. German codetermination has also been in place for decades as part of a large, modern economy, making it the most obvious example of such a system.

The system comprises two facets: (1) shop-level works councils where employees can have input into their working conditions, and (2) employee representation on corporate board of companies with more than 500 employees (in large companies, the employees enjoy something close to parity with the shareholders). Although the system now operates within a legislative framework, it was not originally imposed by the state, but emerged through voluntary agreement in the postwar years (Hayden and Bodie 2020, 176). On the whole it has worked well to complement wage negotiations with the trade unions and to stabilize corporate governance in Germany. But there are reported examples of dysfunctional compliance; in some companies, for instance, shareholders hold separate meetings to avoid disclosing valuable information to other board members (Becht et al. 2003, 38). While codetermination has been a reasonably successful experience in Germany and a few other places, notably Sweden, it has not been scaled up on a global level. In North America in particular, it has been an object of much theoretical debate, but it remains an aspiration rather than a reality.

A giant step toward empowering employees would be to make them the owners of their firms. This is, of course, not a purely hypothetical concept. The idea of creating cooperative enterprises is far from new—at the very least, it can be traced back to the French socialist Joseph Proudhon and a long line of non-Marxist progressive thinkers up to today. And there are several examples of producer cooperatives, especially in the agricultural sector. But in the industrial sector, worker-owned cooperatives are the "exception that confirms the rule." It is not that one cannot find a multiplicity of examples throughout the world, but they are typically small-scale operations;[12] this contrasts, of course, with the more widespread adoption on the cooperative model in the fields of retail distribution, banking (i.e., credit unions), or healthcare. The best example of a rather large-scale operation is the Mondragon corporation that has deep and old roots in the Basque region of Spain. But scale brings up its own problems: as the corporation grew larger, it became arguably less democratic. Cooperatives face a number of obstacles in getting established, notably difficulties in getting access to credit. To solve this problem would require a strong push by governments. The most decisive move in that direction was taken by the French parliament when it passed a law on "the social and solidary economy" on July 31, 2014. The structure set in place by the French government has had a marked effect on the health of the cooperative movement in France, but the relatively modest investments that have been made were used to support cooperatives of all types and not just those active in production. Similar initiatives have been undertaken elsewhere, notably Canada and the EU, but, again, not on a scale that could really transform the status quo. And for all its advantages in terms of democratic participation in the workplace, cooperatives do create their own problems. The most often cited is that the members of a cooperative have little incentives to invest in innovation since it would take away from their shared benefits. They would naturally prefer higher wages to saving for R&D. The empirical evidence for this assertion is not clear-cut. It is true that the worker-controlled firms in what used to be Yugoslavia, which were supposed to be the distinctive feature of this heterodox communist regime, were not innovative as compared to Western European firms in the 1970s and 1980s. But it is far more difficult to generalize about contemporary cooperatives throughout the world. Brat et al. (2016) have found in their large survey of cooperatives that while the business culture in which cooperatives operate is somewhat risk-averse, most of them are well aware of the need to prioritize innovation, and that cooperatives in the financial sector, in particular, have proven quite capable of being innovative.

One possible way of helping workers to start or invest in a cooperative, among many other possible uses of a "stakeholder grant," would be to provide each resident of a country such as the US with a sizable lump-sum payment upon reaching adulthood. The idea was proposed and vigorously defended by the legal scholars Bruce Ackerman and Anne Alstott (1999) as the best way to achieve true equality of opportunity. The sum of $80,000 they suggested as a target in 1999 would have to be at least $100,000 some twenty years later, and possibly quite a lot more if it is to accomplish the sort of things they envisioned then, which have become more expensive in recent decades (e.g., higher education in the US, or buying land practically everywhere). The quid pro quo would be that most of the extant income assistance and social insurance programs would be cut so as not to render the cost of this proposal unfeasible. The risk here is that imprudent recipients of the grant could waste it and find themselves without a safety net. I have already discussed the harshness objection against the luck egalitarian approach and concluded that this is, indeed, a serious objection, but it seems to apply even better to the stakeholder grant, unless it is combined with a minimal safety net (e.g., a negative income tax as explained below). From a theoretical standpoint, however, this proposal is attractive. Economists will appreciate the degree to which it meshes with their concern for efficiency and the protection of property rights. Political philosophers may appreciate its civic republican ethos, that is, the opportunity for free-standing citizens to fully participate in public life once they are able to function effectively in the economic sphere. (On the last point, one could hope that all individuals, but especially those who already possess enough to enjoy a full range of educational and other opportunities, will feel obligated to use at least a portion of their grants for civic-minded purposes, and accept Ackerman and Alstott's suggestion that the grant should be paid back in the form of an inheritance tax.)

The last aspect of predistribution I want to mention at least briefly consists of asset-based approaches to the production and delivery of services in specific areas. One of the most often cited example of this emerging trend is the health sector particularly, albeit certainly not exclusively in the UK. The central idea here is that, instead of treating the users of these services as passive recipients of programs obtained more or less indirectly from something like a Social Welfare Function (SWF), they are involved in the design of these programs and the selection of the priorities that affect them. The disability movement has for quite some time lived by the slogan "nothing about us without us" (Garven et al. 2016, 6). Indeed, the disabilities movement serves as a good example of what progress can be achieved in healthcare and community development more generally when people are empowered to share their experiences, put forward their ideas, and take part in their realization. This is not a new idea. Democratic participation in community development, especially in the area of health, was much discussed in the 1960s already. But it has been rediscovered more recently (Garcia 2020). Some critics argue that the new emphasis on personal responsibility for one's own well-being reflects a "neoliberal" preference for less government intervention and a desire to cut costs. But a more progressive case for an asset-based approach can be articulated from within the capabilities approach. In any event, it is another example of the growing interest in the paradigm of predistribution, and these more focused, nonideal applications are more convincing than some of the more ambitious methods I outlined previously.

To recap, the concept of predistribution is an innovative idea. The proposals discussed above present the advantage of empowering those who find themselves on the lower rungs of society while doing minimum harm to economic freedoms and, in fact, promise to unleash competitive forces in the market rather than restrict the economic liberties of entrepreneurs. In a way, they make it easier for anyone to build up the assets they need to be a more active participant in a market economy functioning on the basis of fairer rules. Unfortunately, this vision can veer toward utopianism. Tong Zhichao (2015) has aptly argued that the Rawlsian notion of property-owning democracy harks back to a deeply rooted pre–New Deal reformist American tradition (see also Jackson 2012). But it has served more as a rhetorical argument for discussing social justice than as a blueprint for actual institutional design. The same can be said about the ways in which property-owning democracy has been treated in other liberal democracies. As for Georgism, it has so far failed to be a viable alternative to the capitalist status quo; home ownership is potentially too risky for low-income families; the scaling-up of cooperative enterprises seems to run into serious obstacles; codetermination works well in specific sociopolitical contexts, but has little chance of being widely adopted in North America. More limited applications to policy areas such as health seem to be more feasible and are gaining traction. But they are hardly the kind of solution that is needed with the immense inequalities of wealth and power that were discussed in Chapter 3. To end on a more optimistic note, one could say that this whole project is still "a work in progress." Much will depend on the mobilization of civil society organizations, from trade unions to philanthropists, and a political willingness to promote new modes of corporate governance.

Trade vs. Aid

So far, I have been concerned mostly with ways of reducing economic inequalities *within* more or less affluent countries. There remains the question of what those who have the means to do so can or should do to alleviate poverty in developing or middle-income countries. In the wake of the decolonization era of the 1950s and 1960s, richer countries committed themselves to contribute to the development of the poorer ones. A UN resolution passed in 1970 committed the richer countries to devote 0.7 percent of their GDP to helping the poorer countries achieve their development objectives; this commitment was renewed in 2002 at the International Conference on Financing for Development and later that same year at the World Summit on Sustainable Development. But few countries have managed to reach even that relatively modest target: according to the Development Assistance Committee (DAC) of the OECD, which acts as the scorekeeper, the average was just under 0.5 percent in 2011 (Deaton 2013, 275). To take just the case of the UK, Parliament passed a law in 2015 committing the country to the 0.7 percent target, but it has not consistently met it since then (largely because of domestic efforts required by the pandemic, the target was lowered to 0.5 percent in 2021). Moreover, it should be noted that at present the majority of people with very low incomes are actually living in middle-income countries who are not the usual beneficiaries of foreign aid (Sumner and Mallet 2013, 2).

Many economists have questioned the wisdom of international aid. The argument is that it is inefficient, especially if the beneficiaries are repressive regimes (Boone 1996); from a public choice perspective, Claudia Williamson (2010) argues that (1) aid is often more beneficial to rent-seeking interests in the donor country (e.g., the agricultural sector) than the recipients; and (2) information about the specific needs of the population in poor countries is not easily accessible, so that projects can be misdirected or redundant. Similar views have been expressed by Nobel Prize recipient Angus Deaton (2013, 274), who notes, "One of the reasons why today's aid does not eliminate global poverty is that it rarely tries to do so." Typically aid flows to government coffers rather than directly to the individuals or communities that need it most. And it often comes with all sorts of conditions that are for the benefits of donor countries. NGOs are preferable in this respect, but Deaton underlines several dysfunctions that diminish their contribution. Clinics operated by these agencies, for example, can divert human resources from the public health systems if they pay higher wages. Moreover, it is difficult to evaluate the *actual* effect of NGO projects because there are no incentives for these agencies to conduct a thorough evaluation of their activities. But moving toward freer trade is more efficient.

> Trade restrictions in rich countries often harm farmers in poor countries. Farming accounts for nearly three-quarters of employment in Africa, and rich countries spend hundreds of billions of dollars each year to support their own farmers. For sugar and cotton, for example, subsidies to producers

in rich countries lower world prices and restrict opportunities for poor farmers.

(Deaton 2013, 323)

Indeed, it is true that the Asian emerging economies have been successful in lifting themselves out of poverty—comparatively, albeit not within their own borders—through their diversified integration into global markets. But many countries in Latin America and Africa are still too dependent on the export of natural resources to fully replicate the Chinese or Vietnamese models. This is the "curse of natural resources" (Sachs and Warner 2001). Deaton (2013, 323–324) also suggests that facilitating migration would have an even greater impact than aid because remittances sent by successful migrants have a beneficial impact on the economic and social structures of the receiving societies. Be it as it may, however, the humanitarian and political crises provoked in Europe by hundreds of thousands of migrants crossing the Mediterranean soon after Deaton published his book show that there are severe limits to this option.

As Deaton (2013, 312–321) himself acknowledges, the aid vs. trade contrast is simplistic. Determining precisely the impact of foreign aid programs is methodologically very challenging, but there is some evidence (Dalgaard et al. 2004; Moreira 2005; Arndt et al. 2016; Galiani et al. 2017) suggesting that aid programs are finally beginning to pay off—perhaps there was too much hope that global inequalities could be dealt with in the short term when in fact they require a very long-term perspective. The hopeful signs could be explained by the fact that lessons have been learned and new more successful practices have emerged, for example, the switch from aid in the form of inputs into sometimes poorly designed projects to an emphasis on rewarding outcomes, that is, "the cash-on-delivery approach" (Birdsall et al. 2010). Moreover, aid *and* trade have not merged into the "aid for trade" strategy pursued by the EU (European Commission 2021; see also Cadot et al. 2014). The central idea here is that poorer countries are not competing on the proverbial level-playing field; they face disadvantages when attempting to integrate their economies into the global economy. Aid for Trade (AfT) aims at (1) removing the various nontariff barriers in the EU that work against poorer trade partners, and (2) assisting developing countries in their efforts to develop the infrastructures they need to compete successfully (e.g., help with the digitalization of financial transactions, governance, data gathering, and so on, and, most importantly, assisting developing countries with respect to trade in services).

But while these developments portend of a brighter future, the global situation is rapidly deteriorating at the time of writing. For some time already, populist leaders have advocated returning to protectionism. The Covid-19 pandemic has severely disrupted supply chains, and the war in Ukraine has unsettled the energy sector, as well as causing harm to countries that depend on the importation of cereals from Eastern Europe. In brief, while the way in which the problem of global poverty is posed has changed, and positive developments have begun to bear some fruits, we are still a long way from resolving it. As the countries that could help the most turn inward, the short-term prognostic appears rather gloomy, all the more so because the threat posed by climate change has yet to be dealt with effectively. In hindsight, it appears as if the much-decried era of "globalization" was a boon that the world cannot afford to carelessly abandon. It is true that it harmed many categories of workers and small businesses in the industrial regions of the developed world while also being unfair to some segments of the population in emerging economies (e.g., "sweatshop" workers lacking any protection against unscrupulous employers). But closed economies and xenophobic politics can only result in a deepening of inequalities that global trade was just beginning to ease. AfT and more outcome-oriented, empowering rather than dependency-inducing forms of aid are pathways that must continue to be developed, while fairer compensation for those whose employment is threatened by global trade flows must be carefully thought through. I suggest that the urgency of addressing the latter challenge is a compelling arguments for a basic income (see below).

Reinventing the Welfare State: More Efficient Income Support and Fairer Taxation

Welfare economics has been concerned with redistribution from its very beginning, but economists have not played a major part in the promotion and actual implementation of the welfare state in the US or other countries. That role initially fell upon social theorists and sociologists,[13] trade unionists, and political leaders, from Chancellor Bismarck to President F. D. Roosevelt to Prime Minister Clement Atlee. No one really "invented" the welfare state. It slowly emerged at the turn of the twentieth century as a complement to the work of charities. Then it gathered speed in the aftermath of World War II and, in the 1960s, took the form to which we are now accustomed, that is, something that is no longer complementary to the works of charitable organizations but an alternative to it. (Note, however, that today the deepening challenges faced by existing welfare states may once again call for greater involvement by what is now called the voluntary sector, in fact, giving rise to doubts about the potential for abuse of power by exceedingly rich donors.[14]) Normative schemes such as those proposed by Ronald Dworkin or John Rawls have been described as *a posteriori* rationalizations of practices that were well anchored in the politics of their times.[15]

The fact that the term "Keynesian" has often been used to describe or qualify the postwar welfare state would suggest that John M. Keynes promoted the idea of such a reform. But that was not truly the case. Keynes reacted favorably to Lord Beveridge's plan to initiate a welfare state in Britain, but he had played no part in its drafting, and arguably Beveridge did not fully comprehend Keynes' economic theory (Carvahlo 2008). What was Keynesian about the welfare state was that it boosted government spending, particularly during periods of low employment (e.g., through unemployment insurance disbursements), and more generally gave governments the means to use fiscal policy in a big way.

During the heydays of Keynesian macroeconomics from the late 1940s to the early 1970s, few economists, with the exception of those who adhered to the Austrian paradigm, were critical of the welfare state, nor was public debt much of an issue. This all changed during the 1970s. A "perfect storm" of events undermined the capacity of all advanced democracies to adequately fund existing programs, let alone continue to expand their reach. The proximate causes were the two oil shocks of 1973 and 1978–79, which resulted in the phenomenon of "stagflation"—an unprecedented combination of economic stagnation and inflation. OECD countries with large welfare states saw their tax revenues shrink at a time when public expenditures were rising, and the cost of borrowing went up quite substantially. With a slowing rate of growth, the question of sustainability of the welfare state was raised. Immediate cuts to social programs appeared unthinkable then, but the problem of increasing debt load of many countries moved up on the policy agenda. Evidently, the problem of public debt has become even more acute in the twenty-first century, although not to the same degree and in the same way for all countries.

Of course, writing about "the welfare state" as if it were a universal and unchanging reality is a simplification. It ignores the significant differences that exist among countries or even across time; federal countries, such as the US or Canada, administer social programs in a much more decentralized manner than France or Sweden, to give just one example. It is common in the policy studies literature to make a distinction between three types of welfare state "regimes": the liberal welfare state regime of English-speaking countries, the conservative/corporatist regime of continental Europe and Japan, and the social democratic regime of the Scandinavian countries (Esping-Andersen 1990). While useful as a starting point, this typology is unsatisfactory in several ways. As time goes on, hybrid types emerge (the Swedish model, for example, is not quite as "social democratic" as it used to be after moving in the direction of the supposedly market-oriented liberal regime), and it leaves aside many political systems (e.g., the ex-communist countries of Central and Eastern Europe). In any event, while these differences are important to keep in mind, I am using "welfare state" here as a generic term for dealing with (more or less fully) tax-funded social insurance programs and needs-based redistributive schemes that in one form or another have been in place in practically all OECD countries for decades. My focus is on so-called advanced welfare states. The question I am essentially concerned with is: in the eyes of economists, or those who take economic arguments seriously, does this set of institutions and programs continue to best address the problems of inequality? Is it in a "crisis"? And if so, should the way out of this crisis be to strengthen, and reinvest in, these institutions, or to reinvent the welfare state altogether?

Significant changes took place through the 1990s and the early 2000s when social policy in many countries shifted from guaranteeing "welfare" in the form of passive income assistance to "workfare" that requires recipient to (re)join the labor market.[16] This was accompanied by a new, and still rather common, political economic discourse that disparages habitual reliance on social assistance and promotes greater flexibility in the labor market (Brodsky 1994). The best examples can be found in the policy pronouncements of "New Labour" in Britain, or the Clinton administration that signaled a growing awareness of the looming danger posed by debt accumulation, a willingness to more closely tie income support to active participation in the world of work. Emblematic of this policy shift was the Personal Responsibility and Working Opportunity (PRWO) Act signed into law by President Clinton on August 22, 1996. The title of the act conveys its intent quite well: it made the transfer of federal funds conditional upon the states' adoption of measures encouraging recipients of income assistance benefits to actively seek employment. In the US, the transition to participation in the labor market was also made smoother by the tax refundable credit known as the Employment Income Tax Credit (EITC) for workers with low wages. Not surprisingly, a comparable move toward "workfare" took place in the 1990s in Canada[17] (the Canadian Child Tax Credit, which was very significantly hiked in 2016, can be described as a variant of the EITC) and in the UK where Prime Minister Tony Blair's "New Labour" approach was based on the idea that the state's social goals should as much as possible be consistent with a well-functioning market economy, meaning, of course, that state expenditures on social programs must be kept under control. More surprisingly perhaps is the fact that the typically social democratic Swedish welfare system moved in the same direction in 1998 (Kananen 2014, 107–109).

The impact of these reforms has been significant. In the US, for example, single (i.e., never married, divorced, and widowed) mothers began to be much more involved in labor market—the rate of participation of never married category, in particular, went from 44 percent in 1993 to 66 percent in 2000. As expenditures on "welfare" began to level off, budgetary deficits in the countries pursuing these policies decreased—in fact from the mid-1990s to 2009, Canada experienced a long series of budgetary surpluses. But the overall effect on poverty reduction and inequality was not very impressive. Many of the jobs that income assistance recipients were able to find were low-paying ones, and those unable to find jobs ended up in a worse situation. The most obvious weakness of the workfare approach is that in many jurisdictions the tax regime has not been sufficiently amended to allow disadvantaged individuals to cumulate wage income with some degree of still-needed income assistance—in other words, the fairest approach would consist of a well-balanced combination of traditional "welfare" and "workfare" instead of implementing the latter primarily as an alternative to the former.

The trend toward workfare across most OECD countries was well underway until it was derailed by the 2008–10 crisis. With rising unemployment and other social problems looming large, priorities changed, at least for a while. In 2012, for example, the Obama administration eased the constraints imposed by the PRWO Act. It appeared as if Keynesian macroeconomic had come back, even if the bulk of government expenditures were earmarked for purposes other than reinvesting in the welfare state (e.g., bailing out the banks). But after 2010, especially in the Eurozone, the pendulum swung back, and "austerity" became the new imperative in the 2010s. Spending cuts were more severe during that period than in any previous era, especially in southern Europe. This reprioritization of debt reduction took place against the background of a heated debate about the significance of, and risks posed by, the rise of "neoliberalism." And yet, austerity itself came to an end, partly because the recovery had finally lessened the need for it, but mostly because in 2020 the pandemic once again necessitated massive public spending to prevent a catastrophic depression. A broad consensus in political and business circles formed around the notion that income support, rather than debt reduction, is what is required under the circumstances. Not only did it become necessary to spend more on long-standing programs such as unemployment insurance, but new and extraordinary measures were also required. With hindsight, it became clear that the policy pursued in many countries—and most forcefully in the UK—of controlling expenditures in the public health sector (e.g., by reorganizing or closing hospitals) were penny-wise but pound-foolish. At the time of writing, however, it appears that this massive spending has contributed to a return of inflation after a forty-year absence, even though the catalyst for this shift were external shocks (the effect of the pandemic on the global supply chains, and the war in Ukraine).

The welfare state has survived and is not going away. But one must consider emerging long-term threats such as an aging population, which will put more stress on public pensions and on publicly funded health systems; the still unpredictable effects of climate change on food supplies; and even more unmanageable migration flows than they already are, as some regions may become uninhabitable. All this is happening against an increasingly unstable political background. Peter Taylor-Gooby (2013, 98) perceptively identifies the "trilemma" faced by "those committed to a more generous and inclusive welfare state": "higher taxes are disliked, the poor are viewed with suspicion and effective, inclusive services demand higher spending." For some time now, analysts have proposed more or less profound structural reforms (Mooij 2006; Van Kersbergen and Vis 2014; Hannesson 2015). But the pandemic crisis has revealed the extent to which public health, social inequalities, economic performance, and the legitimacy of the state are deeply interconnected. Hereafter, I map out the concepts and paradigms that are available for undertaking this rebuilding effort.

Tax Reform

The future of the welfare state is evidently linked to budgetary revenues. But taxation is also in itself a way of correcting inequalities. Progressive taxation was used extensively for that very purpose in what now looks a rather distant past. This was more typically the case in English-speaking democracies (e.g., the marginal tax rate for high earners was exceptionally high in the US in the 1950s and 1960s). Thus, one strategy for dealing with economic inequalities would consist in revisiting the issue of progressive taxation; as we have seen, this is precisely Piketty's preferred option.[18]

Decades of tinkering with public finance have resulted in a complicated web of deductions and tax credits that benefit tax lawyers and accountants more than the people or firms they are meant to assist. This is a recurring theme in the politics of most countries, but the problem seems to be easier to spot than to fix. (There are too many interested parties for the task of reform to be politically rewarding in practically all political contexts.) Taxation is a subject about which the economic literature has much to say. That literature can be divided into two branches: one that is policy-oriented and empirical; the other that is concerned with the formulation of a "theory of optimal taxation." I focus more on the latter because the question of how reducing inequalities through tax reform can be done without causing undue inefficiencies is obviously a large piece of the puzzle I am dealing with in this chapter. However, I admit that the use of optimal tax theory for redistributive purposes is more of an academic exercise than a practical option for policymakers who, incidentally, are less interested in maximizing social welfare than in who wins or loses from changing existing tax laws. And ultimately what economic theory treats as "optimal" with respect to social welfare is not necessarily the most desirable outcome from the standpoint of fairness; very few economists have tried to bridge that gap (but see Kolm 2004; Fleurbaey and Maniquet 2018).[19]

The modern theory of optimal taxation owes much to the seminal work of J A. Mirrlees (1971,, 1986). It is no exaggeration to say that Mirrlees' 1971 article serves as its cornerstone. But credit should also go to the brilliant Cambridge polymath Frank P. Ramsey (1927); Ramsey limited the problem to the search for an efficient sales tax—one that would minimally affect the behavior of consumers. Mirrlees (1971) addressed the more important problem of designing an optimal income tax that is typically the most significant revenue source for the modern welfare state and can double as a powerful instrument for reducing inequalities.[20] The problem that the Mirrleesian tradition addresses is how to design a taxation system that maximizes the social benefits of the state's redistributive policies without unduly distorting the allocation of labor inputs (e.g., by creating disincentives to using one's skills as effectively as possible). As Emmanuel Saez and Stefanie Santcheva (2013, 1) explain:

> The dominant approach in optimal tax theory is to use the standard welfarist framework in which the government sets taxes and transfers to maximize a social welfare function which is an explicit function of individual utilities and solely of individual utilities. Social welfare is maximized subject to a government budget constraint and taking into account how individuals respond to taxes and transfers.

This involves (1) formulating a social welfare function according to criteria defined by policymakers; (2) maximizing it subject to several constraints, such as ensuring that taxes at least cover government expenditures (Saez and Santcheva 2013 6), and maximizing a consumers' utility function that includes both the taxes they pay and the benefits they receive from government expenditures

(Mirrlees 1986, 1201–1209). In principle, an optimal income tax would be the first step toward an overall optimal economic policy such that "there is no change in it which will leave total welfare unchanged and at the same time generate a new addition to government revenue" (Mirrlees 1976, 254).

Paradoxically, the upshot of this ambitious model is that the income tax proves to be a weak instrument for addressing inequalities. Among the noteworthy conclusions reached by Mirrlees (1971, 208), the following is arguably the most significant: "The income tax is a much less effective tool for reducing inequalities than has often been thought." That is because imposing steeply increasing marginal tax rates on high-income earners creates disincentives to work at one's fullest level of abilities and, therefore, results in inefficiencies. Ultimately, such inefficiencies negatively affect social welfare. (In any event, global competition and mobility, especially for highly skilled income earners, make it increasingly difficult to adopt steeply progressive tax schedules.) An alternative could theoretically take the form of "a tax schedule that depends on time worked as well as upon labour-income" (these are respectively the variables y and z, which are central to Mirrlees' optimization model). Unfortunately, "such a tax would not be fully practicable" because of the planners' lack of information on the tax payers' skills and, therefore, the labor-income they can be expected to generate.[21] A lump-sum tax is another alternative. In principle, it would be easy to calculate: if G is the budget expenditure that is intended to be financed by the poll tax, then that tax should be set at G/N, where N is the population, but it is obviously unfair and potentially very unpopular. Margaret Thatcher's imposition in 1989 of a "community charge," more commonly known as the "poll tax," contributed to her downfall—it was a flat tax paid by all residents, landowners, and renters of towns and cities to fund local governments and not actually a tax on the act of going to the polls to vote, but the name stuck because the principle was identical: the same rate applied to everyone, whether they lived in large or small, cheap or expensive dwellings;[22] violent protest riots erupted in March 1990. This was, however, something of an anomaly. Gregory Mankiw et al. (2009) provide interesting data that suggest that to a noticeable extent policymakers in OECD countries have heeded the recommendations of optimal tax theory: marginal tax rates on higher incomes have come down and incomes tax schedules have become flatter.[23] Thus, instead of steeply increasing tax rates to reduce inequalities, Mirrlees (1971, 208) recommended a negative income tax—that is, transferring to individuals who earn less than a certain threshold an amount corresponding to the difference between that threshold and their income; incomes above that threshold are, of course, taxed. I return to this concept in the next subsection on "basic income."

The mathematical problems analyzed by Mirrlees, and others who have followed his theoretical lead, bypass many of the concrete challenges facing policymakers.[24] One reason being that, as Joel Slemrod (1990, 157) remarks, tax theory "is incomplete as a guide to action because it has not yet come to term with taxation as a system of coercively collecting revenues from individuals who will tend to resist." Slemrod and colleagues have produced a rather large literature on tax evasion to fill this gap (see Slemrod 2007). There are ways of adding this dimension to optimal taxation theory, but the technical problems become even more intractable, and for economists specializing in these issues the elusive target of being able to provide useful policy advice has moved even farther down the road.

Several critics go further and question the utilitarian normative foundations upon which this whole theory rests. The normative axiom inherent in utilitarian welfarist models is that individuals have identical utility functions, balancing consumption with some degree of inequality aversion. While different models propose their own way of dealing with the efficiency–equity trade-off, the underlying normative assumption remains the same. But in complex societies, individuals typically hold different preferences over a range of social outcomes. The interpersonal comparisons required for defining a socially optimal taxation scheme "involve much more difficult questions, which … are generally addressed in terms of fair allocation of resource or opportunities" (Fleurbaey and Maniquet 2018, 1030). But as the previous chapter made clear, fairness in such matters is subject to many conflicting interpretations. One question that is now looming larger is how to address the growing problem of intergenerational fairness, as an aging population in Europe, North America, and Japan places an increasing burden on younger generations; are we looking toward a future where employed individuals will have to pay more and more taxes to fund programs from which they will not benefit themselves—at least not for several decades?

Saez and Santcheva (2013) use a shortcut to bring in a multidimensional component in the conventional optimal taxation model; they attach a weighting factor to individual utilities. This allows them to factor in different values that policymakers and citizens may hold about paying taxes, redistribution, and the provision of public goods, fairness, and so on. This can be expressed in mathematical terms. The social planner's goal is to maximize a social welfare function:

$$\max SWF = \max \int_i w_i u_i$$

where w_i is a weighting factor applied to individual utilities. Utilitarians typically assume that for any individual i, we have $w_i = 1$. Saez and Santcheva, however, propose to treat it as a variable called a "generalized social welfare weight" that can take an entire range of values. These values can be logically deduced from existing philosophical theories, such as Rawls' privileging of the least well-off members of society, or adjusted on the basis of empirical evidence about what people tend to believe about distribution, responsibility, and so on. To be a little more specific, Saez and Santcheva propose the following example of what a "marginal generalized social welfare weight" could look like ("marginal" here meaning the social value associated with an additional \$1 transfer as a result of a tax change). It is formally denoted as $g_i(c_i, T_i)$, where c_i stands for i's consumption and T_i stands for the net taxes paid by *i* on his or her income *z*. In this illustration, two opposite normative standpoints are taken into account. A Pigouvian utilitarian approach assumes that $g(c, T)$ decreases in *c* because as consumption increases, people derive less and less utility from more consumption—the egalitarian corollary of this premise is that resources should be distributed equally, hence those who are able to consume more (but derive comparatively less satisfaction from it than those who consume a lesser amount) should be taxed more. Inversely, from a libertarian standpoint, $g(c, T)$ increases in *T* because from that standpoint, individuals who pay higher taxes either deserve to pay less (because they are fully entitled to their income, regardless of its level) or to receive more services (and not contribute to a redistributive scheme). Then they propose the following definition: "A Tax system $T(z)$ is defined as optimal if and only if, for any budget neutral, small tax reform $dT(z)$, we have $\sum_i g_i dT(z_i) = 0$" (Saez and Santcheva 2013, 8).

As Saez and Santcheva recognize, this method does not take into account the behavioral responses (e.g., tax avoidance) that taxpayers can be expected to display in response to a tax increase of this sort. They do go on to refine their model to take the latter problem into account, but there is no need for my purpose here to go into these complicated details. The point is simply this: Mirrlees' often repeated conclusion that the optimal tax schedule looks more or less flat is not the only conclusion that a rigorous application of economic analysis necessarily yields. This is not to say that efficiency considerations can be brushed aside. Behavioral responses to severe tax increases can still result in a "leaky bucket." But if a societal consensus emerges around the desirability of filling up a large bucket in the first place so as to, for instance, help the working poor, taxes can still go up. Inversely, if a libertarian consensus takes hold, not only should the tax schedule look flat, but it can be expected to move down to the lowest possible rate. There are, in other words, many options to choose from, and economics does not suggest a single "optimal" taxation system. Choosing among these options is a political or philosophical problem, not one that can be solved by economic theory alone. However, once that choice has been made, economists can work out the conditions that need to be met in order to make it as nearly "optimal" as possible. Considering that a quasi-libertarian aversion to higher taxes (on anybody other than the much reviled 0.1 percenters) is spreading, the optimal tax should probably be designed to be more progressive toward the bottom rather than the top of the income scale; this is precisely what a negative income tax (NIT) can help to achieve.

A Basic Income Guarantee

The easy-to-grasp idea behind the NIT is that individuals are unconditionally entitled to a minimum income. This need not be an income they can live on, although it could, depending on how the scheme is implemented. In essence, those declaring an income below a certain amount receive the full or weighted (e.g., 50 percent) amount of the difference between their income and that threshold. The Wikipedia entry on this topic provides a numerical example (based on Friedman [1962] 2002, 192): assuming that the threshold is set at $30,000 and that a 50 percent discount is applied, someone with no income would receive a payment of $15,000; someone earning $25,000 would receive $2,500, and someone earning $30,000 would receive no payment and would pay no income tax; but someone earning $100,000 would pay $35,000 in income tax. This example looks like a flat tax with a high rate that would probably result in inefficiencies. For that reason, a somewhat more complicated system might be preferable, for example, deferring the effect of a full 50 percent rate for incomes above $30,000 up to another threshold and imposing a lower rate between $30,000 and that second threshold. Alternatively, one could set the cut-off point at a much higher level (e.g., $60,000) and settle for a lower tax rate (e.g., 25 percent). The problem becomes, however, that as one raises the threshold, the proportion of the population who pays no income tax—but is far from being poor—increases significantly. This could threaten the legitimacy of the scheme. The NIT is not a new idea—it was first proposed in the 1940s by the British economist Juliet Rhys-Williams (1943) and was advocated by Milton Friedman (1962, 1980), among other well-known economists,[25] but it has never been fully implemented. Nevertheless. as I explain below, it has been tested, and some recent tax reforms adopted in the US and a few other countries can be seen as advances toward that goal.

One of the most obvious advantages of a NIT is that it would be less patronizing than the means-tested "welfare programs" in place in most nations, particularly in North America.[26] All that would be required from a potential recipient of a benefit would be to fill out an income tax form. On the face of it, it would be easier and less costly to implement than already existing programs. Writing in the 1960s before the turn to "workfare" mentioned in a previous section, Friedman argued that the NIT would create less disincentives to return to work than the social assistance programs he was then familiar with. As mentioned previously, these perverse disincentives have largely been remedied since the 1990s.

Several pilot studies have been conducted. While there are methodological issues that make it somewhat difficult to interpret the empirical results of these studies (it was not possible to ensure that individuals in the test cases were receiving *only* the benefits of an NIT-like pilot program), it would seem that the NIT creates a weak disincentive to work especially for those who have no employment. But from a normative standpoint, it could be argued that this particular behavior is not detrimental to the well-being of the recipients of social assistance: it provides them with the means to find a better-paying and/or more satisfying job.[27]

As mentioned, a full implementation of the NIT has never been attempted.[28] From a political standpoint, the NIT is ambiguous. On the one hand, it can be presented as a scheme for helping the working poor, which is usually a popular idea. However, if those with no employment income at all would receive the maximum benefit under this plan, many voters will probably object. There is a prejudice against providing social assistance without requiring some sort of reciprocal contribution, for example, in terms of finding employment. This tends to discourage policy entrepreneurs and elected officials from aggressively advocating the NIT. A few significant steps in the direction of a NIT have nevertheless been put into effect, all in the name of helping the working poor. One such example is the EITC in the US, or the Working Income Tax Benefit (WITB) in Canada. Although childless workers older than twenty-five and earning less than a very low annual income (around $14,500 in 2015) qualify for a small tax credit, the EITC is designed to help low-income families with children. The actual mechanism is more complicated than the way in which the NIT theoretically works (as described above), but the principle is the same: below a certain income level, households get a *refundable* tax credit; "refundable" here means that the credit is payable in full, even if applying only a fraction of it to the amount of taxes owed suffices to bring the tax to zero. In fact, this concept could advantageously be extended to all tax credits for individuals or households earning less than a certain cut-off income deemed to be appropriate for maintaining a decent standard of living and/or raising children.

An improvement upon the NIT has been proposed by Serge-Christophe Kolm as a building block of his theory of "macrojustice" (2005, 2007). Kolm (2005, 66) rejects the conventional version of the NIT on the ground that taxing income is not justifiable; taxes on elastic items—such as earned income—induce inefficiencies but, more fundamentally, taxing what are essentially an individual's choices is a violation of that person's right to use their talents as they please. If some people decide to work long hours and give up opportunities for leisure and other activities in order to earn more, save for retirement, and so on, it is not a choice for which they ought to be penalized by the taxman. Kolm proposes to find a way of reconciling a liberal conception of freedom as choice with a moral obligation to treat people as equal with respect to those aspects of life in society where equality is appropriate. Effort is not one such dimension—there is no reason to redistribute from enterprising individuals to the less motivated ones. But productive capacities—one's productivity, one's ability to get the job done, one's technical knowledge and level of training, and so on—is another matter. To a significant degree productive capacities are given to an individual by the society in which he or she lives. It is, therefore, fair to expect some contribution in return in order to help improve the standard of living of those with lower productive capacities. Individuals who fall into this category are likely to earn less when spending the same or even a higher degree of effort. To put it another way, productive capacities, like all resources, produce rent; they must be shared in some measure (Kolm 2007, 71–72). In a way, it is as if we were leasing our productive capacities.

This can all be expressed formally as follows: Assume that society is composed of n individuals indexed as i, with $1 \leq i \leq n$. An individual i chooses to work for a duration l_i at a wage rate of w_i, and thus the average wage rate will be $\overline{w} = 1/n\ \Sigma w_i$. For the purpose of fair redistribution, society will select a labor duration

k during which individuals will contribute their productive capacities to social transfers. Let $t_i = k(\overline{w} - w_i)$, then t_i will a tax if $w_i > \overline{w}$, or a transfer if $w_i < \overline{w}$. Kolm calls this redistributive mechanism the Equal Labor Income Equalization (ELIE). The choice of k reflects societal norms. For example, if a society leans toward libertarianism, then $k = 0$; in an egalitarian society, it would be close or equal to 1. (For unemployed individuals, a coefficient $p > k$ could be applied in order to raise the income support up to what an individual with no income needs to maintain a decent standard of living while looking for a job [Kolm 2007, 82–83]). Individuals are, of course, free to work beyond k, so that an individual's disposable income will *be* $y_i = l_i wi + t_i$. Now ELIE is similar to the NIT, but the crucial difference is that it bears only on what individuals justifiably owe to society, corresponding to the fraction of their higher productivity, which is not due to their own merits alone. In other words, rather than being taxed on their whole income, a large proportion of which society has no claim upon (e.g., their willingness to take risks, work longer hours), they are taxed on the rents they derive from talents they owe merely to luck or, as is often the case, to societal assets that have helped them to acquire or perfect such talents.[29] It is less likely to produce disincentives to work. But questions can be raised as to the availability of the information necessary to calculate ELIE.[30] There is also the issue that affects all negative income-type schemes that recipients could have to wait a year to get the lump-sum payment they are entitled to instead of receiving a steady stream of income support. A basic income, among other vaunted advantages, does not suffer from this inconvenience.

The strongest push in the direction of providing an *unconditional* minimal income to all members of a political community is the Basic Income Guarantee (BIG), also called Universal Basic Income (UBI). The NIT and Kolm's ELIE are still tied in some measure to the world of work, but BIG/UBI is completely divorced from it. Leaving aside some practical, albeit potentially thorny, issues having to do with exactly *who* qualifies (e.g., all residents or citizens only), BIG/UBI is made available to all members of a political community where the policy is in place, regardless of their employment status or income. Involuntarily as well as voluntarily unemployed adults, "stay-at-home mothers," homeless individuals, and so on, as well as, in some version of the scheme, children (although presumably at a lower level) are entitled to the benefit just as anyone else. Everyone without exception is expected to become a recipient. Even the "0.1 percenters" are entitled in principle, although in some versions of the proposal a ceiling is put in place.

BIG/UBI has only become a topic of sustained debate in policy circles and academics since the 1990s, but the idea itself is not new. Thomas Paine had proposed something similar in the eighteenth century already (see his *Agrarian Justice* 1797). President Nixon presented a Family Assistance Plan in 1969, which was essentially a basic income scheme but with a rather low ceiling (i.e., only low-income families qualified); it passed in the House of Representatives but died in the US Senate. In Canada, the Croll report (1971) issued by a Special Senate Committee on Poverty recommended a guaranteed income of

CAN$3,500 for a family of four (about CAN$20,000 today). This recommendation was never enacted into law, but a pilot study (the Mincome project) affecting 1,300 families was run in the town of Dauphin, Manitoba, between 1974 and 1979. Valuable data were obtained thanks to this project.[31] But then the idea went "under the radar" of policymakers. Philippe Van Parijs can be credited for putting it back at the forefront when he published *Real Freedom for All* (1995).

Van Parijs (1995, 1) asserts that freedom is not merely a matter of rights but also of means. Providing the means to achieve some essential life goals—such as being able to find a rewarding job rather than being constrained to take any job for fear of ending up unemployed or to meet the requirements of "workfare"—does not commit one to the most comprehensive and far-reaching interpretation of "positive liberty," let alone to a perfectionist moral standpoint. An unconditional BIG/UBI is not meant to be the first step in an endless series of government-supported and -funded steps toward the realization of every individual's aspiration. It is the one and only departure from the ideal of negative liberty that Van Parijs allows. In most other respects, he defends a libertarian social philosophy. The outcome of a basic income would be "real freedom for all." He justifies this assertion by appealing to an argument we have already encountered, namely, that individuals are not entitled to benefit from whatever rents they have been able to capture even if, for efficiency purposes, it may not make sense to try to recover the entirety of these rents. In Van Parij's terms, we are all entitled to enjoy what we can derive from our "internal endowments" but not to get more than our equal share of what the wealth produced from "external endowments," that is, those resources we get from nature or society. Contrary to most "left libertarians" (but in line with Kolm), Van Parijs (1995, 101) does not think it is necessary to restrict external endowments to natural resources; societal endowments include not only material assets but also cultural ones (e.g., the work ethic). But Van Parijs goes even further by insisting that employment should be included among external endowments. Because jobs are scarce, he claims, they can be treated as rent-generating assets. This is, of course, open to criticism. Admittedly, there will at any time be a mismatch between those who seek employment and the number and types of available jobs. However, a significant and lasting scarcity of jobs—of the kind that could plausibly be the *main* source of rents—is not necessarily an inherent feature of market economies. Whether artificial intelligence will some day produce job scarcity on a massive scale is still a purely hypothetical prediction. All the same, economic rents of many kinds are indeed a fundamental problem. Thus I agree with Van Parijs (1995, 99) that "there is a nonarbitrary and generally positive legitimate level of basic income that is determined by the per capita value of society's external assets and must be entirely financed by those who appropriate these assets."

One can also find advocates of the concept of a BIG/UBI among more traditional or "right-wing" libertarians. Even though they concede that the legitimacy of a market economy probably necessitates guaranteeing a minimum income to all, they are not interested in social justice per se. Their reasons for supporting a BIG/UBI are more practical. They simply view it as a potentially cheaper and less intrusive alternative to the welfare state, which they regard as far too bureaucratic, costly, and cumbersome (e.g., Murray [2006] 2016; Weber 2013).[32]

It was necessary to start with the early proponents. But today the literature on BIG/UBI, which includes the journal *Basic Income Studies*, is enormous. I certainly do not pretend to be able to review exhaustively all the pros and cons arguments that have been debated, but I summarize hereafter some of the most salient under two rubrics: normative justifications and critiques, on the one hand, and practical problems, on the other.

Let me begin with the more attractive aspects. In different ways perhaps, both classical and progressive liberals value the autonomy of individuals. They also value self-respect. And on both counts, providing every adult with an unconditional income is a step in the right direction. They could much more freely decide for themselves to invest in their education, take time off work to take care of their dependents, or otherwise pursue their own sense of what happiness means. And as far as self-respect is concerned, not having to prove that one is in need of assistance, which can be demeaning, is a definitive advantage. But classical liberals/libertarians are more impressed with the potential impact that a BIG/UBI could have on the role of the state and the degree of coercion or dependence that in various degrees all citizens experience. Income assistance recipients would be freed from bureaucratic chicanery, and if significant savings can be achieved by adopting the plan (more on this below), it could translate into tax cuts. Progressive supporters are more prone to see advantages in the freedom vis-à-vis employers that a BIG/UBI would provide. Applicants could afford to be more selective in choosing the job they prefer if they have the means to wait for it. And employers might become less averse to paying higher wages to attract more demanding applicants. Inversely, people motivated to work for NGOs or civil society organizations unable to offer high wages could choose to contribute their talents to these causes. But communitarian progressives who prioritize solidarity are less impressed. Anna Coote and Andrew Percy think that "giving money to individuals to spend as they wish does nothing to bring them together or to build a sense of common purpose" (cited by Hodgson 2021, 238). But that is debatable. Poverty also isolates people, and giving them the means to escape poverty should also make it easier for them to play a more active role in their community. Perhaps a more convincing but not totally unrelated philosophical argument concerns the lack of a reciprocal exchange between givers (i.e., taxpayers) and recipients, especially those who prefer leisure over work. Could a BIG/UBI become conducive to what G. van Donselaar (2009, 4), drawing from ideas originally developed by the philosopher David Gauthier, calls "parasitism," that is, a relationship in which one of the parties—in this case a wage earner—is worse-off because of the very existence of another—in this case Van Parij's famous example of Lazy, the hedonistic beach surfer? It is one thing to say that jobs are scarce, and therefore, those who are employed owe something to those who would like to have one but for whatever reason, including physical disability, cannot find employment. But it is another to say that someone who is simply not interested in working even part time, who, in other words, only value leisure, is entitled to "exploit" wage earners. This is not a risk that is very likely to pose a serious problem in practice—after all, few people will decide to be completely inactive, whether being active means being employed or volunteering, providing care, and so on—but it is still morally troubling. A possible answer would be to deny the grant to able-bodied adult under the age of sixty-five who have not declared any income from employment for a given number of years.

For all its theoretical advantages, the BIG/UBI scheme faces rather daunting practical obstacles and well-argued objections.[33] This is the reason why in spite of countless experiments and pilot projects, reports, and academic studies, no major OECD country has fully implemented it. There are, however, many partial applications on a more or less limited scale at the national (e.g., Brazil, Iran) or subnational (e.g., Alaska) levels.[34] The most obvious problem is costs. If pegged at a high enough level to function at least as a temporary living income (e.g., approximately US$18,000), and if all other subsidies, social insurance payments, or other social services are not entirely phased out, then the cost would be prohibitive and taxes would have to be raised far above their current level. For example, in their report to the British Columbia provincial government about the feasibility of a basic income program for the province, the economists David Green, Jonathan Kesselman and Lindsay Tedds (2020) estimate that paying C$20,000 to every adult resident under the age of sixty-five *without* drastically eliminating all other assistance programs (e.g., disability benefits, rental assistance) would cost the equivalent of the entire budget of the province (338). If most existing programs are kept, then the only option would be a NIT with a rather high benefit reduction rate (BRR), that is to say the method used to calculate the point on the income scale where a person starts paying a tax rather than receiving a benefit. But, of course, the cost estimates vary greatly from author to author depending on how much of the existing assistance programs are kept or rolled into the basic income. As mentioned above, Murray argues that a BIG/UBI would achieve savings but that is because he pegs the grant at a relatively low level (US$13,000 at 2014 parity) and recommends winding down the welfare state altogether. In Canada's case, Richard Pereira (2017) has calculated that a national basic income paying C$15,000 is feasible by eliminating only some redundant social assistance programs but, importantly, *not* the Medicare program, the single-payer, publicly funded health insurance plan that is considered to be sacrosanct by the majority of Canadian voters. It is also argued by defenders of a BIG/UBI that implementing it would be economically efficient in a variety of ways, such as improving the health of the general population, thereby lowering hospitalization and other medical cost. In brief, it is difficult *a priori* to accurately estimate the cost of a BIG/UBI. It is undeniably a very costly proposition but could still be feasible if most existing tax subsidies and assistance programs are replaced by the monthly grant. But the more such programs are cut, the fiercer the political resistance to a BIG/UBI is likely to be.

Then there is the question of eligibility. Should all residents in a country be eligible or just citizens? The latter would be politically more feasible, that is, less likely to spark a negative populist response but would be socially much less effective. Moreover, there is the risk that a widely available and generous grant would encourage more migrants to move to (for now) the rather exceptional country where this BIG/UBI would be implemented. Should minors also be included, possibly at a lower rate? This would help families to raise their children; but this runs the risk of making the program unaffordable. Should very affluent households be cut off, as Eyal (2010) proposes? This would be a double-edged sword: on the one hand, it would address a political concern—why should public money be wasted on individuals who definitely do not need the grant; but, on the other hand, if a cap is put in place, it is quite plausible that it could be deliberately lowered to cover only the "deserving poor," thereby reintroducing the social stigma that a BIG/UBI is supposed to do away with. Finally, there is the question of how to track homeless families or individuals. They would obviously be entitled to the grant—indeed one of the strongest arguments for it is that it would solve homelessness—but there could be significant administrative costs involved (De Wispelaere and Stirton 2011).

A question often raised by economists concerns the potential impact of a BIG/UBI on the labor market. Would it be a disincentive to find employment or to work full time? In a sense, this is another way of stating the concern that led to calls to replace welfare with "workfare" (see above). But there is ample empirical evidence that the disincentive effect would be weak (Hodgson 2021, 234; Pinto et al. 2021).

But probably the biggest obstacle to the plan is the lack of solid political support. This is less true of the Global South where the idea is gaining traction, but no OECD country has fully adopted it. Politically, BIG/UBI suffers from two public perception challenges. The first is the issue of cost. This plays in two ways. Some people are mostly concerned about potential tax increases; others fear that to compensate for that cost, cherished social programs would be eliminated. The other is an increasing populist reaction to the notion of providing assistance to those who are perceived as the "undeserving" poor ("foreigners," drug addicts, etc.). Political parties (e.g., Green parties in Germany or Canada) or leadership candidates (e.g., Andrew Yang in the US) who have run their campaigns on this idea have not fared particularly well electorally. Even if the Covid-19 pandemic might have made more people realize that they may themselves be more at risk of a sudden change of circumstances than they had previously thought, all the arguments listed above are likely to deter many voters. In brief, BIG would be a leap of faith that short-term-oriented political strategists tend to recommend against even if the long-term benefits would probably be positive.

Conclusion

To recap, the most promising strategy for moving in the direction of equality of opportunity without losing sight of economic efficiency is to prioritize asset-based approaches and, insofar as there would still be a need for redistribution, to combine these approaches with a basic income or, more realistically, some sort of NIT or, at the very least, expanding the range of refundable tax credits. This sketchy recommendation falls short of an "ideal theory." The goal is not to define a perfect standard of justice but to be able to carry out debates in a fair and reasonable manner.

In the end, though, practical reforms will have to be democratically debated and passed into law. Since there could be many options to choose from, it may be objected that Arrow's impossibility theorem (see Chapter 2) would lead to irrational outcomes. But that is only a very hypothetical problem. Moreover, in order to avoid running into the cycling problem, Sen suggests that one promising way of relaxing the conditions on rational choice imposed by Arrow is to not insist on complete orderings. For a variety of reasons, including "unbridgeable gaps in information, and judgmental unresolvability involving disparate considerations that cannot be completely eliminated" (Sen 2009, 103), "persistent incompleteness may be a hardy feature of judgments of social justice" (105). Thus, "there is need for accommodation not only of different individuals' respective partial rankings but also of the extent of incompleteness that may exist in a shared partial ranking on which different individuals may reasonably agree" (Sen 2009, 396). In any event, I agree with Sen (399) that

> to be useful, a social ranking must have some substantive coverage but need not be complete. A theory of justice has to rely fundamentally on partial orderings based on the intersection—or commonality—of distinct rankings drawing on different reasons of justice that can all survive the scrutiny of public reasoning.

Regrettably, the present climate of political polarization, which has spread across many liberal democracies in recent years, makes the sort of public reasoning that Sen wishes to see increasingly less likely to happen by closing the door to a productive democratic debate before it has even begun.

Assuming, however, that political polarization is not an inescapable fate, it remains for me to briefly elaborate on how moving toward a predistributive strategy fits within the analytical framework that has taken shape in the previous chapters of this book. As I explained in Chapter 2, economists first confronted economic inequalities through the lenses of welfare economics; this was the origin of the efficiency vs. equity dilemma. Moving from theory to practice, economists also formulated indices for measuring inequalities and more recently found innovative ways of gathering relevant historical data (see Chapter 3). But this research also revealed the complexity of the subject: all the available indices are biased in some way (e.g., the Gini coefficient provides little information about the structure of the income distribution and hence about the more or less fair share of national income controlled by the "one-percenters"); should we focus on income (easier to measure) or wealth (somewhat less easy to measure), and so on? Indeed, the complexity of the subject becomes even more apparent as we attempt to move away from the relatively simplistic notion of equality of welfare to take into account equality of opportunity. For a long time, mainstream economists defended a bare-bone notion of equality of opportunity according to which all that is required is to ensure that property rights are well defined and no one is discriminated against; if so, all economic agents are competing on the same "level playing field" (Chapter 4). But (see Chapter 5) a long list of more or less egalitarian philosophers have challenged this reductionist vision. However, the range of opinions on how to balance all the societal dysfunctions and biases that cause economic inequalities and how best to remedy them is immense. In view of these difficulties, it is advisable to settle for a pragmatic approach that does not pretend to pave the way toward an ideally just society and can be revised in the light of ever-changing circumstances and political conflicts.[35] This pragmatic outlook also implies that the discourse of economists should accommodate a more diverse range of criteria than efficiency alone. I hope to have shown that there has been modest progress in this regard.

Two more issues that further illustrate the complex nature of economic inequalities need to be briefly considered. The first concerns the challenges that are involved in moving from theory to practice. When, after debating feasible options, a final decision has to be made, is the problem raised by Arrow's impossibility theorem (see Chapter 2) going to render the whole process irrational? This would only be the case if it is strictly true that voters cannot converge toward a workable compromise that reflects at least a limited capacity to empathize with the needs and aspirations of the less well-off. While one could take this possibility for granted in earlier decades, it seems that the deepening political polarization that is taking place in many liberal democracies, such as the US, the UK, or France, does not augur well for the future of a balanced and pragmatic social (or environmental) policy.

The second issue concerns the role of the state in alleviating economic inequalities. In much of what was discussed in previous chapters, the focus was on the choice of appropriate public policies. The reason being that ever since World War II, it has been assumed that only the state apparatus had the resources to promote the ideal of equality of opportunity on a large scale. But even then, the voluntary sector continued to play a significant role; nowadays, because of the urgency of budget constraints practically everywhere, the voluntary sector is called upon to play a greater role. This can be seen in the health sector, drug addiction, youth intervention, the insertion of immigrants in the labor market, environmental protection, and so on. But what is needed, and would arguably be efficient, is for the state to work cooperatively with civil society. The point I am trying to make here is not that the state should abdicate its responsibilities nor that all social services should be privatized but rather that all avenues for partnership and dialogue between these two spheres should be explored in a transparent manner; that institutional mechanism for ensuring accountability be revisited and improved; that means of fairly sharing resources be examined.[36] This sort of bottom-up approach should also prove valuable in addressing the severe legitimation crisis that policymakers are increasingly experiencing, not least of all in their attempts to reduce the impact of worsening economic inequalities. Economists, for the most part, are already convinced that decentralization is the best way to achieve efficiency; but whether they or their interlocutors in other fields can agree that the requirements of fairness can also be met by relying more extensively on civil society is a question that I foresee will become more and more salient in the foreseeable future as the limits of state action become increasingly evident.

Notes

1 In 2021, approximately 58 million children of primary school age are still not attending school: https://ourworldindata.org/children-not-in-school.

2 The libertarian economist Bryan Caplan (2018) has made the case that university degrees are overrated but in a way that is too polemical and overgeneralizing; a better approach, I would suggest, is to examine why some higher education systems are less affected by the problem of disproportional differences in the reputation of different institutions (and hence undeserved rents), such as those of Canada or Finland. There are probably lessons to be drawn from these cases, but space lacks here to explore this question further.

3 By singling out public funding, I do mean to imply that there ought not be any opportunities for private schools to compete with public schools; in fact, competition of this sort is healthy and ought to be encouraged. But access to private schools ought not be restricted to well-off families; public funding is needed to equalize opportunities for parents of all backgrounds to choose the schools to which they wish to send their children. Public funding can be given directly to students (a voucher system) or, as is far more common, to the schools themselves.

4 At the federal level in the US, the National Minimum Wage Act was passed in 1998, replacing the New Deal–era Fair Labor Standards Act (FLSA), which had been passed in 1938. But Congress has for decades failed to increase the federal minimum wage to keep with the cost of living; Presidents Obama and Biden have used executive orders to raise the wages of federal employees and of workers in companies contracting with the US government, but this affects only a relatively small proportion of wage earners. The legislated minimum wages vary significantly from state to state. In 2022, the minimum wage in Washington was a little more than double what it was in Texas. Canada does not have a minimum wage at the federal level, but each province or territory regulates wages in their jurisdictions.

5 Some countries, for example, the UK, apply different rules depending on the age of the employees. The rationale being that young workers who generally have low skills, something which would deter employers from hiring them if they had to pay more for their labor, benefit from the experience of holding a job.

6 For an eloquent plea to move toward social policies that do away with the stigmatization and "othering" of the poor, see Lister (2021, chapter 4).

7 Thomas Piketty, however, has argued that predistribution and redistribution are better thought of as complementary rather than substitutes (cited by O'Neil 2020, 65).

8 The economic theory of rent was first formulated by David Ricardo (see Dobuzinskis 2022, 54–63).

9 From today's standpoint, it is very doubtful that a single tax on land rent would be sufficient to cover the costs of existing social programs, even accounting for the fact that it in itself would somewhat reduce the need for income assistance by, for example, making housing more affordable.

10 Considering that the very idea of a single tax on land rents can be traced back to the eighteenth-century French political economist François Quesnay, the history of its practical failure is even longer!

11 For a forceful argument to that effect, see Hayden and Bodie (2020; 2021).

12 In the US, for example, enterprises owned and operated by their employees employ only about 8,000 people (https://uwcc.wisc.edu/resources/worker-cooperatives).

13 The British sociologist T. H. Marshall played a key role in that respect.

14 On this point, see Saunders-Hastings (2022).

15 But, as already pointed out, Rawls' favorite option was something else than the welfare state. Rawls (2001, 136) distinguishes between five regimes: "(a) laissez-faire capitalism; (b) welfare-state capitalism; (c) state socialism with a command economy; (d) property-owning democracy; and finally, (e) liberal (democratic) socialism." Contrary to what is sometimes assumed, Rawls did not intend to simply provide a philosophical justification for the welfare state; his preference was for "property-owning democracy," which he claims (135) "realizes all the main political values expressed by [his] two principles of justice." Unfortunately, he said little more about the practical implications of this idea.

16 In the US, when combined with the Earned Income Tax Credit, "workfare" amounts to replacing welfare with subsidized low-wage labor.

17 In Canada, the shift can also be dated back to 1996 when the Canada Assistance Plan (which was funded by the federal government separately from health-targeted transfers) was replaced with the new amalgamated Canada Health and Social Transfer Program, which made it imperative for the provinces to find ways of economizing on their welfare expenditures to maintain their health system at the level where public opinion expects it to remain.

18 Piketty and colleagues estimate that there is lots of room at the very top of the income scale for additional taxes on wealthy individuals without having a noticeable effect on their economic behavior; see Gruber and Saez (2002), Piketty, Saez, and Santcheva (2014).

19 Robert Nozick (1974), of course, thought the gap is unbridgeable.

20 There are significant variations. According to the OECD, "Taxes tend to be less progressive in the Nordic countries, France, and Switzerland" (cited in Obinger and Wagschal 2010, 345). That is because, at least in the case of Nordic countries and France, middle-income earners are themselves heavily taxed.

21 However, Kolm (2004) thinks that this is not an unsurmountable difficulty, and his ELIE model (see next subsection) is designed to equalize labor income.

22 There were some exceptions to this principle: students and the registered unemployed were taxed at a much lower rate.

23 Mankiw et al. (2009, 165) also note with respect to indirect taxes that the optimal design consists of only taxing the final product (and not the components that enter

into its production). The so-called value-added tax (VAT) aims to meet this criterion; with the sole exception of the US, all OECD countries have adopted a national VAT.

24 It could be added that Mirrlees' approach in terms of working out an elegant mathematical solution derived from restrictive assumptions is somewhat outdared. Computer-based simulation techniques could be used advantageously to work out more flexible models, yielding a broader range of options to choose from (see Columbino 2009).

25 Walter Heller, a contemporary of Friedman, but who stood to his left politically (he served as chairman of the Council of Economic Advisers under Presidents Kennedy and Johnson), also supported the idea of a negative income tax.

26 To add insult to injury, some jurisdictions require welfare applicants to get rid of most of their assets before they can be eligible for social assistance.

27 Supporting evidence can be found in Pinto et al. (2021)—which is a meta-study of more than seventy experiments, a good proportion of which, if not all, are about NIT— and Widerquist (2019).

28 But the level at which Canada's refundable child tax credit has been pegged in 2016 is a significant step in that direction.

29 Kolm does not claim that ELIE would result in something that could be described as optimally just. At the level of what he calls "microjustice," that is, in more localized settings or particular circumstances, there would be room for gift-giving and reciprocal arrangements that could result in even fairer allocations. Indeed, in many of his writings, Kolm (1984, 2000a, 2006) has emphasized the moral imperative of compassion and the importance of reciprocity in human relations; these more or less altruistic dispositions create opportunities for philanthropic organizations to do their immensely important work. However, social policy in complex societies cannot aim at achieving utopian ideals. It must realistically set "second best" standards of fairness.

30 Kolm (2009, 92) retorts that the exemption built into the French tax system for overtime labor over the thirty-five-hour work week is proof that taxing wage rates is not strictly impossible.

31 Experiments have also been conducted in Brazil and India.

32 For a debate on the merits of a BIG among more or less libertarian economists within the Austrian school, see Nell (2013).

33 In what follows, I rely largely on Hodgson's (2021, 233–241) carefully presented review of the major issues faced by the proponents of a basic income.

34 In terms of scale, the Citizen's Account Program adopted by Saudi Arabia in 2017 comes the closest to what I have discussed so far. But its purpose is rather different. Whereas the primary goal of a BIG/UBI is to eliminate poverty, the Saudi program is intended to become an alternative to the current practice of giving to the majority of Saudi citizens a job in the public service (paid for by oil revenues). The generally much poorer and disadvantaged foreign workers who play an essential part in the Saudi economy and society do not qualify for these payments.

35 There is a vast literature on "policy learning" conveniently summarized by Antje Witting (2017). Much of that literature, however, is exhortatory rather than empirical, by which I mean that, although there is some evidence of actual learning taking place, policymakers still have a long way to go to fulfill the expectations theorists

have raised about what a turn to a more evidence-based style of policymaking could achieve.

36 I am not reinventing the wheel here. There is growing academic interest in these matters (see Laforest 2011 and, more generally, relevant articles in the *Nonprofit and Voluntary Sector Quarterly*).

Works Cited

Aaberge, Rolf. 2008. "Ranking Intersecting Lorenz Curves." Discussion Paper no. 3852. Bonn: Forschungsinstitut zur Zukunft der Arbeit/Institute for the Study of Labor (IZA).

Abbey, Ruth, ed. 2013. *Feminist Interpretations of John Rawls*. University Park, PA: The Pennsylvania State University Press.

Acemoglu, Daron, and James A. Robinson. 2015. "The Rise and Decline of General Laws of Capitalism." *Journal of Economic Perspectives* 29, no. 1: 3–28.

Ackerman, Bruce and Anne Alstott. 1999. *The Stakeholder Society*. New Haven: Yale University Press.

Adler, Matthew D. 2013. "The Pigou–Dalton Principle and the Structure of Distributive Justice." Duke University Working Paper. http://scholarship.law.duke.edu/faculty_scholarship/3065.

Adler, Matthew D. 2019. "Social Welfare Functions." In O. F. Norhelm, E. J. Emmanuel, and J. Millum, eds., *Global Health Priority-Setting: Beyond Cost-Effectiveness*. Oxford: Oxford University Press.

Ahmad, Mahyudin. 2017. "Economic Freedom and Income Inequality: Does Political Regime Matter?" *Economies* 5, no. 2: 1–28.

Aivazian, Varouj A., and Jeffrey L. Callen. 2003. "The Core, Transaction Costs, and the Coase Theorem." *Constitutional Political Economy* 14: 287–299.

Albertsen, Andreas, and Lasse Nielsen. 2020. "What Is the Point of the Harshness Objection?" *Utilitas* 32: 427–443.

Albertsen, Andreas. 2019. "Markets, Distributive Justice and Community: The Egalitarian Ethos of G. A. Cohen." *Political Research Quarterly* 72, no. 2: 376–388.

Alchian, Armen A. and Harold Demsetz. 1973. "The Property Rights Paradigm." *The Journal of Economic History* 33, no. 1: 16–27.

Altman, Morris. 2008. "How Much Economic Freedom Is Necessary for Economic Growth? Theory and Evidence." *Economics Bulletin* 15, no. 2: 1–20.

Andersen-Gott, M., G. Ghinea, and B. Bygstad. 2012. "Why Do Commercial Companies Contribute to Open Source Software?" Brunel University Research Archive, http://bura.brunel.ac.uk/bitstream/2438/6981/5/Fulltext.pdf.

Anderson, Elizabeth S. 1999. "What Is the Point of Equality?" *Ethics* 109: 287–337.

Anderson, Elizabeth S. 2008. "How Should Egalitarians Cope with Market Risks?" *Theoretical Inquiries in Law* 9: 239–270.

Anderson, Elizabeth. 2010. *The Imperative of Integration*. Princeton: Princeton University Press.

Argentiero, A., S. Casal, L. Mittone and A. Morreale, eds. 2021. Special Issue: "Tax Evasion and Economic Inequality: New Insights and Policy." *Economics of Governane* 22, no. 4.

Armitage, Faith. 2006. *The Ideal of Equality: Luck Egalitarianism and Its Critics*. PhD dissertation. Ann Arbor, MI: ProQuest.

Armstrong, Chris. 2006. *Rethinking Equality: The Challenge of Equal Citizenship*. Manchester: University of Manchester Press.

Arndt, Channing, Sam Jones, and Finn Tarp. 2016. "What Is the Aggregate Economic Rate of Return to Foreign Aid?" *World Bank Economic Review* 30, no. 3: 446–474.

Arneson, Richard J. 1989. "Equality and Equal Opportunity for Welfare." *Philosophical Studies: An International Journal for Philosophy in the Analytic Tradition* 56, no. 1: 77–93.

Arneson, Richard J. 1995. "Equality." In R. F. Goodin and P. Pettit, eds., *A Companion to Political Philosophy*. Oxford: Blackwell. 389–507.

Arneson, Richard J. 2008. "Rawls, Responsibility, and Distributive Justice." In M. Fleurbaey, M. Salles, and J. Weymark, eds., *Justice, Political Liberalism, and Utilitarianism: Themes from Harsanyi and Rawls*, Cambridge: Cambridge University Press. 80–107.

Arneson, Richard. 2018. "Egalitarian Perspectives on Paternalism." In K. Grill and J. Hanna, eds., *The Routledge Handbook of Paternalism*. London: Routledge. 194–205.

Arrow, Kenneth J. 1951. "An Extension of the Basic Theorems of Classical Welfare Economics." In *Proceedings of the Second Berkeley Symposium on Mathematical Statistics and Probability*. Berkeley and Los Angeles: University of California Press. 507–532.

Ashworth, Jared, and Tyler Ransom. 2019. "Has the College Wage Premium Continued to Rise? Evidence from Multiple U.S. Surveys." *Economics of Education Review* 69: 149–154.

Aslanbeigui, Nahid, and Guy Oakes. 2015. *Arthur Cecil Pigou*. London: Palgrave.

Aslanbeigui, Nahid, and Guy Oakes. 2019. "The Ethics of Political Economy: Pigou in the Public Sphere." *Œconomia* 9, no. 2: 237–263.

Aslanbeigui, Nahid. 1987. "Some Inconsistencies in Lionel Robbin's Methodology." *Review of Social Economy* 45, no. 3: 325–335.

Atkinson, Anthony B. 2001. "The Strange Disappearance of Welfare Economics." *Kyklos* 54, nos. 2–3: 193–206.

Atkinson, Anthony B. 2008. "More on the Measurement of Inequality." *Journal of Economic Inequality* 6, no. 3: 277–283.

Avent, Ryan. 2014. "A Piketty Problem?" *The Economist*, May 24.

Ayal, E. B., and G. Karras. 1998. "Components of Economic Freedom and Growth: An Empirical Study." *Journal of Developing Areas* 32: 327–338.

Barclay, Linda. 2007. "Feminist Distributive Justice and the Relevance of Equal Relations." In N. Holtug and K. Lippert-Rasmussen, eds., *Egalitarianism: New Essays on the Nature and Value of Equality*. Oxford: Clarendon Press. 196–210.

Barro, Robert J. 1997. *Determinants of Economic Growth: A Cross-Country Empirical Study*. Cambridge, MA: MIT Press.

Barro, Robert J. 2002. *Nothing Is Sacred: Economic Ideas for the New Millennium*. Cambridge, MA: MIT Press.

Barry, Brian. 1986. "Lady Chatterley's Lover and Doctor Fischer's Bomb Party: Liberalism, Pareto Optimality, and the Problem of Objectionable Preferences." In J. Elster and A. Hylland, eds., *Foundations of Social Choice Theory*. Cambridge: Cambridge University Press. 11–44.

Barry, Brian. 1995. *Justice as Impartiality*. Oxford: Clarendon Press.

Baujard, Antoinette. 2016. "Welfare Economics." In G. Faccarello and H. D. Kurz, eds., *Handbook of the History of Economic Analysis*, vol. 3. Cheltenham: Edward Elgar. 611–623.

Becht, Marco, Patrick Bolton, and Ailsa Röell. 2003. "Corporate Governance and Control." In G. M. Constantinides, M. Harris, and R. Stulz, eds., *Handbook of the Economics of Finance*. Amsterdam: Elsevier. 1–109.

Belman, Dale, and Paul J. Wolfson. 2014. "The New Minimum Wage Research." *Employment Research Newsletter* 21, no. 2: 4–6.

Bergson, Abram (Burk). 1938. "A Reformulation of Certain Aspects of Welfare Economics." *Quarterly Journal of Economics* 52, no. 2: 310–334.

Bergson, Abram. 1948. "Socialist Economics." In H. S. Elis, ed., *A Survey of Contemporary Economics*, Philadelphia: Blakiston. 193–236.

Bergson, Abram. 1954. "On the Concept of Social Welfare." *Quarterly Journal of Economics* 68: 233–252.

Bergson, Abram. 1983. "Pareto on Social Welfare." *Journal of Economic Literature* 21, no. 1: 40–46.

Berrgren, Niclas. 2003. "The Benefits of Economic Freedom: A Survey." *Independent Review* 8, no. 2: 193–211.

Bethell, Tom. 1998. *The Noblest Triumph: Property and Prosperity through the Ages*. New York: St. Martin's Press.

Bhagwati, Jagdish, and Arvind Panagariya. 2013. *Why Growth Matters: How Economic Growth in India Reduced Poverty and the Lessons for Other Developing Countries*. New York: Public Affairs.

Bhagwati, Jagdish. 2007. *In Defense of Globalization*. Oxford: Oxford University Press.

Binmore, Ken. 1998. *Just Playing: Game Theory and the Social Contract II*. Cambridge, MA: MIT Press.

Binmore, Ken. 2005. *Natural Justice*. Oxford: Oxford University Press.

Binmore, Kenneth. 2014. "Bargaining and Fairness." *PNAS* 111, suppl. 3: 10785–10788.

Block, Walter. 1998. "A Libertarian Case for Free Immigration." *Journal of Libertarian Studies* 13 (Summer): 167–186.

Boniwell, Ilona, Susan A. David, and Amanda Conley Ayers, eds. 2013. *Oxford Handbook of Happiness*. Oxford: Oxford University Press.

Boone, Peter. 1996. "Politics and the Effectiveness of Foreign Aid." *European Economivc Review* 40, no, 2: 289–329.

Boudreaux, Donald J., and Mark J. Perry. 2013. "The Myth of a Stagnant Middle Class." *Wall Street Journal*. www.wsj.com/articles/SB10001424127887323468604578249723138161566.

Bourguignon, François, Francisco H. G. Ferreira, and Michael Walton. 2007. "Equity, Efficiency and Inequality Traps: A Research Agenda." *Journal of Economic Inequality* 5, no. 2: 235–256.

Boushey, Heather. 2019. *Unbound: How Inequality Constricts Our Economy and What We Can Do about It*. Cambridge, MA: Harvard University Press.

Bowles, Samuel and Wendy Carlin. 2020. "What Students Learn in Economics 101:Time for a Change." *Journal of Economic Literature* 58, no. 1: 176–214.

Bowles, Samuel, and Herbert Gintis. 1990. "Contested Exchange: New Microfoundations for the Political Economy of Capitalism." *Politics and Society* 18, no. 2: 165–222.

Bowles, Samuel, and Herbert Gintis. 1998. "Is Equality Passé?" *Boston Review*, December 1, http://bostonreview.net/samuel-bowles-herbert-gintis-is-equality-passe.

Bowles, Samuel, and Herbert Gintis. 2011. *A Cooperative Species: Human Reciprocity and Its Evolution*. Princeton: Princeton University Press.

Bowles, Samuel. 2012. *The New Economics of Inequality and Redistribution*. Cambridge: Cambridge University Press.

Boyle, James. 2008. *The Public Domain: Enclosing the Commons of the Mind*. New Haven: Yale University Press.

Brat, Eric, Inmaculada Buendía Martínez, and Nabila Ouchene. 2016. *Innovation: Priorities and Practices in Cooperatives*. Montreal: Alfonse and Dorimène Desjardins International Institute for Cooperatives.

Brennan, Geoffrey, and Philip Pettit. 2004. *The Economy of Esteem: An Essay on Civil and Political Society*. Oxford: Oxford University Press.

Brennan, Geoffrey. 1993. "The Contribution of Economics." In R. E. Goodin and P. Pettit, eds., *A Companion to Contemporary Political Philosophy*. Oxford: Blackwell. 123–156.

Brewer, Anthony. 1995. "A Minor Ricardian? Marx as an Economist." *History of Political Economy* 27: 111–146.

Brighouse, Harry, and Ingrid Robeyns, eds. 2010. *Measuring Justice: Primary Goods and Capabilities*. Cambridge: Cambridge University Press.

Brodsky, Melvin. 1994 "Labor Market Flexibility: A Changing International Perspective." *Monthly Labor Review* 117: 53–60.

Bruni, Luigino, Allesandra Smerilli, and Dalila De Rosa, eds. 2021. *A Modern Guide to the Economics of Happiness*. Cheltenham: Edward Elgar.

Bruni, Luigino, and Pier Luigi Porta, eds. 2007. *Handbook on the Economy of Happiness*. Cheltenham: Edward Elgar.

Bruni, Luigino, and Stefano Zamagni. 2016. *Civil Economy: Another Idea of the Market*. Newcastle upon Tyne: Agenda Publishing.

Bruni, Luigino. 2009. "Pareto's Methodological Project." In L. Bruni and A. Montesano, eds., *New Essays on Pareto's Economic Theory*. London: Routledge. 5–29.

Bruni, Luigino. 2012. *The Genesis and Ethos of the Market*. London: Palgrave,

Buchanan, James and Gordon Tullock. 1962. *The Calculus of Consent*. Ann Arbor: University of Michigan Press.

Buchanan, James M. 1987. "Towards the Simple Economics of Natural Liberty: An Exploratory Analysis." *Kyklos* 40: 3–20.

Buchanan, James M., and Roger D. Congleton. 1998. *Politics by Principle, Not Interest*. Cambridge: Cambridge University Press.

Buchanan, James M., and Yong J. Yoon. 2000. "Symmetric Tragedies: Commons and Anticommons," *Journal of Law and Economics* 43: 1–13.

Buchanan, James. M. 1969. "External Diseconomies, Corrective Taxes and Market Structure." *American Economic Review* 59, no. 1: 174–177.

Burczak, Theodore. 2006. *Socialism after Hayek*. Ann Arbor: University of Michigan Press.

Cadot, Olivier, Ana Fernandes, Julien Gourdon, Aaditya Mattoo and Jaime de Melo. 2014. "Evaluating Aid for Trade: A Survey of Recent Studies," *The World Economy*: 516–529.

Campbell, Richmond. 2014. "Reflective Equilibrium and Moral Consistency Reasoning." *Australasian Journal of Philosophy* 92, no. 3: 433–451.

Canto-Sperber, Monique. 2004. "Proudhon, the First Liberal Socialist." In M. J. Parrine and Mary Jane, eds., *A Vast and Useful Art: The Gustave Gimon Collection on French Political Economy*. Stanford: Stanford University Press, 1–16.

Caplan, Bryan. 2018. *The Case against Education*. Princeton: Princeton University Press.

Cappelen, Alexander W., James Konow, Erik O. Sorensen, and Bertil Tungodden. 2013. "Just Luck: An Experimental Study of Risk-Taking and Fairness." *American Economic Review* 103, no. 4: 1398–1413.

Card, David and Alan B. Krueger. 1994. "Minimum Wages and Employment: A Case Study of the Fast-Food Industry in New Jersey and Pennsylvania." *The American Economic Review*. 84, no. 4: 772–793.

Card, David. 1992a. "Using Regional Variation in Wages to Measure the Effects of the Federal Minimum Wage." *Industrial and Labor Relations Reuiew* 46, no. 1: 22–37.

Card, David. 1992b. "Do Minimum Wages Reduce Employment? A Case Study of California, 1987–89." *Industrial and Labor Relations Review* 46, no. 1: 38–54.

Carlsson, Frederick, and Susanna Lunström. 2002. "Economic Freedom and Growth: Decomposing the Effects." *Public Choice* 112: 335–344.

Carvahlo, Fernando Cardim de. 2008. "Keynes and the Reform of the Capitalist Social Order." *Journal of Post Keynesian Economics* 31, no. 2: 191–211.

Checchi, Daniele. 2004. "Does Educational Achievement Help Explain Income Inequality?" In G.A. Cornia, ed. *Inequality Growth and Poverty in an Era of Liberalization and Globalization*. Oxford: Oxford University Press.

Chirinko, Robert S. 2008. "σ: The Long and Short of it." *Journal of Macroeconomics* 30, no. 2: 671–686.

Chong, Alberto, and Cesar Calderon. 1997. *Institutional Change and Poverty, or Why Is It Worth to Reform the State?* Washington, DC: World Bank.

Church, Tom, Chris Miller, and John B. Taylor, eds. 2015. *Inequality and Economic Policy: Essays in Honor of Gary Becker*. Stanford: Hoover Institution Press.

Clark, Andrew. 2018. "Four Decades of the Economics of Happiness: Where Next?" *Review of Income and Wealth* 64, no. 3: 245–269.

Coase, Ronald. 1960. "The Problem of Social Cost." *Journal of Law and Economics* 3, no. 1: 1–44.

Coase, Ronald. 1988. *The Firm, The Market and the Law*. Chicago: University of Chicago Press.

Cohen, Gerald A. 1989. "On the Currency of Egalitarian Justice." *Ethics* 99, no. 4: 906–944.

Cohen, Gerald A. 1993. "Equality of What? On Welfare, Goods, and Capabilities." In M. Nussbaum and A. Sen, eds., *The Quality of Life*. Oxford: Oxford University Press. 9–29.

Cohen, Gerald A. 2000. *If You Are an Egalitarian, How Come You're So Rich?* Cambridge, MA: Harvard University Press.

Cohen, Gerald A. 2004. "Expensive Taste Rides Again." In J. Burley, ed., *Dworkin and His Critics*. Oxford: Blackwell Publishing. 81–115.

Cohen, Gerald A. 2008. *Rescuing Justice and Equality*. Cambridge, MA: Harvard University Press.

Collins, Stephanie. 2015. *The Core of care Ethics*. London: Palgrave.

Columbino, Ugo. 2009. "Optimal Income Taxation: Recent Empirical Applications." *Rivista italiana degli economisti* XIV, no. 1: 47–70.

Conard, Edward. 2016. *The Upside of Inequality: How Great Intentions Undermine the Middle Class*. New York: Random House/Penguin.

Cooter, Robert and Peter Rappoport. 1984. "Were the Ordinalists Wrong About Welfare Economics?" *Journal of Economic Literature* XXII: 507–530.

Corak, Miles. 2013. "Income Inequality, Equality of Opportunity, and Intergenerational Mobility." *Journal of Economic Perspectives* 27, no. 3: 79–102.

Correia, Isabel H. 1999. "On the Efficiency and Equity Trade-Off." *Journal of Monetary Economics* 44: 581–603.

Cowell, F. A. 2000. "Measurement of Inequality." In A. B. Atkinson and F. Bourguignon, eds., *Handbook of Income Distribution*, vol. 1. Amsterdam: Elsevier. 87–166.

Dalgaard, Carl-Johan, Henrik Hansen, and Finn Tarp. 2004. "On the Empirics of Foreign Aid and Growth." *Economic Journal* 114: F191–F216.

Dalingwater, Louise. 2019. "Linking Health and Wellbeing in Public Discourse and Policy: The Case of the UK." *Revue Interventions Economiques* 62: 1–20.

Dari- Mattiacci, Giuseppe and Nuno Garoupa. 2008. "The Unsolvable Dilemma of a Paretian Policymaker," *Supreme Court Economic Review* 16, no. 1: 117–126.

Davidov, Guy. 2009. "A Purposive Interpretation of the National Minimum Wage Act." *Modern Law Review* 72, no. 4: 581–606.

Davidov, Guy. 2018. "Distributive Justice and Labour Law." In H. Collins, G. Lester, and V. Mantouvalou, eds., *Philosophical Foundations of Labour Law*. Oxford: Oxford University Press. 141–155.

Davidson, Donald. 1986. "Judging Interpersonal Interests." In J. Elster and A. Hylland, eds., *Foundations of Social Choice Theory*. Cambridge: Cambridge University Press. 195–211.

Davies, James, and Michael Hoy. 1995. "Making Inequality Comparisons When Lorenz Curves Intersect." *American Economic Review* 85, no. 4: 980– 986.

Dayton-Johnson. 2001. *Social Cohesion and Economic Prosperity*. Toronto; James Lorimer.

De Nardi, Martacritina, Giulo Fella and Fang Yang. 2017. "Macro Models of Wealth Inequality." In H. Boushey, J. B. DeLong, and M. Steinbaum, eds., *After Piketty: The Agenda for Economics and Inequality*. Cambridge, MA: Harbard University Press. 322–354.

De Wispelaere, Jurgen, and Lindsay Stirton. 2011. "The Administrative Efficiency of Basic Income." *Policy and Politics* 39, no. 1: 115–132.

Deaton, Angus. 2003. "Inequality, and Economic Development." *Journal of Economic Literature* 41, no. 1: 113–158.

Deaton, Angus. 2013. *The Great Escape: Health, Wealth and the Origins of Inequality*. Princeton: Princeton University Press.

Debreu, Gerard. 1959. *Theory of Value: An Axiomatic Analysis of Economic Equilibrium*. New Hacen: Yale University Press.

Demsetz, Harold. 1967. "Toward a Theory of Property Rights." *American Economic Review* 57, no. 2: 347–359.

Demsetz, Harold. 2008. "Fischmann's View of 'Toward a Theory of Property Rights.'" *Review of Law and Economics* 4, no. 1: 127–132.

Dewey, John. 2008. *The Collected Works of John Dewey, The Later Works. Volume 2: Essays, Review, Miscellany and* The Public and Its Problems. Carbondale: Southern Illinois University Press.

Di Tella, Rafael and Robert L. MacCullogh. 2008. "Gross National Happiness as an Answer to the Easterlin Paradox?" *Journal of Development Economics* 86: 22–42.

Di Tella, Rafael, Robert J. MacCulloch, and Andrew J. Oswald. 2003. "The Macroeconomics of Happiness." *Review of Economics and Statistics* 85, no. 4: 809–827.

Dobuzinskis, Laurent. 2010. "Non-Welfarism *Avant la Lettre*: Alfred Fouillée's Political Economy of Justice." *European Journal of the History of Economic Thought* 17, no. 4: 837–864.

Dobuzinskis, Laurent. 2020. "Justice in the City: Georgist Insights and Their Limits." *Cosmos+Taxis* 8, nos. 8–9: 90–107.

Dobuzinskis, Laurent. 2022. *Moral Discourse in the History of Economic Thought*. London: Routledge.

Donath, Susan. 2000. "The Other Economy: A Suggestion for a Distinctively Feminist Economics." *Feminist Economics* 6, no. 1: 115–123.

Donselaar, Gijs van. 2009. *The Right to Exploit: Parasitism, Scarcity, Basic Income*. Oxford; Oxford University Press.

Doucouliagos, Hristos and T.D. Stanley. 2009. "Publication Selection Bias in Minimum-Wage Research? A Meta-Regression Analysis." *British Journal of Industrial Relations* 47, no. 2: 406–428.

Drakopoulos, Stavros A. 1989. "The Historical Perspective of the Problem of Interpersonal Comparisons of Utility." *Journal of Economic Studies* 16, no. 4: 35–51.

Drennan, Matthew P. 2015. *Income Inequality: Why It Matters and Why Most Economists Didn't Notice*. New Haven: Yale University Press.

Drèze, Jean, and Amartya Sen. 2002. *India: Development and Participation*. Oxford: Oxford University Press.

Dutt, Amitava Krishna and Benjamin Radcliff, eds. 2009. *Happiness, Economics and Poliics: Toward a Multi-Disciplinary Approach*. Cheltenham: Edward Elgar.

Dworkin, Ronald. 2000. *Sovereign Virtue: The Theory and Practice of Equality*. Cambridge, MA: Harvard University Press.

Dworkin, Ronald. 2011. *Justice for Hedgehogs*. Cambridge, MA: Harvard University Press.

Dwyer, Rachel. 2013. "The Care Economy? Gender, Economic Restructuring, and Job Polarization in the U.S. Labor Market." *American Sociological Review* 78, no. 3: 390–416.

Easterlin, Richard. 1974. "Does Economic Growth Improve the Human Lot? Some Empirical Evidence." In Paul A. David and Melvin W. Reder, eds., *Nations and Households in Economic Growth: Essays in Honor of Moses Abramovitz*. New York: Academic Press.

Elster, Jon, and John E. Roemer. 1991. "Introduction." In J. Elster and J. R. Roemer, eds., *Interpersonal Comparisons of Well-Being*. Cambridge: Cambridge University Press. 1–16.

Ernst & Young. 2011. Entrepreneurs Speak Out—China. www.ey.com/Publication/wwLUAssets/G20_Entrepreneurship_barometer_-_China_report/$FILE/barometer_G20_China.pdf.

Esping-Andersen, Gøsta. 1990. *The Three Worlds of Capitalism*. Princeton: Princeton University Press.

European Commission. 2021. *EU Aid for Trade: Progress Report 2021*. Brussels: Office of the European Union.

Evensky, John. 2003. "Review of *The Moral Conditions of Economic Efficiency*." *History of Political Economy* 35, no. 3: 575–577.

Eyal, Nir. 2010. "Near Universal Basic Income." *Basic Income Studies* 5, no. 1: 1–26.

Farrelly, Colin. 2007. "Justice in Ideal Theory: A Refutation." *Political Studies* 55: 844–864.

Feldman, Allan M., and Roberto Serrano. 2006. *Welfare Economics and Social Choice Theory*, 2nd ed. New York: Springer.

Feser, Edward. 2005. "There Is No Such Thing as an Unjust Initial Acquisition." In Ellen Frankel Paul, Fred D. Miller, and Jeffrey Paul, eds., *Natural Rights Liberalism from Locke to Nozick*. Cambridge: Cambridge University Press. 56–80.

Fleurbaey, Marc, and François Maniquet. 2018. "Optimal Taxation Theory and Principles of Fairness." *Journal of Economic Literature* 56, no. 3: 1029–1079.

Fleurbaey, Marc, and Peter Hammond. 2004. "Interpersonally Comparable Utility." In S. Barbera, P. Hammond, and C. Seidl, eds., *Handbook of Utility Theory, Volume II: Extensions*. Boston: Kluwer Academic Press. 1181–1285.

Fleurbaey, Marc, and Philippe Mongin. 2005. "The News of the Death of Welfare Economics Is Greatly Exaggerated." *Social Choice and Welfare* 25: 381–418.

Fleurbaey, Marc, and Vito Peragine. 2013. "*Ex Ante* versus *Ex Post* Equality of Opportunity." *Economica* 18: 118–130.

Fleurbaey, Marc, Bertil Tungodden, and Howard F. Chang. 2003. "Any Non-Welfarist Method of Policy Assessment Violates the Pareto Principle: A Comment." *Journal of Political Economy* 111: 1382–1385.

Fleurbaey, Marc. 2008. *Fairness, Responsibility, and Welfare*. Oxford: Oxford University Press.

Fleurbaey, Marc. 2012. "Economics and Economic Justice." *Stanford Encyclopedia of Philosophy*. http://plato.stanford.edu/archives/sum2012/entries/economic-justice.

Folbre, Nancy. 1994. *Who Pays for the Kids? Gender and the Structure of Constraint*. London: Routledge.

Fourie, Carina, Fabian Schuppert, and Ivo Wallimann-Helmer, eds. 2015. "The Nature and Distinctiveness of Equality: An Introduction." In *Social Equality: On What It Means to Be Equals*. Oxford: Oxford University Press. 1–17.

Fourie, Carina. 2015. "To Praise and to Scorn: The Problem of Inequality of Esteem for Social Egalitarians." In Carina Fourie, Fabian Schuppert, and Ivo Wallimann-Helmer, eds., *Social Equality: On What It Means To Be Equal*. Oxford: Oxford University Press.

Frankfurt, Harry G. 2015. *On Inequality*. Princeton: Princeton University Press.

Frey, Bruno S. 2008. *Happiness: A Revolution in Economics*. Cambridge: MIT Press.

Frey, Bruno S., and Alois Stutzer. 2001. *Happiness and Economics: How the Economy and Institutions Affect Human Well-being*. Princeton: Princeton University Press.

Frey, Bruno S., and Alois Stutzer. 2013. "Economics and the Study of Individual Happiness." In I. Boniwell, S. A. David, and A. C. Ayers, eds., *Oxford Handbook of Happiness*. Oxford: Oxford University Press. 431–447.

Friedman, Milton, and Rose Friedman. 1980. *Free to Choose: A Personal Statement*. New York: Harcourt Brace Jovanovich.

Friedman, Milton. [1962] 2002. *Capitalism and Freedom*. Chicago: University of Chicago Press.

Friesen, Jane. 2003. "Communities and Economic Prosperity: Exploring the Links." In L. Osberg, ed., *The Economic Implications of Social Cohesion*. Toronto: University of Toronto Press. 183–212.

Frisch, Ragnar. 1959. R. "On Welfare Theory and Pareto Regions." *International Economic Papers* 9: 39–92.

Fukuyama, Francis. 1995. *Trust: The Social Virtues and the Creation of Prosperity*. New York: Free Press.

Fumagalli, Roberto. 2020. "Buyer Beware: A Critique of Leading Virtue Ethics Defense of Markets." *Journal of Social Philosophy* 51, no. 3: 457–482.

Furubotn, Erik G. 1971. "Economic Organization and Welfare Distribution." *Swedish Journal of Economics* 73, no. 4: 409–416.

Galiani, Sebastian, Stephen Knack, Lixin Colin Xu, and Ben Zou. 2017. "The Effect of Aid on Growth: Evidence from a Quasi-Experiment." *Journal of Economic Growth* 22: 1–33.

Garcia, Ivis. 2020. "Asset-Based Community Development (ABCD): Core Principles." In Rhonda Phillips, Eric Trevan, and Patsy Kraeger, eds., *Research Handbook on Community Development*. Cheltenham: Elgar. 67–75.

Garven, Fiona, Jennifer McLean, and Lisa Pattoni. 2016. *Asset-Based Approaches: Their Rise, Role and Reality*. Edinburgh: Dunedin.

Gaus, Gerald. 2011. *The Order of Public Reason*. Cambridge: Cambridge University Press.

Gaus, Gerald. 2016. *The Tyranny of the Ideal: Justice in a Diverse Society*. Princeton: Princeton University Press.

George, Henry. [1879] 1935. *Progress and Poverty: An Inquiry into the Cause of Industrial Depressions and of Increase of Want with Increase of Wealth, the Remedy*, 50th anniversary ed. New York: Robert Schalkenbach Foundation.

Georges-Tudo, Frédéric. 2015. *Piketty au piquet! Le Capital au XXIe siècle—Enquête sur une imposture*. Paris: Editions du Moment.

Gewirth, Alan. 1982. *Human Rights: Essays on Justification and Applications*. Chicago: University of Chicago Press.

Giles, Chris and Ferdinando Giugliano. 2014. "Thomas Piketty's Exhaustive Inequality Data Turn Out to Be Flawed." *Financial Times* (23 May).

Gintis, Herbert. 2009. *The Bounds of Reason: Game Theory and the Unification of the Behavioral Sciences*. Princeton: Princeton University Press.

Girard, René. 1987. *Things Hidden since the Foundation of the World* (trans. S. Bann and M. Metter). Stanford: Stanford University Press.

Glaeser, Edward L and Charles Redlick. 2009. "Social Capital and Urban Growth." *International Regional Science Review* 32, no. 3: 264–299.

Gorman, W.M. 1955. "The Intransitivity of Certain Criteria Used in Welfare Economics." *Oxford Economic Papers* 7: 25–35.

Gotoh, Reiko. 2021. *The Ethics and Economics of the Capability Approach*. Singapore: Springer Nature.

Graafland, Johan, and Bart Compen. 2012. "Economic Freedom and Life Satisfaction: A Cross Country Analysis." Discussion Paper 2012-038. Tilburg: Tilburg University Center for Economic Research.

Graafland, Johan. 2020. "When Does Economic Freedom Promote Well Being? On the Moderating Role of Long-Term Orientation." *Social Indicators Research* 149: 127–153.

Graeber, David, and David Wengrow. 2021. *The Dawn of Everything: The History of Humanity*. London: Penguin Books.

Graham, Carol. 2011. *The Pursuit of Happiness*. Washington, DC: Brookings Institution Press.

Green, David A., Jonathan Rhys Kesselman, and Lindsay M. Tedds. 2020. *Covering All the Basics: Reforms for a More Just Society*, Final Report of the Expert Panel on Basic Income. Victoria, BC: Government of British Columbia.

Grindle, Merilee S. 2007. "Good Enough Governance Revisited." *Development Policy Review* 25, no. 5: 553–574.

Gruber, Jon, and Emmanuel Saez. 2002. "The Elasticity of Taxable Income: Evidence and Implications." *Journal of Public Economics* 84: 1–32.

Gründler, Klaus, and Philipp Scheuermeyer. 2018. "Growth Effects of Inequality and Redistribution: What Are the Transmission Channels?" *Journal of Macroeconomics* 55: 293–313.

Gustav Tinghög, David Andersson, Daniel Västfjäll. 2017. "Are Individuals Luck Egalitarians? An Experiment on the Influence of Brute and Option Luck on Social Preferences." *Frontiers in Psychology* 8, article 460.

Gwartney, James, Robert Lawson, and Joshua Hall. 2012. *Economic Freedom of the World, Annual Report 2021*. Vancouver: Fraser Institute.

Gwartney, James, Robert Lawson, Joshua Hall, and Ryan Murphy. 2021. *Economic Freedom of the World, Annual Report 2021*. Vancouver: Fraser Institute.

Haber, Stephen, Douglass C. North, and Barry R. Weingast. 2008. "Political Institutions and Financial Development." In S. Haber, D. C. North, and B. R. Weingast, eds., *Political Institutions and Financial Development*. Stanford: Stanford University Press. 1–9.

Hall, Joshua, and Robert Lawson. 2008. "Theory and Evidence on Economic Freedom and Growth: A Comment." *Economics Bulletin* 15, no. 18: 1–6.

Hanke, Steve H. 2014. "Raise Minimum Wage, Kill Jobs." *Cato at Liberty*. www.cato.org/blog/raise-minimum-wage-kill-jobs.

Hannesson, Rögnvaldur. 2015. *Debt, Democracy and the Welfare State: Are Modern Democracies Living on Borrowed Time and Money?* London: Palgrave.

Harris, Colin, Meina Cai, Ilya Murtazashvili, and Jennifer Brick Murtazashvili. 2020. *The Origins and Consequences of Property Rights: Austrian, Public Choice, and Institutional Economics Perspectives*. Cambridge: Cambridge University Press.

Harsanyi, John C. 1955. "Cardinal Welfare, Individualistic Ethics, and Interpersonal Comparisons of Utility." *Journal of Political Economy* 63, no. 4: 309–321.

Harsanyi, John C. 1977. *Rational Behavior and Bargaining Equilibrium in Games and Social Situations*. Cambridge: Cambridge University Press.

Harsanyi, John C. 2008. "Interpersonal Utility Comparisons." In S. N. Durlauf and L. E. Blume, eds., *New Palgrave Dictionary of Economics*, 2nd ed., vol. 4. New York: Palgrave Macmillan. 529–532.

Hayden, Grant M., and Matthew T. Bodie. 2021. "Codetermination in Theory and Practice." *Florida Law Review* 73, no. 2: 1–42.

Hayden, Grant M., and Matthew T. Brodie. 2020. *Reconstructing the Corporation: From Shareholder Primacy to Shared Governance*. Cambridge: Cambridge University Press.

Hayek, Friedrich A. 1973. *Law, Legislation and Liberty*, vol. 1: *Rules of Order*. Chicago: University of Chicago Press.

Heath, Joseph. 2004. "Dworkin's Auction." *Politics, Philosophy & Economics* 3, no. 3: 313–335.

Heller, Michael. 2008. *The Gridlock Economy: How Too Much Ownership Wrecks Markets, Stops Innovation, and Costs Lives*. New York: Basic Books.

Henry, John F. 1999. "John Locke, Property Rights and Economic Theory." *Journal of Economic Issues* XXXIII, no. 3: 609–624.

Hetzer, Moritz, and Didier Sornette. 2013. "The Co-Evolution of Fairness Preferences and Costly Punishment." *Plos One* 8, no. 3: e54308.

Hicks, John R. 1975. "The Scope and Status of Welfare Economics." *Oxford Economic Papers*, New Series 27, no. 3: 307–326.

Hicks, John R. 1976. "Some Questions of Time in Economics." In A. M. Tang, F. M. Westfield, and J. S. Worley, eds., *Evolution, Welfare and Time in Economics: Essays in Honor of Nicholas Georgescu-Roegen*. Lexington: Heath-Lexington Books.

Hill, Marianne T. 2003. "Development as Empowerment." *Feminist Economics* 9: 117–135.

Hobbes, Thomas. 1949. *De Cive or the Citizen*, edited by S.P. Lamprecht. New York: Appleton-Century-Crofts.

Hodgson, Geoffrey M. 2021. *Liberal Solidarity: The Political Economy of Social Democratic Liberalism*. Cheltenham: Elgar.

Hongo, Ryo. 2013. "Some Aspects of the Formation of Pigou's Welfare Economics: Charity, Poor Law Reform, and Unemployment." *International Workshop on Welfare Economics and the Welfare State: Historical Re-evaluation*, Hitotsubashi University.

Hoobes, Thomas. 2008. *Leviathan*, edited by M. Missner. London: Routledge.

Hoppe, Hans-Hermann. 1989. *A Theory of Socialism and Capitalism*. Boston: Kluwer Academic.

Horwitz, Steven. 2021. "Growth, Inequality, and Unfairness: Comparing the Progressive and Classical Liberal Perspectives." In G.P. Manish and S.C. Miller, eds., *Capitalism and Inequality: The Role of State and Market*. London: Routledge.

Hovenkamp, Herbert. 2009. "The Coase Theorem and Arthur Cecil Pigou." *Arizona Law Review* 51: 633–649.

Howson, Colin, and Peter Urbach. 2006. *Scientific Reasoning: The Bayesian Approach*, 3rd ed. Chicago: Open Court.

Hume, David. 2009. *A Treatise of Human Nature.* The Floating Press,

Hunggerbühler, Mathias and Etienne Lehmann. 2009. "On the Optimality of a Minimum Wage: New Insights from Optimal Tax heory." *Journal of Public Economics* 93: 464–481.

Igersheim, Herrade. 2019. "The Death of Welfare Economics: History of a Controversy." *History of Political Economy* 51, no. 5: 827–865.

Jackson, Ben. 2012. "Property-Owning Democracy: A Short History." In M. O'Neill and T. Williamson, eds., *Property-Owning Democracy: Rawls and Beyond.* Oxford: Blackwell. 33–52.

Jacobs, Jane. 1961. *The Death and Life of Great American Cities.* Ne York: Random House.

Johns, Helen, and Paul Ormerod. 2007. *Happiness Economics and Public Policy.* London: The Institute of Economic Affairs.

Kahneman, Daniel, Jack L. Knetsch, and Richard H. Thaler. 1986. "Fairness and the Assumptions of Economics." *Journal of Business* 59, no. 4: S285–S300.

Kaiser, Caspar F. and Maarten C.M. Vendrik. 2019. "Different Versions of the Easterlin Paradox: New Evidence for European Countries." In M. Rojas, ed. *The Economics of Happiness How the Easterlin Paradox Transformed Our Understanding of Well-Being and Progress.* Cham, Switzerland: Springer.

Kakwani, Nanak. 1980. *Income Inequality and Poverty.* Oxford: Oxford University Press.

Kananen, Johannes. 2014. *The Nordic Welfare State in Three Eras: From Emancipation to Discipline.* London: Routledge.

Kaplow, Louis and Steven Shavell. 2001. "Any Non-welfarist Method of Policy Assessment Violates the Pareto Principle." *Journal of Political Economy* 109, no. 2: 281–286.

Katz, Lawrence F. and Alan B. Krueger. 1992. "The Effect of the Minimum Wage on the Fast Food Industry." Industrial and Labor Relations *Review* 46, no.1: 6–21.

Kersbergen, Kees Van and Barbara Vis. 2014. *Comparative Welfare State Politics: Development, Opportunities, and Reform.* Cambridge: Cambridge University Press.

Kim, Hee-Kang. 2010. "Luck and the Gendered Social Structure." *Journal of Women, Politics & Policy* 31, no. 1: 87–92.

King, Loren A. 2011. "Exploitation and Rational Choice." *Canadian Journal of Political Science* 44, no. 3: 635–661.

Klassen, Stephan and Francesca Lamanna. 2009. "The Impact of Gender Inequality in Education and Employment on Economic Growth: New Evidence for a Panel of Countries." *Feminist Economics* 15, no. 3: 91–132.

Klassen, Stephan. 2002. "Low Schooling for Girls, Slower Growth for All? Cross-Country Evidence on the Effect of Gender Inequality in Education on Economic Development." *World Bank Economic Review* 16, no. 3: 345–73.

Klein, Peter G. 1996. "Economic Calculation and the Limits of Organization." *Review of Austrian Economics* 9, no. 2: 3–28.

Knack, Stephen, and Philip Keefer. 1995. "Institutions and Economic Performance: Cross-Country Tests Using Alternative Institutional Measure." *Economics and Politics* 7, no. 3: 202–227.

Knight, Carl. 2013. "Luck Egalitarianism." *Philosophy Compass* 8, no. 10: 924–934.

Knight, Carl. 2021. "An Argument for All-Luck Egalitarianism." *Philosophy and Public Affairs* 49, no. 4: 350–378.

Knight, Karen Lovejoy. 2018. *A. C. Pigou and the "Marshallian" Thought Style*. London: Palgrave.

Knoop, Todd A. 2020. *Understanding Economic Inequality: Bigger Pies and Just Desserts*. Cheltenham: Edward Elgar.

Kogelmann, Brian. 2020. "The Future of Political Philosophy: Non-Ideal and West of Babel." *Review of Austrian Economics* 33: 237–252.

Kohn, Margaret. 2016. "The Critique of Possessive Individualism: Solidarism and the City." *Political Theory* 44, no. 5: 603–628.

Kolm, Serge-Christophe. [1971] 1997. *Justice and Equity* (trans. H. F. See). Cambridge, MA: MIT Press.

Kolm, Serge-Christophe. 1984. *La bonne économie: La réciprocité générale*. Paris: Presses Universitaires de France.

Kolm, Serge-Christophe. 1994. "Rational Normative Economics vs 'Social Welfare' and 'Social Choice.'" *European Economic Review* 38: 721–730.

Kolm, Serge-Christophe. 1996. *Modern Theories of Justice*. Cambridge, MA: MIT Press.

Kolm, Serge-Christophe. 2000a. "Introduction: The Economics of Reciprocity, Giving and Altruism." In L.-A. Gérard-Varet, S.-C. Kolm, and J. Mercier-Ethier, eds., *The Economics of Reciprocity, Giving and Altruism*. New York: Palgrave Macmillan. 1–44.

Kolm, Serge-Christophe. 2000b. "The Theory of Reciprocity." In L.-A. Gérard-Varet, S.-C. Kolm, and J. Mercier-Ethier, eds., *The Economics of Reciprocity, Giving and Altruism*, New York: Palgrave Macmillan. 115–141.

Kolm, Serge-Christophe. 2005. *Macrojustice: The Political Economy of Fairness*. Cambridge: Cambridge University Press.

Kolm, Serge-Christophe. 2006. "Introduction to the Economics of Giving, Altruism and Reciprocity." In S.-C. Kolm and J. Mercier-Ethier, eds., *Handbook of the Economics of Giving, Altruism and Reciprocity*, vol. 1. Amsterdam: Elsevier. 1–122.

Kolm, Serge-Christophe. 2007. "Macrojustice: Distribution, Impôt et transferts optimaux." *Revue d'économie politique* 117, no. 1: 61–89.

Kolm, Serge-Christophe. 2009. "A Response to Erik Schokkaert on *Macrojustice*." *Economics and Philosophy* 25: 85–98.

Kolm, Serge-Christophe. 2009. "Inequality." In *J. Peil and I. van Staveren*, eds. *Handbook of Economics and Ethics*. Cheltenham: Edward Elgar. 267–275.

Krugman, Paul. 2021. "Why We're in a New Gilded Age." *New York Review of Books* 61, no. 8 (May 8).

Kumekawa, Ian. 2017. *The First Serious Optimist: A. C. Pigou and the Birth of Welfare Economics*. Princeton: Princeton University Press.

Kuznets, Simon. 1955. "Economic Growth and Income Inequality." *American Economic Review* 45, no. 1: 1–28.

Laforest, Rachel. 2011. *Voluntary Sector Organizations and the State*. Vancouver: UBC Press.

Lambert, Peter J, 1993. *The Distribution and Redistribution of Income*, 2nd ed. Manchester: Manchester University Press.

Lange, Oscar, and Fred M. Taylor. 1938. *On the Economics Theory of Socialism*. Minneapolis: University of Minnesota Press.

Lange, Oscar. 1936. "On the Economic Theory of Socialism." *Review of Economic Studies* 4: 53–71.

Langrill, Ryan and Virgil Storr. "The Moral Meaning of Markets." *Journal of Markets and Morality* 15, no. 2: 347–362.

Lawson, R. A., and J. R. Clark. 2010. "Examining the Hayek-Friedman Thesis on Economic and Political Freedom." *Journal of Economic Behavior and Organization* 74, no. 3: 230–239.

Layard, Richard. 2005. *Happiness: Lessons from a New Science*. New York: Penguin.
Levy, Jacob T. 2016. "There Is No Such Thing as Ideal Theory." *Social Philosophy & Policy* 33, nos. 1–2: 312–333.
Lindblom, Lars. 2015. "Equality of Resource, Risk, and the Ideal Market." *Erasmus Journal for Philosophy and Economics* 8, no. 1: 1–23.
Lindley, Joanne, and Stephen Machin. 2012. "The Quest for More and More Education: Implications for Social Mobility." *Fiscal Studies* 33, no. 2: 265–286.
Lipton, Michael. 2009. *Land Reform in Developing Countries: Property Rights and Property Wrongs*. London: Routledge.
Lister, Ruth. 2021. *Poverty*, 2nd ed. London: Polity.
Locke, John. 2003. *Two Treatise of Government and a Letter on Toleration*. I. Shapiro, ed. New Haven: Yale University Press.
Lockwood, B. 2008. "Pareto Efficiency." In S. N. Durlauf and L. E. Blume, eds., *The New Palgrave Dictionary of Economics*, 2nd ed. Volume 6, New York: Palgrave. 292–295.
Long, Douglas. 2006. "Adam Smith's Politics." In K. Haakonssen, ed. *The Cambridge Companion to Adam Smith*. Cambridge: Cambridge University Press.
Lucas, Robert. 2003. "The Industrial Revolution: Past and Future." *Federal Reserve Bank of Minneapolis*. www.minneapolisfed.org/article/2004/the-industrial-revolution-past-and-future.
Mackie, Gerry. 2003. *Democracy Defended*. Cambridge: Cambridge University Press.
Macpherson, C.B. 1962. *The Political Theory of Possessive Individualism*. Oxford: Oxford University Press.
Mahon, Rianne, and Fiona Robinson, eds. 2011. *Feminist Ethics and Social Policy: Towards a New Global Political Economy of Care*. Vancouver: UBC Press.
Manish, G.P. and S.C. Miller, eds. *Capitalism and Inequality: The Role of State and Market*. London: Routledge.
Mankiw, N. Gregory, Matthew Weinzierl, and Danny Yagan. 2009. "Optimal Taxation in Theory and Practice." *Journal of Economic Perspectives* 23, no. 4: 147–174.
Mankiw, N. Gregory. 2013. "Defending the One Percent." *Journal of Economic Perspectives* 27, no. 3: 21–34.
Maskin, Eric. 2014. "Why Haven't Global Markets Reduced Inequality?" *Annual Conference on Development Economics*, World Bank, June. 48–52.
Mathis, Klaus. 2009. *Efficiency Instead of Justice? Searching for the Philosophical Foundations of the Economic Analysis of Law*, transl. D. Shannon. Dordrecht: Springer.
Mayer, Karl Ulrich, Walter Müller, and Reinhard Pollack. 2007. "Germany: Institutional Change and Inequality of Access in Higher Education." In Y. Shavit, R. Arum, and A Gamoran, eds., *Stratification in Higher Education*. Stanford: Stanford University Press. 240–265.
McCain, Roger A. 2019. *Welfare Economics: An Interpretive History*. London: Routledge.
McCloskey, Deirdre Nansen. 2006. *The Bourgeois Virtues: Ethics for an Age of Commerce*. Chicago: University of Chicago Press.
McCloskey, Deirdre Nansen. 2010. *Bourgeois Dignity: Why Economics Can't Explain the Modern World*. Chicago: University of Chicago Press.
McCloskey, Deirdre Nansen. 2016. *Bourgeois Equality: How Ideas, Not Capital or Institutions, Enriched the World*. Chicago: University of Chicago Press.
McCloskey, Deirdre Nansen. 2021. *Bettering Humanomics: A New, and Old, Approach to Economic Science*. Chicago: Chicago University Press.
McCloskey, Deirdre Nansen. 2022. *Beyond Positivism, Behaviorism, and Neoinstitutionalism in Economics*. Chicago: Chicago University Press.

McCracken, M. C. 2003. "Social Cohesion and Macroeeconomic Performance." In L. Osberg, ed., *The Economic Implications of Social Cohesion*. Toronto: University of Toronto Press. 213–230.

Medema, Steven G., and Richard O. Zerbe. 2000. "The Coase Theorem." In B. Bouckert and G. De Geest, eds., *Encyclopedia of Law and Economics*. Cheltenham: Edward Elgar. 836–892.

Meijers, Huub. 2011. "A Short Note on the Elasticity of Substitution." http://meijers.unu-merit.nl/index.php?pagename=ces.

Mian, Atif, and Amir Sufi. 2014. *House of Debt: How They (and You) Caused the Great Recession, and How We Can Prevent It from Happening Again*. Chicago: University of Chicago Press.

Milanovic, Branko. 2010. *The Haves and the Have-Nots: A Brief and Idiosyncratic History of Global Inequality*. New York: Basic Books.

Milanovic, Branko. 2011. *Worlds Apart: Measuring International and Global Inequality*. Princeton: Princeton University Press. 235–258.

Milanovic, Branko. 2016. *Global Inequality: A New Approach for the Age of Globalization*. Cambridge, MA: Harvard University Press.

Milanovic, Branko. 2017. "Increasing Capital Share and Its Effect on Personal Income Inequality." In H. Boushey, J. B. DeLong, and M. Steinbaum, eds., *After Piketty: The Agenda for Economics and Inequality*. Cambridge, MA: Harvard University Press.

Miller, David. 2014. "The Incoherence of Luck Egalitarianism." In Alexander Kaufman, ed. *Distributive Justice and Access to Advantage: G.A. Cohen's Egalitarianism*. Cambridge, Cambridge University. 131–150.

Mirrlees, James A. 1971. "An Exploration in the Theory of Optimal Income Taxation." *Review of Economic Studies* 38, no. 114: 175–208.

Mirrlees, James A. 1976. "Optimal Tax Theory: A Synthesis." *Journal of Public Economics* 6:327–358.

Mirrlees, James A. 1986. "The Theory of Optimal Taxation." In K.J. Arrow and M.D. Intriligator, eds. *Handbook of Mathematical Economics*, vol. III. Amsterdam: Elsevier.

Mises, Ludwig von. 1936. *Socialism: An Economic and Sociological Analysis*. London: Jonathan Cape.

Mises, Ludwig von. 1990. *Economic Calculation in the Socialist Commonwealth*. Auburn, AL: Ludwig von Mises Institute.

Mongin, Philippe. 2000. "Does Optimization Imply Rationality?" *Synthese* 124:73–111.

Mooij, Ruud de. 2006. "Reinventing the Welfare State." Working Paper no. 60. The Hague: CPB Netherlands Bureau for Economic Policy Analysis.

Moreira, Sandrina. 2005. "Evaluating the Impact of Foreign Aid on Economic Growth: A Cross-Country Study." *Journal of Economic Development* 30, no. 2: 25–48.

Mueller, Dennis C. 2003. *Public Choice III*. Cambridge: Cambridge University Press.

Murray, Charles. [2006] 2016. *In Our Hands: A Plan to Replace the Welfare State*, 2nd ed. Washington, DC: AEI Press.

Nagel, Thomas. 2002. *Concealment and Exposure: And Other Essays*. Oxford: Oxford University Press.

Nell, Guinevere. 2013. *Basic Income and the Free Market: Austrian Economics and the Potential for Efficient Redistribution*. London: Palgrave.

Ng, Yew-Kwang. 1983. *Welfare Economics: Introduction and Development of Basic Concepts*. London: Macmillan.

Ng, Yew-Kwang. 2004. *Welfare Economics: Towards a More Complete Analysis*. Houndmills: Palgrave.

Nikolaev, Boris. 2014. "Economic Freedom and Quality of Life: Evidence from the OECD's Your Better Life Index." *Journal of Private Enterprise* 29, no. 3: 61–96.

Noah, Timothy. 2012. *The Great Divergence: America's Growing Inequality Crisis and What To Do about it*. New York: Bloomsbury.

North, Douglass C., John J. Wallace, and Barry Weingast. 2009. *Violence and Social Orders: A Conceptual Framework for Interpreting Human History*. Cambridge: Cambridge University Press.

Novak, Mikayla. 2018. *Inequality: An Entangles Political Economy Perspective*. London: Palgrave.

Nozick, Robert. 1974. *Anarchy, State and Utopia*. Oxford: Blackwell.

Nussbaum, Martha. 2011. *Creating Capabilities: The Human Development Approach*. Cambridge, MA: Harvard University Press

O'Boyle, Edward J. 1998. *Personalist Economics: Moral Convictions, Social Realities, and Social Action*. Amsterdam: Kluwer.

O'Donnell, Margaret G. 1979. "Pigou: An Extension of Sidgickwian Thought." *History of Political Economy* 11, no. 4: 588–605.

O'Neill, Martin. 2020. "Power, Predistribution, and Social Justice." *Philosophy* 95: 63–91.

O'Neill, Martin. 2021. "Justice, Power, and Participatory Socialism: On Piketty's *Capital and Ideology*." *Analyse & Kritik* 43, no. 1: 89–124.

O'Sullivan, John ("Butterworth"). 2021. "Why Capital Will Become Scarcer in the 2020s." *The Economist* (December 28).

Obinger, Herbert, and Uwe Wagschal. 2010. "Social Expenditures and Revenues." In F. C. Castles, S. Leibfried, J. Lewis, H. Obinger, and C. Pierson, eds., *The Oxford Handbook of the Welfare State*. Oxford: Oxford University Press. 333–352.

OECD. 2015. *In It Together: Why Less Inequality Benefits All*. Paris: OECD Publishing.

Okun, Arthur M. 1975. *Equality and Efficiency, The Big Tradeoff*. Washington, DC: Brookings Institution.

Olson, Kristi. 2020. *The Solidarity Solution: Principles for a Fair Income Distribution*. Oxford: Oxford University Press.

Oprea, Alexandra. 2019. "Democracy as Game of Trust: The Limits of the Generality Constraint." *Homo Economicus* 36: 227–248.

Ostrom, Elinor. 1990. *Governing the Commons: The Evolution of Institutions for Collective Action*. Cambridge: Cambridge University Press.

Ostry, Jonathan D., Prakash Longani, and Andrew Berg. 2019. *Confronting Inequality: How Societies Can Choose Inclusive Growth*. New York: Columbia University Press.

Otsuka, Michael. 2003. *Libertarianism without Inequality*. Oxford: Clarendon Press.

Otteson, James. 2019. "The Misuses of Egalitarianism." In R. M. Whaples, M. C. Munger, and Christopher J. Coyne, eds., *In all Fairness: Equality, Liberty and the Quest for Human Dignity*. Oakland, CA: Independent Institute. 25–36.

Parfit, Derek. 2000. "Equality or Priority?" In M. Clayton and A. Williams, eds., *The Ideal of Equality*. London: Palgrave. 81–125.

Parijs, Philiipe van. 1995. *Real Freedom for All. What (if Anything) Can Justify Capitalism?*. Oxford: Oxford University Press.

Peart, Sandra, and David M. Levy. 2005. "A Discipline without Sympathy: The Happiness of the Majority and Its Demise." *Canadian Journal of Economics* 38, no. 3: 937–954.

Pereira, Richard. 2017. "The Cost of Universal Basic Income: Public Savings and Programme Redundancy Exceed Cost." In R. Pereira, ed., *Financing Basic Income: The Cost Objection*. Cham: Springer Nature. 9–45.

Perena, Mathieu, and Caludia Senik. 2020. *Le Bien-être en France: Rapport 2020.* Paris: CEPREMAP.

Pickett, Kate E., Oliver W. James, and Richard G. Wilkinson. 2006. "Income Inequality and the Prevalence of Mental Illness: A Preliminary International Analysis." *Journal of Epidemiology and Community Health* 60: 646–647.

Piereson, James. 2015. "Background Facts." In T. Church, C. Miller and J.B. Taylor, eds. *Inequality and Economic Policy : Essays In Honor of Gary Becker.* Stanford: Hoover Institution Press. 1–16.

Pigou, Arthur Cecil. [1952] 2002. *The Economics of Welfare*, 4th ed. London: Routledge.

Piketty, Thomas, Emmanuel Saez, and Stefanie Santcheva. 2014. "Optimal Taxation of Top Labor Incomes: A Tale of Three Elasticities." *American Economic Journal: Economic Policy* 6, no. 1: 230–271.

Piketty, Thomas. 2014. *Capital in the Twenty First Century* (trans. A. Goldhammer). Cambridge, MA: Belknap Press.

Piketty, Thomas. 2015b. "A Practical Vision of a More Equal Society." *New York Review of Books* (June 25).

Piketty, Thomas. 2015c. "About *Capital in the Twenty First Century*." *American Economic Review: Papers and Proceedings* 105, no. 5: 1–6.

Piketty, Thomas. 2020. *Capital and Ideology* (trans. A. Goldhammer). Cambridge, MA: Belknap Press.

Pinker, Steven. 2011. *The Better Angels of Our Nature: Why Violence Has Declined.* New York: Viking.

Pinto, Andrew D., Melissa Perri, Cheryl L. Pedersen, Tatiana Arantagy, Ayu Pinky Hapsari, and Stephen W. Wang. 2021. "Exploring Different Methods to Evaluate the Impact of Basic Income Interventions: A Systematic Review." *International Journal for Equity in Health* 20: 142.

Preston, Samuel H. 1975. "The Changing Relations between Mortality and Level of Economic Development." *Population Studies* 29, no. 2: 231–248.

Protzer, Eric and Paul Summerville. 2022. *Reclaiming Populism: How Economic Fairness Can Win Back Disenchanted Voters.* London: Polity.

Proudhon, Pierre-Joseph. 1868. *Œuvres complètes de P.-J. Proudhon.* Paris: Librairie Internationale.

Przeworski, Adam. 2004a. "Institutions Matter." *Government and Opposition* 39, no. 2: 527–540.

Przeworski, Adam. 2004b. "Democracy and Economic Development." In Edward D. Mansfield and Richard Sisson, eds., *The Evolution of Political Knowledge.* Columbus: Ohio State University Press. 300–324.

Putnam, Robert D. 1993. "What Makes Democracy Work?" *National Civic Review* Spring 1993: 101–107.

Putnam, Robert D. 2000. *Bowling Alone: The Collapse and Revival of American Community.* New York: Simon & Schuster.

Putnam, Robert D., ed. 2002. *Democracy in Flux: The Evolution of Social Capital in Contemporary Society.* Oxford: Oxford University Press.

Qizilibash, Mozaffar. 2011. "Sugden's Critique of the Capability Approach." *Utilitas* 23, no. 1: 25–51.

Radkiewicz, Piotr, and Thomas Jarmakowski-Kostrzanowski. 2021. "Liberals Versus Communitarians: Psychosocial Sources of the Conflict over Democracy in Today's Poland." *SAGE Open* (January–March): 1–14.

Rauh, Joshua. 2015. "The Broad-Based Rise in the Return of the Talents." In T. Church, C. Miller, and J. B. Taylor, eds., *Equality and Economic Policy: Essays in Honor of Gary Becker*. Stanford: Hoover Institution Press. 17–48.

Rawls, John. [1971] 1999. *A Theory of Justice*, rev ed. Cambridge, MA: Harvard University Press.

Rawls, John. 1958. "Justice as Fairness." *Philosophical Review* 67, no. 2: 164–194.

Rawls, John. 1985. "Justice as Fairness: Political not Metaphysical." *Philosophy and Public Affairs* 14, no. 3: 226–230.

Rawls, John. 1993. *Political Liberalism*. Cambridge, MA: Harvard University Press.

Rawls, John. 1999. *The Law of Peoples*. Cambridge, MA: Harvard University Press.

Rawls, John. 2001. *Justice as Fairness: A Restatement*. Cambridge, MA: Harvard University Press.

Rhys-Williams, Juliet Evangeline. 1943. *Something to Look Forward To: A Suggestion for a New Social Contract*. London: MacDonald.

Robbins, Lionel. 1935. *An Essay on the Nature and Significance of Economic Science*, 2nd ed. London: Macmillan and Co.

Robbins, Lionel. 1938. "Interpersonal Comparisons of Utility: A Comment." *Economic Journal* 48, no. 192: 635–641.

Robeyns, Ingrid. 2017. *Wellbeing, Freedom and Social Justice: The Capability Approach Re-Examined*. Cambridge: Open Book Publishers.

Roemer, John E. 2012. "On Several Approaches to Equality of Opportunity." *Economics & Philosophy* 28: 165–200.

Roemer, John E., and Alain Trannoy. 2015. "Equality of Opportunity." In A. B. Atkinson and F. Bourguignon, eds., *Handbook of Income Distribution*, vol. 2A. Amsterdam: Elsevier. 217–300.

Roemer, John E., and Richard J. Arneson. 1996. *Equal Shares: Making Market Socialism Work*. London: Verso.

Rognlie, Matthew. 2014. "A Note on Piketty and Diminishing Return on Capital." www.mit.edu/~mrognlie/piketty_diminishing_returns.pdf.

Rognlie, Matthew. 2015. "Deciphering the Fall and Rise of Net Capital Share." Brookings Papers on Economic Activity Conference Draft (March 19–20). Washington, DC: Brookings Institution.

Rosefielde, Steven and Ralph W. Pfouts. 2015. *Inclusive Economic Theory*. Singapore: World Scientific.

Rossi, Mauro. 2011. "Transcendental Arguments and Interpersonal Utility Comparisons." *Economics and Philosophy* 27: 273–295.

Rousseau, Jean-Jacques. 2012. *The Major Political Writings of Jean-Jacques Rousseau: The Two Discourses and the Social Contract*, transl. J.T. Scott. Chicago: University of Chicago Press.

Sachs, Jeffrey D., and Andrew M. Warner 2001. "The Curse of Natural Resources." *European Economic Review* 45: 827–838.

Saez, Emmanuel, and Stefanie Santcheva. 2013. "Generalized Social Marginal Welfare Weights for Optimal Tax Theory." National Bureau of Economic Research Working Paper no. 18835.

Samuelson, Paul. 1947. *Foundations of Economic Analysis*. Cambridge, MA: Harvard University Press.

Samuelson, Paul. 1950. "Evaluation of Real National Income." *Oxford Economic Papers*, New Series 2, no. 1: 1–29.

Sandel, Michael J. [1982] 1998. *Liberalism and the Limits of Justice*, 2nd ed. Cambridge: Cambridge University Press.

Sanmartin, Claudia Grant Schellenberg, Jennifer Kaddatz, Joelle Mader, Guy Gellatly, Sean Clarke, and Danny Leung. 2021. *Moving Forward on Well-Being (Quality of Life) Measures in Canada*. Ottawa: Statistics Canada.

Saunders-Hastings, Emma. 2022. *Private Virtues, Public Vices: Philanthropy and Democratic Equality*. Chicago: University of Chicago Press.

Schultz, Walter J. 2001. *The Moral Conditions of Economic Efficiency*. Cambridge: Cambridge University Press.

Schumpeter, Joseph. [1954] 2006. *History of Economic Analysis*. London: Routledge.

Scitovky, Tibor. 1941. "A Note on Welfare Propositions in Economics." *Review of Economic Studies* 9: 77–88.

Scitovky, Tibor. 1992. *The Joyless Economy: The Psychology of Human Satisfaction*, rev. ed. Oxford: Oxford University Press.

Scully, Gerald W. and Daniel J. Slottje. 1991. "Ranking Economic Liberty across Countries." *Public Choice* 69: 121–152.

Segall, Shlomi. 2010. *Health, Luck and Justice*. Princeton: Princeton University Press.

Sen, Amartya, Angus Deaton, and Tim Besley. 2020. "Economics with a Moral Compass? Welfare Economics: Past, Present, and Future." *Annual Review of Economics* 12: 1–21.

Sen, Amartya. [1973] 1997. *On Economic Inequality*, expanded ed. Oxford: Oxford University Press.

Sen, Amartya. 1970. "The Impossibility of a Paretian Liberal." *Journal of Political Economy* 78, no. 1: 152–157.

Sen, Amartya. 1980. "Equality of What?" In S. McMurrin, ed., *Tanner Lectures on Human Values*, vol. 1. Cambridge: Cambridge University Press.

Sen, Amartya. 1987. *On Ethics and Economics*. Oxford: Basil Blackwell.

Sen, Amartya. 1993. "Capability and Well-Being." In M. Nussnaum and A. Sen, eds., *The Quality of Life*. Oxford: Clarendon Press.

Sen, Amartya. 1995. "Rationality and Social Choice." *The American Economic Review* 85, no. 1: 1–24.

Sen, Amartya. 1999. *Development as Freedom*. New York: Anchor Books.

Sen, Amartya. 2009. *The Idea of Justice*. Cambridge, MA: The Belknap Press.

Sidgwick, Henry. 1901. *The Methods of Ethics*, 6th ed. London: Macmillan.

Sigmund, Karl, Ernest Fehr, and Martin A. Nowak. 2002. "The Economics of Fair Play." *Scientific American* (January): 83–87.

Simmons, A. John. 1995. "Historical Rights and Fair Share." *Law and Philosophy* 14: 149–184.

Simpson, A. W. Brian. 1996. "'Coase v. Pigou' Re-Examined." *Journal of Legal Studies* 25, no. 1: 53–97.

Slemrod, Joel. 2007. "Cheating Ourselves: The Economics of Tax Evasion." *Journal of Economic Perspectives* 21, no. 1: 25–48.

Smith, Adam. [1776] 1981. *An Inquiry into the Nature and Causes of the Wealth of Nations*. Indianapolis, IN: Liberty Fund.

Smith, Vernon L. and Bart J. Wilson. 2019. *Humanomics: Human Sentiments and the Wealth of Nations for the Twenty-First Century*. Cambridge: Cambridge University Press.

Sober, Elliott. 2008. *Evidence and Evolution: The Logic Behind the Science*. Cambridge: Cambridge University Press.

Sreenivasan, Gopal. 1995. *The Limits of Lockean Rights in Property*. Oxford: Oxford University Press.

Steiner, Hillel. 1994. *An Essay on Rights*. Oxford: Blackwell.
Stiglitz, Joseph E. 2009. "Moving beyond Market Fundamentalism to a More Balanced Economy." *Annals of Public and Cooperative Economics* 80, no. 3: 345–360.
Stiglitz, Joseph E. 2013. *The Price of Inequality*. New York: W. W. Norton.
Stiglitz, Joseph E. 2015. *The Great Divide: Unequal Societies and What We Can Do about Them*. New York: W. W. Norton.
Sugden, Robert. 2015. "Team Reasoning and Intentional Cooperation for Mutual Benefit." *Journal of Social Ontology* 1, no. 1: 143–166.
Sugden, Robert. 2018. *The Community of Advantage: A Behavioural Economist's Defence of the Market*. Oxford: Oxford University Press.
Sumner, Andy and Richard Mallet. 2013. *The Future of Foreign Aid: Development Cooperation and the New Geography of Global Poverty*, Cham, Switzerland: Springer.
Tachibanaki, Toshiaki, and Sayaka Sakoda. 2016. "Comparative Study of Happiness and Inequality in Five Industrialized Countries." In T. Tachibanaki, ed., *Advances in Happiness Research: Comparative Perspectives*. Cham: Springer. 97–118.
Taylor, Fred M. 1929. "The Guidance of Production in a Socialist State." *American Economic Review* 19: 1–8.
Taylor-Gooby, Peter. 2013. *The Double Crisis of the Welfare State and What We Can Do about It*. Houndmills: Palgrave.
Temkin, Larry. 2011. "Justice, Equality, Fairness, Desert, Rights, Free Will, Responsibility and Luck." In C. Knight and Z. Stemplowska, eds., *Responsibility and Distributive Justice*. Oxford: Oxford University Press. 51–76.
Tomasi, John. 2012. *Free Market Fairness*. Princeton: Princeton University Press.
Trotsky, Leon. 2006. *Literature and Revolution* (ed. William Keach). Chicago: Haymarket Books.
Tully, James. 1980. *A Discourse on Property: John Locke and His Adversaries*. Cambridge: Cambridge University Press. 51–76.
Valentini, Laura. 2012. "Ideal vs. Non-ideal Theory: A Conceptual Map." *Philosophy Compass* 7, no. 9: 654–664.
Vallentyne, Peter. 2009. "Left-Libertarianism and Liberty." In T. Christiano and J. Christman, eds., *Contemporary Debates in Political Philosophy*. Chichester: Wiley-Blackwell. 137–151.
Van der Linden, Marcel, and Elisa Reis. 2018. "Social Trends and New Geographies." In *Rethinking Society for the 21st Century: Report of the International Panel on Social Progress, Volume 1: Socio-Economic Transformations*. Cambridge: Cambridge University Press. 9–39.
Van der Veen, Robert. 2002. "Equality of Talents: Procedures or Outcomes?" *Ethics* 113: 55–81.
Varian, Hal R. 1985. "Dworkin on Equality of Resources." *Economics and Philosophy* 1: 110–125.
Vaughn, Karen I. 1980. *John Locke, Economic and Social Scientist*. Chicago: University of Chicago Press.
Veblen, Thorstein. [1899] 2007. *The Theory of the Leisure Class*. Oxford: Oxford University Press.
Vienney, Claude. 1994. *L'Economie sociale*. Paris: La Découverte.
Vivarelli, Roberto. 2000. "Political Freedom and Economic Freedom." *European Review* 8, no. 2: 185–191.
Voigt, K. 2007. "The Harshness Objection: Is Luck Egalitarianism Too Harsh on the Victims of Option Luck?" *Ethical Theory and Moral Practice* 10: 389–407.

Wagner, Richard E. 2016. *Politics as a Peculiar Business: Insights from a Theory of Entangled Political Economy*. Cheltenham: Edward Elgar.

Waldron, Jeremy. 2005. "Nozick and Locke: Filling the Space of Rights." *Social Philosophy and Policy* 22, no. 1: 81–110.

Wallison, Peter J. 2009. "Cause and Effect: Government Policies and the Financial Crisis." *Critical Review* 21, nos. 2–3: 365–376.

Walras, Léon. [1907] 1987. "La paix par la justice sociale." In P. Dockès, P.H. Goutte, C. Hébert, C. Mouchot, J.P. Potier, and J.M. Serveteds, *Mélanges d'économie politique et sociale*. Paris: Economica. 467–503.

Walzer, Michael. 1983. *Spheres of Justice: A Defense of Pluralism and Equality*. Oxford: Blackwell.

Watson, William. 2015. *The Inequality Trap: Fighting Capitalism Instead of Poverty*. Toronto: University of Toronto Press.

Weber, Cameron. 2013. "Taming Leviathan with a Basic Income." In G. L. Nell, ed., *Basic Income and the Free Market*. Basingstoke: Palgrave Macmillan. 81–96.

Weber, Michael. 2019. "The Persistence of the Levelling Down Objection." *Erasmus Journal for Philosophy and Economics* 12, no. 1: 1–25.

Weil, David. 2015. "A Review of Angus Deaton's *The Great Escape: Health, Wealth, and the Origins of Inequality*." *Journal of Economic Literature* 53, no. 1: 102–114.

Weingast, Barry R. 2016. "Exposing the Neoclassical Fallacy: McCloskey on Ideas and the Great Enrichment." *Scandinavian Economic History Review* 64, no. 3: 189–201.

West, Edwin G. 2003. "Property Rights in the History of Economic Thought." In T. L. Anderson and F. S. McChesney, eds., *Property Rights: Cooperation, Conflict and Law*. Princeton: Princeton University Press. 259–281.

White, Mark D. 2019. "More Harm Than Benefit: The Implications of the Neglect of Rights in Economics." In W. Dolfsma and I. Negru, eds., *The Ethical Formation of Economists*. London: Routledge. 77–91.

Widerquist, Karl. 2019. "The Negative Income Tax Experiments of the 1970s." In M. Torry, ed., *The Palgrave International Handbook of Basic Income*. Cham: Springer Nature. 303–318.

Wilkinson, Richard G., and Kate E. Pickett. 2006. "Income Inequality and Population Health." *Social Science and Medicine* 62, no. 7: 1768–1784.

Wilkinson, Richard G., and Kate E. Pickett. 2009. *The Spirit Level: Why More Equal Societies Almost Always Do Better*. New York: Allen Lane.

Williamson, Claudia. 2010. "Exploring the Failure of Foreign Aid: The Role of Incentives and Information." *Review of Austrian Economics* 23, no. 1: 17–33.

Winters, Jeffrey A. 2017. "Wealth Defense and the Complicity of Liberal Democracy." *NOMOS* 58: 158–225.

Witting, Antje. 2017. "Insights from 'Policy Learning' on How to Enhance the Use of Evidence by Policymakers." *Palgrave Communications* 3, no. 49. https://doi.org/10.1057/s41599-017-0052-x.

Wolff, Jonathan. 2015. "Social Equality and Social Inequality." In C. Fourie, F. Schuppert, and I. Wallimann-Helmer, eds., *Social Equality: On What It Means To Be Equal*. Oxford: Oxford University Press. 209–225.

Yunker, James A. 2001. *On the Political Economy of Market Socialism*. London: Routledge.

Zak, Paul J., ed. 2008. *Moral Markets: The Critical Role of Values in the Economy*. Princeton: Princeton University Press.

Zhichao, Tong. 2015. "Rawlsian Property-Owning Democracy: An American Historical Interpretation." *American Political Thought* 4, no. 2: 289–310.

Index

Note: Page numbers in *italics* indicate a figure on the corresponding page. Page numbers followed by 'n' indicate a note.